TRIATHLON

TRIATHLON
TRAINING FUNDAMENTALS

A Beginner's Guide to
Essential Gear, Nutrition, and Training Schedules

Will Peveler

LYONS PRESS
Guilford, Connecticut
An imprint of Globe Pequot Press

Lyons Press is an imprint of Globe Pequot Press.

All photos are the author's unless otherwise noted.

Text design/layout: Mary Ballachino
Project editor: Ellen Urban

Library of Congress Cataloging-in-Publication Data is available on file.

ISBN 978-0-7627-8664-0

Printed in the United States of America

10 9 8 7 6 5 4 3 2 1

Medical Disclaimer:

The programs in this book are designed for athletes with either a healthy-to-high level of fitness or the physiology to attain a healthy-to-high level of fitness. Readers should consult a physician before beginning any of the programs or workouts suggested herein. If you experience any pain or difficulty with these exercises, stop and consult your healthcare provider.

I dedicate this book to Grayson and Garrett,
two of the best sons a father could ever hope for.

Contents

PART II Training

PART III Racing

Acknowledgments

I would like to thank all of those who have educated, mentored, and put up with me through my educational years. I would like to specifically acknowledge: Dr. Phil Bishop, Dr. Matt Green, Dr. Mark Richardson, Dr. Frank Wyatt, Dr. Thad Crews, and Dr. Joe Smith. The guidance and friendship I have received from these individuals and others have been invaluable.

I would also like to thank those who have provided photos for the book: Cannondale, Advanced Sport International, Profile Design, Polar, Vasa, Hammer Nutrition, Rudy Project, Aqua Sphere, Nathan Kortuem, and Milay Galvez. I would also like to thank those who allowed me to photograph them for the book: Samantha Brey, Kayla Wright, Quinton Dunn, Gabe Sanders, Scott Brock, Raymond Gardinier, Josh Volpenhein, and Connie Vaughn.

Last but not least, I would like to thank all those at Globe Pequot Press who have worked hard to make this book a success. I would like to especially thank Katie Benoit and Ellen Urban.

Introduction

Throughout my career, both as a competing triathlete and a collegiate cycling and triathlon coach, I have spent a lot of time answering questions regarding training for triathlons. This book, written with the beginning athlete in mind, is an attempt to answer all of those questions in an easy-to-use and straightforward manner. In short, this book contains all of the information that I wish I had known prior to my first triathlon.

Sport of Triathlon

Triathlons are relatively new. The first US triathlon was held in 1974, and it was not until the 2000 Olympics that the triathlon was introduced as an Olympic sport. The popularity of the sport has grown exponentially. Today triathlons consist of a swim followed by a bike ride and finished off with a run.

People become involved in the sport of triathlon for a variety of reasons, but mainly for the challenge and the resultant feeling of accomplishment that comes from completing that first race. There's also a national increase in awareness of the positive impact of physical activity on health and aging, which results in people becoming more active and looking for alternate and challenging methods of exercise. And some triathletes get involved to give back to the community through charitable organizations. Regardless of the rationale, one truth is universal: Once you complete the race, you are a triathlete for life.

Challenge and Competition

Many people become involved in triathlon because of the physical and mental challenge that the sport provides. It allows you to push your perceived limits to discover what you are made of and what you can accomplish. For many, just completing a triathlon is a challenge in and of itself and reward enough. For others, the drive is the competition, competing against fellow athletes to determine who is faster.

But to be a triathlete, all you have to do is finish in the allotted amount of time. One of the unique aspects of triathlon is that it is an individual sport. This allows individuals of varying ages and fitness levels to become involved.

The sport of triathlon has grown exponentially during the last ten years.

You can train in all three disciplines at your own pace and on your own schedule (although it is always fun to train and race with friends!).

Health

Improved health is a great motivator for triathletes, many of whom become involved in triathlon during their pursuit of a healthier lifestyle. Individuals who are physically active are four times less likely to develop cardiovascular disease than those who do not participate in regular physical activity. This fact is so strongly supported by available research that the American College of Sports Medicine recently implemented the Exercise Is Medicine initiative, which is officially supported by the surgeon general and USA Triathlon.

Triathlon provides a challenging but attainable goal for those who wish to get in shape for health or personal reasons. To maximize the health benefits of exercise, 30 minutes of physical activity per day is recommended for most days of the week. During triathlon training you will exceed those minimum recommendations and be well on your way to the development of a lifelong healthy lifestyle.

While cardiovascular activity has a strong positive impact on your health, you need to first ensure that you are healthy enough to begin an exercise program with no restrictions. Exercise takes your body out of *homeostasis* (the maintenance of balance within the human body: body temperature, blood glucose levels, etc.) and therefore increases the risk of a cardiovascular incident in those with undiagnosed or unknown heart conditions. You should seek a physician's clearance prior to beginning an exercise program in order to confirm that you are healthy enough to begin. This is especially true for sedentary individuals, older individuals, those that have not had a recent physical, and those that possess risk factors for the development of cardiovascular disease or signs of cardiovascular disease.

Charity Events

Some individuals become involved in triathlons in order to raise money for specific causes or organizations. The Wounded Warrior Project works with triathlon race directors to raise money for wounded veterans coming home from war. As a war veteran I feel very strongly about this organization. The Leukemia and Lymphoma Society's Team in Training helps prepare you for your first triathlon by providing coaching and motivation throughout training, while also raising money to support cancer research. I have previously worked as a Team in Training coach, and it is a very rewarding experience.

Triathlon provides an excellent opportunity to raise money for charities.

Racing

In the sport of triathlon there are three basic race categories: sprint, Olympic, and ultra-distance. These categories are specifically defined by the distance of the race, with the shortest being sprint and the longest being ultra-distance. While the actual length of the swim, bike, and run varies from race to race, each triathlon can be placed in one of the three categories. This book focuses on sprint and Olympic-distance races. For more information on ultra-distance races, read *Be Iron Fit* by Don Fink. Part III of this book covers everything you need to know to succeed on the day of the race.

Sprint

Sprint races are the shortest and most abundant of the three distances. While the other two race categories have very specific distances for the swim, bike, and run, the sprint triathlon has greater variation. The typical distances will be anchored somewhere around 600 m (0.37 mile) for the swim, 20 km (12.43 miles) for the bike, and 5 km (3.11 miles) for the run. The sprint is the most raced of all the distances because it is shorter and therefore less intimidating.

Olympic

The Olympic-distance races are the next step up from the sprint distance. Variations in distances are much less prevalent in the Olympic races than they are for the sprint distance. An Olympic-distance race consists of a 1500 m (0.93 mile) swim, 40 km (24.86 miles) bike, and a 10 km (6.21 mile) run.

Ultra-Distance

Ultra-distance races are long and extremely challenging. The most common ultras are the Ironman distance races consisting of a 3,862.43 m (2.4 miles) swim, a 180.25 km (112 miles) bike, and a 42.16 km (26.2 miles) run. "Ironman" is the trademark name for a specific group of ultra-endurance races. Ultra-endurance races of the same length are typically referred to as "ironman distance," but do not use the trademark name Ironman. The shortest of the ultra-endurance races is the half ironman distance, which consists of a 1,931.21 m (1.2 miles) swim, a 90.12 km (56 miles) bike, and a 21.08 km (13.1 miles) run. For those that really want a challenge, there are also double and triple ironman distance races. Additionally, there are many variations on distances in ultra-endurance races. For example, the Leadman Tri consists of a 5 km (3.11 miles) swim, a 223 km (138.57 miles) bike, and a 22 km (13.67 miles) run.

Off-Road

In recent years off-road triathlons have become very popular. Off-road triathlons increase the level of challenge by adding mountain biking and trail running to the mix. While there are races that are longer, most off-road triathlons are variations on sprint distances. Keep in mind that in most cases a 13-mile mountain ride is more difficult than a 13-mile road ride. The Xterra race series is currently the most popular off-road triathlon series in the United States.

Variations on Race Format

If you are not yet ready for a traditional triathlon, there are still several ways to get involved in a multisport activity. The most common variation is the duathlon, which consists of a run, a bike ride, and another run. Duathlons are perfect for those not yet comfortable with swimming long distances.

The aquabike is another variation that allows individuals who cannot run—due to injury or other reasons—to participate in a multisport race. The aquabike involves the swim and bike portions of a triathlon. Many of

Joining a local triathlon club is an excellent way to become involved in the sport.

the aquabike races are set up as part of a normal triathlon; finish times are recorded at the end of the bike for aquabikers, while those competing in the triathlon continue on with the run. An aquathlon—run-swim-run—allows those who do not currently possess a bike to participate in a multisport activity.

How to Get Involved

While a large number of people would like to compete in triathlons, many do not get involved simply because the sport can be intimidating, and they do not know where to begin. Triathletes, as a whole, are very accepting and supportive of beginners, and most seasoned racers go out of their way to help out those just getting started. Finding a local group of triathletes to start working with is much easier than you think.

Local Triathlon Clubs

One of the first places to look to for knowledge and support is your local triathlon club. Most areas have a club that gets together weekly for training sessions. Local club members can provide some level of coaching, as well as knowledge on local races and shops, and where to swim, bike, and run locally.

Most important, they provide a social support group for your involvement in the sport. If you have more than one local triathlon club, find the one that best fits your needs. For example, one group may focus more on optimizing performance and racing while another will focus more on enjoying the sport first and look at optimizing performance second. You can usually find information on triathlon clubs at your local triathlon shop, bike shop, or running store, or online at USA Triathlon (see below). If your area does not currently have a triathlon club, the local running or cycling club will typically have a subgroup of triathletes—or consider starting a new club.

USA Triathlon

USA Triathlon (USAT) is the governing body of triathlon in the United States. USAT is primarily concerned with sanctioning races, development and enforcement of rules and regulations, development of individual athletes, World Championship and Olympic teams, and overall support for the growth and development of triathlon. Most US triathlons are USAT-sanctioned and require a USAT license to participate. Getting involved with USAT is a great way to familiarize yourself with the sport.

Collegiate Triathlon

For those of you in college, one of the best ways to get involved with the sport of triathlon is through a collegiate team. Collegiate triathlon is a club sport and does not fall under NCAA jurisdiction, which means that you can earn money and prizes during races, seek direct sponsorship, and work as many hours as you like, and, because there are few (if any) scholarships, triathletes of all levels can join. The downside is that there is very little monetary support from universities and very few programs have scholarships. If your school does not currently have a collegiate triathlon team, consider starting one through your local recreation department and USAT. The process is fairly easy and does not require too much work or money.

Paratriathlon

There are multiple means for individuals with disabilities to participate in the sport of triathlon. USAT currently has six different categories for paratriathletes that are based upon the individual's disability, both type and extent. While there are slight variations to the race rules, paratriathletes race right alongside their able-bodied counterparts. USAT provides information and support for paratriathletes on its website—www.usatriathlon.org.

Triathlon requires specialized gear.

Triathlon Gear

Now that you have decided to participate in triathlon, you need to obtain the appropriate gear. Choosing triathlon gear can be a daunting and expensive experience, but with the right information it does not have to be. Part I of this book covers the necessary equipment for the swim, bike, run, and transition. Note that there is a difference between required equipment and equipment that would be nice to have. This section also covers how and where to purchase equipment as well as advice on how much to spend. Maintenance of your triathlon equipment is also extremely important to prevent expensive repairs or replacement of your equipment down the road. Keep in mind the more maintenance that you can do for yourself, the less you have to pay to have done.

Training and Nutrition

To successfully complete your first triathlon, it is vital that you develop and maintain a sound training and nutrition plan. Unfortunately, training is not as simple as just swimming, biking, and running. Since you work with three different modes of racing, you need to develop a plan that allows you to optimally work all three into your schedule without overtraining. If you do not know how to develop a training plan, it may be beneficial to work with a coach.

While most triathletes spend a lot of time developing their training plan, they commonly ignore their nutrition plan. To optimize training you must not only eat specific types of food, but also consider the amount of food and the timing of meals. Training and nutrition is covered in Part II of the book.

Part I
EQUIPMENT

CHAPTER ONE

Swim Gear and Maintenance

The swim is the first leg of the triathlon and requires very specific gear to safely and competently compete. Unless you have a swimming background, you probably are not familiar with the necessary equipment required to competently train for this leg of the race. This chapter provides information on basic swim gear so you can make educated decisions when purchasing equipment. While swimming does not require a large amount of equipment, your choice of equipment can mean the difference between an enjoyable or miserable swim. Due to the corrosive nature of pool and ocean water, specific care of swim gear is required to prevent premature equipment failure.

Goggles/Masks

One of the most important pieces of swimming equipment that you will purchase is your swim goggles or mask. Most open water swim courses occur in water with very limited visibility. It is very rare that an open water swim will be held in crystal clear water, and unfortunately there are never lane lines at the bottom of a lake. As such, you need to be able to periodically sight swim buoys to maintain a correct course. The better your visibility, the faster you will be able to sight buoys and stay on course. To pick the best path through crowded waters, it also helps to be able to see other swimmers around you. There are two basic options. The first is the traditional Swedish goggles (Swedish-style goggles are also placed in this category), and the second is the swim mask that looks like a dive mask, but does not cover the nose. If you choose a mask, find one that provides a good seal that is maintained throughout your swim session, fits comfortably to your face, and provides superior visibility. Because heads and faces are shaped differently, there is no one mask that will fit everyone the same.

Many swimmers, especially those with a pool background, prefer Swedish-style goggles, which have cups that fit individually over each eye socket and are the preferred choice of most competitive pool swimmers. These goggles

Cincinnati Triathlon swim start

come unassembled so that you can customize the fit to your specific needs. They are relatively inexpensive and typically cost between $5 and $10. The downside to Swedish-style goggles is that many people find them uncomfortable, and they tend to leak during prolonged swims.

Traditional Swedish-style goggles *Aqua Sphere*

Swim masks are less likely to leak and provide great visibility. *Aqua Sphere*

I tend to lean toward a swim mask, such as the Aqua Sphere Seal. This type of swim mask fits more like a dive mask, but does not cover your nose. For most individuals this type of mask provides a better seal and a more comfortable fit. This is especially true for beginners. Because the lens wraps around the face, it also provides a better field of vision. The downside to swim masks is that they will typically cost around $20 to $30.

You want to consider optimizing your visibility when purchasing your eyewear. Swim masks provide a much wider field of view, which is extremely important for open water swimming. Be sure the mask is tinted for bright, sunny day swims so you can spot swim buoys when lifting your head out of the water. Smoke or mirrored masks seem to work the best. Avoid blue-tinted goggles because they fade out red and orange buoys, making them very difficult to spot. Keep a clear set of goggles for overcast days or days where the orientation of the sun will not affect your vision.

Sometimes the glass on your mask will fog up from water condensation and negatively impact vision. This situation occurs when moisture in the air makes contact with the glass surface, which is much cooler, causing water to form on the glass. How the water forms determines whether noticeable "fogging" occurs or not. If the surface is smooth, then the water will uniformly spread across the glass instead of binding together to form fog on the lens; this will not greatly affect visibility. Most swim goggles/masks come from the factory with an anti-fog coating on the lens. This allows the water to smoothly form over the glass and therefore not reduce visibility.

Inevitably the original coating will wear off and the goggles or mask will then begin to fog. Once the factory anti-fog coating ceases to work, you can help prevent fogging by creating a surface that allows the water to form smoothly over the glass. Anti-fogging solution can be purchased at any local swim, triathlon, or dive shop. There are specific application instructions for each brand. There is also the spit method: You just spit into your dry mask, rub the spit around the glass, rinse, and then wear. Or, use baby shampoo: Rub a small amount of baby shampoo onto a dry lens, rinse, and then use.

If you have corrective vision, there are a couple of options. The cheapest and easiest option is to wear your contacts with a swim mask, which is perfectly okay unless your doctor tells you otherwise. You could lose a contact if your mask is flooded or knocked from your eyes, but this risk is minimal. The other option is to purchase prescription goggles, which can be costly.

Clothing

Clothing choices vary depending on if you are racing or training. Due to the expense of triathlon racing suits and the fact that pool chemicals and repeated washing wears the material down, just wear a swimsuit during normal swim training. Also, riding in a pair of cycling shorts on a training ride is more comfortable than riding in your triathlon shorts.

Race Suit

Triathlon race suits are designed to optimize performance through all three legs of the triathlon. They come in one- and two-piece suits and are designed to optimize hydrodynamics by reducing drag during the swim. Reduction in drag is accomplished mainly by material type and streamlining shape. The material of modern triathlon suits is designed so that water flows more smoothly over the material. The trick is that this material also needs to be breathable on hot days for the bike and run. A good race suit should fit snug, but not be so tight as to be uncomfortable. A loose-fitting race suit increases drag and therefore increases the difficulty of the swim.

One of the key components of a triathlon race suit is the chamois, commonly referred to as the bike pad. The pad, located in the shorts, is designed to move with your skin across the saddle and move moisture away from the skin so that chafing is minimized. The chamois in a triathlon short will be much thinner than the chamois found in cycling shorts and, therefore, provides less protection from chafing, but the thin material holds less water, which is better and more comfortable for the race. Wearing underwear with the chamois is not necessary and may actually increase chafing. Shorts with longer legs, as opposed to "Speedo" style, are also recommended to prevent chafing of the inside of the legs on the saddle.

Shown: One-piece and two-piece triathlon suits *Hammer Nutrition*

One-piece suits provide the best hydrodynamics during the swim and best aerodynamics during the ride. Men can unzip the top on hot runs, or, with two-piece suits, take off the top. Always wear a top for the bike leg to help protect against road rash in the event of a crash.

Skin suits, specialized one-piece triathlon suits, are designed to improve performance by optimizing hydrodynamics. Some skin suits are not currently approved by USAT for racing, so be sure to check prior to purchasing one (www.usatriathlon.org).

The cost of triathlon suits varies depending on the type, brand, and material. Triathlon shorts typically range from $50 to $100, tops range from $50 to $100, and one-piece suits typically run between $100 and $200. Because of the cost, most individuals save their triathlon suits for race day and brick days (two workouts in one day, typically a bike followed by a run).

Training Suit

It is not necessary to train in your triathlon suit. While it is important to become accustomed to your triathlon suit to ensure that it works for you, frequent pool swimming will deteriorate the fabric. Most people purchase suits specifically for swim training.

Swimsuits for lap swim will fit tight and close to the body to optimize hydrodynamics. The one exception to this rule is the drag suit. This suit is designed to intentionally increase drag in order to increase resistance during a workout. Do not use a drag suit every time you swim. For men, avoid swimming laps in the trunks you wear at the beach. The mesh lining in the suit will lead to chafing. For women, beach swimsuit tops may not fit snugly and therefore not stay in place as they should during lap swim. Find a swimsuit that is comfortable and functional.

Wetsuit

Consider these factors when purchasing a wetsuit: type, insulating properties, comfort, movement, buoyancy, cost, and USAT rules. Triathlon wetsuits are not designed to the same specifications as scuba diving or surfing wetsuits. Triathlon wetsuits allow for greater movement of the shoulder to optimize movement during the swim. They are also designed to optimize buoyancy and, therefore, body position during the swim by altering thickness to affect flotation. Increased buoyancy is very beneficial for novice swimmers. However, keep in mind that while a wetsuit does increase buoyancy, it will not keep the average person afloat. The outer skin is also designed to optimize hydrodynamics by decreasing drag in the water. The increased buoyancy, combined with the decreased drag, results in much faster swim times.

There are three basic types of wetsuits: full, sleeveless, and shorty. A full wetsuit provides the greatest insulation and buoyancy but does affect movement at the shoulder joint. A sleeveless wetsuit provides less insulation but greater movement at the shoulder. A shorty provides the least insulation but greater mobility. When purchasing a wetsuit, make sure you select one that fits appropriately. Suits can range from $200 to $600

Shown: Full-sleeve and sleeveless wetsuit
Profile Design

depending on the brand and model, so it is important to be properly fit in one by an expert. Wetsuits are designed to fit snug against the body. The suit should not sag around the shoulders or between the legs and fit tight enough to keep the boundary layer of water against the skin, but not so tight as to prevent movement.

While wetsuits have the potential to increase swim performance, getting in and out of them quickly takes knowledge and practice. There are two main tricks that allow for ease of donning: The first is to leave your socks on, which decreases friction between your skin and the wetsuit as you push your foot through. The second is to use a lubricant, such as BodyGlide, around the forearms, wrist, hands, lower legs, ankles, and feet (if you are not wearing socks) to allow the limbs to smoothly pass through. Do not use lubricants that are petroleum based, as this will deteriorate the neoprene. To be safe, use a lubricant designed for this purpose. Lubrication also gives the added bonus of easing removal of the wetsuit later and decreasing chafing in areas such as the armpits. Once your wetsuit is on and zipped, remember to attach the zipper leash to your wetsuit so that it does not interfere with your swimming.

Practice removing your wetsuit prior to race day. The last thing that you want to do is flail around transition for 5 minutes working your wetsuit off your body. With practice you will be able to remove your wetsuit in just seconds. Begin by unzipping and removing the top as you leave the water. Once you reach your transition spot, remove the rest of your wetsuit. Some races will have volunteers who assist with wetsuit removal.

USAT has specific regulations governing the use of wetsuits for age-group athletes (non-professional triathletes). Wetsuits are permitted for water temperatures of 78°F or less with no restrictions. For water temperatures between 78 and 84°F, age-group triathletes can wear wetsuits but are not eligible to receive awards. At water temperatures between 80 and 83.9°F, you will get hot in your wetsuit. Use of a wetsuit in water that is 84°F or higher is not permitted. Wearing a wetsuit in water that is too warm can lead to overheating and, in long or hot races, can result in the development of a heat-related illness. The official water temperature that will determine the use of wetsuits will be taken on race day—make sure you have an alternative plan if wetsuits are not permitted. Regulations on the use of wetsuits for professional-level triathletes may differ in relation to age-group athletes and are determined by the USAT.

Quickly removing a wetsuit takes practice.

Swim Cap

Swim caps provide various benefits, including reducing drag and improving hydrodynamics, especially for those with long hair, protecting your hair against pool chemicals and tangles, and most importantly increasing the swimmer's visibility during open water swims. For improved visibility wear a bright-colored swim cap with a strong contrast to the water. Some race directors will designate a specific color for beginners so that lifeguards and other officials can pay extra attention to those swimmers during the race.

The swim cap provides visibility during the swim.

Training Gear

You may want to consider additional equipment to enhance your swim training. Each piece of equipment can either add to your training experience if used properly, or decrease performance and cause overuse injuries if used incorrectly. While there are many valuable training tools that can be used to increase swim performance, this section will only cover the basics. Check with your pool prior to purchasing equipment, as many pools have some equipment that you can use.

Pull Buoy

Pull buoys are used to float the lower body without kicking. By placing the pull buoy between your legs, you can concentrate on upper body movement—arm movement and breathing patterns. The pull buoy also allows you to feel how the body should be positioned while swimming. Many beginners swim "uphill" with their legs too far down in the water.

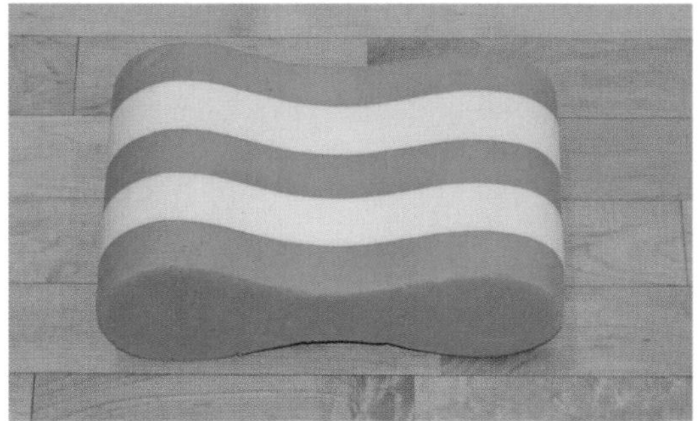

Pull buoys allow you to focus on upper body swim stroke.

Hand Paddles

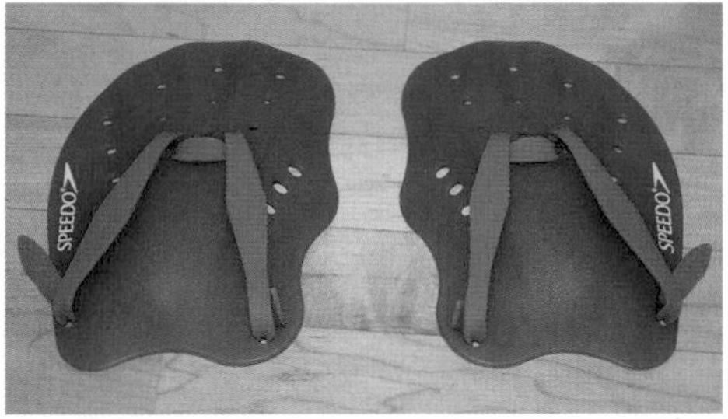

Hand paddles are typically used in conjunction with a pull buoy to work on technique.

Often used in conjunction with a pull buoy, hand paddles are designed to increase resistance and improve feel during the swim stroke. They allow you to notice when you are performing an incorrect hand entry and stroke. A correct water entry and stroke will feel smooth when using a hand paddle, while improper technique will "grab" the paddle and will be very noticeable. Hand paddles also increase strength by adding resistance to the stroke and therefore acting as a sport-specific resistance workout for swimmers. Because of the added stress placed on the muscles of the shoulder joint and shoulder girdle, implement hand paddles slowly and only as a small portion of your overall workout. Using swim paddles with poor swim stroke technique can lead to injury. For this reason swim paddles are not recommended for beginners.

Kickboard and Fins

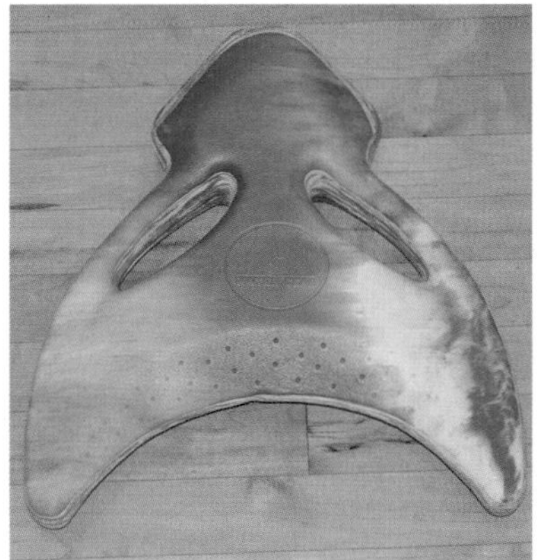
As the name implies, kickboards allow you to focus on your kick.

A kickboard is mainly used to allow you to focus on kicking. Too often novice swimmers possess a very weak kick. Using a kickboard requires you to move through the water powered only by your kick. To increase both the speed and resistance, you can also combine a kickboard with swim fins. A kickboard should be used only as a small portion of your workout because it alters body position in the water.

Swim Bag

You will need a swim bag to haul all of your gear to and from the pool. You will need a mesh bag that allows the water to easily evaporate and your equipment to finish drying. The bag needs to be large enough to hold all of your gear and built strong enough to handle the water and the abuse of regular use. Gear bags start at around $15.

A swim bag should be breathable to allow your gear to dry.

Care of Equipment

Care and maintenance of swim gear is relatively easy—rinse, rinse, and rinse again. Both the chemicals used in pools and the salt water from the ocean can be very corrosive and eventually lead to deterioration of your gear. While fresh water found in lakes and rivers is not as corrosive as pool or ocean water, it still contains many types of bacteria. Always rinse your gear thoroughly in clean water after every session to increase longevity.

While goggles, kickboards, and similar equipment hold up relatively well, suits are another story. Suits are more delicate and should be rinsed with fresh water after use, even if you are planning on washing the suit the same day. Triathlon suits are somewhat expensive and extra caution should be taken in the care of your suit. After rinsing your triathlon suit, either hand wash or machine wash on gentle. After washing, hang your suit to dry and do not machine dry.

Individual manufacturers typically provide specific instructions on wetsuit care. However, there are general guidelines followed by all manufacturers: Wetsuits should be rinsed thoroughly after every use and periodically cleaned with a wetsuit cleaner. If bacteria is allowed to build in the wetsuit, it will begin to stink. Rinse the outside of the wetsuit and then turn it inside out and rinse the inside. Thoroughly rinse the zipper, dry, and apply zipper lube or beeswax to prevent corrosion and allow for smooth operation of the zipper mechanism. When cleaning is complete, leave the suit inside out and hang on a wetsuit hanger to dry.

No matter how careful you are with your suit, you will eventually puncture or rip the neoprene. When this occurs you should repair the tear immediately to prevent it from becoming larger. You can find repair kits at your local triathlon or dive shop. They are relatively easy to use and work extremely well.

Wetsuits should be stored at room temperature and inside out to protect the outer layer. Do not store your suit folded, as this will cause permanent creases if left for too long. Instead, store your wetsuit flat or on a wetsuit hanger designed specifically for this purpose. For prolonged storage, keep in mind that neoprene does shrink as it dries out. So if you pull your suit out the following season and it fits tighter than normal, do not freak out because it may not be a result of an increase in your waistline (unless of course it is). Soaking the wetsuit in warm water for a few hours and then hanging to dry will help.

CHAPTER TWO

Cycling Gear and Maintenance

This chapter covers the necessary equipment used when training for and racing the bike leg of the triathlon. Due to the nature of cycling, there will be more time spent covering cycling gear in relation to swim or run gear. It is not that cycling is more important, but it does require more gear, which requires greater care and maintenance. Of the three sports, cycling also creates the greatest challenges when it comes to equipment choice. Cycling is expensive, and you want to ensure that you do not buy the incorrect gear. The first part of this chapter provides you with information on the purchase of your first triathlon bike and bike fit. The remainder of the chapter covers related equipment and bike maintenance.

Bike/Triathlon Shop

Naturally, you need a bike to participate in triathlon. One of the most important decisions to make when looking for a bike is where to buy your bike. It is rare that you will find a triathlon-specific store unless you live in a large city with a sizeable triathlon population. Your local bike shop may have a small area that caters specifically to triathletes. I strongly suggest that you visit more than one store to find one that will work best for you.

Purchasing a bike is a big investment and you want to work with a shop that will work with you. While pricing is important, there is much more to a shop than finding the one with the least expensive bike. Most important, a good shop is the one that you find yourself in regularly just to hang out and talk with friends. The shop is where you can learn a lot of information on racing, training, equipment, and maintenance. If you have a good relationship with your local shop, it will bend over backward to help you out when you need it.

When pricing bikes keep in mind that the profit margin on a bike is very small and shops do not have a large amount of room or freedom to drop prices. Many manufacturers actually limit how low the bike shop can drop the prices through the dealership agreement. The one exception to this rule

A basic understanding of cycling gear and maintenance is vital for a triathlete.

is when the shops purchase deals on close-out models at the end of the year, typically in the fall, which is one of the best times to look for a new bike.

A good shop will spend time to ensure that you get the bike and accessories you need. The staff should ask about your short- and long-term goals, riding experience, and budget. These questions will allow you and the expert to work together to come up with the best bike that fits your current needs and budget. If the staff does not seem eager to help you, then it is time to visit another shop.

Choosing a Bike

The bike is the single most expensive piece of required equipment that you will purchase as a triathlete and, therefore, budget is going to be a major factor for most individuals. An entry-level road bike will cost between $500 and $600, a good beginning race bike will cost between $1,000 and $1,500, and professional triathlete–level bikes start at around $4,000 and increase from there. It is common for professional triathletes to ride bikes that start at around $6,000. There are significant differences in performance between an entry-level and a professional-level bike. There is an inverse relationship between cost and weight; as cost increases, weight decreases. Highly skilled labor and better material are required to make a bike lighter while still maintaining structural integrity, which in turn increases manufacturing costs. Also, as price increases performance, reliability, and durability increases. However, a $6,000 bike is not required to participate in a triathlon. It just requires a bike. Keep in mind that, when you are losing by minutes, spending an extra $2,000 for a lighter bike to shave seconds off your time is not overly cost-effective. Work on the engine first, and then worry about the bike second.

Due to the cost of new bikes, many people look to purchase a used bike for their first triathlon bike to get more bike for their money. Bikes are similar to cars in that the value drops immediately after purchase. You can typically find a used entry-level race bike that is a few years old for the same price as an entry-level road bike. As long as the bike has been well maintained, then it will be a good first purchase. I advise having a bike mechanic look over the bike prior to purchase to ensure that it is in working order. Do not be afraid to work with your local shop when purchasing a used bike. Shops know that you will come in to buy accessories and for maintenance of your used bike and will treat you right. You can look up the original specifications and price of the used bike on the manufacturer's website. If the price is not listed, you can check at www.bikepedia.com.

Of course there are benefits to buying new as opposed to used. Typically the warranty on a used bike does not transfer to the new owner. Frame warranties range from 5 years to lifetime, depending on the company. Components, forks, and wheel sets typically have only a 1-year warranty from defect, starting the day of purchase. Also, some shops offer free or discounted basic maintenance with the purchase of a new bike.

Buying a bike online can be somewhat complicated, especially for beginners. If the bike is used, then you cannot be sure of the condition of the frame and components. Regardless of whether it is new or used, it will be somewhat difficult to determine the correct size to purchase. There are differences in geometry and measurement methods between manufacturers. For example, I ride a 56 cm bike by one manufacturer and a 58 cm bike by another. When buying from a local shop, the staff will take the time to properly fit you to the bike.

Proper fit should be the most important deciding factor during your purchase. A bike that does not fit properly will be uncomfortable to ride, may be difficult to handle properly, and could lead to overuse injuries. Saving money on a bike that does not fit properly may lead to greater cost in the long run. Some bike shops will provide a standard fit for free with purchase of a bike, but charge extra for a full in-depth micro fit.

Types of Bikes

You will see three basic types of bikes at a triathlon: triathlon, road bike, and mountain bike. A dedicated triathlon bike is the optimal choice. Triathlon bikes possess frames with bladed tubing to reduce drag by optimizing aerodynamics. This will be discussed in further detail later in this chapter. The cockpit on a triathlon bike, consisting of

Dedicated triathlon bikes are ideal for optimal triathlon performance. *Cannondale® is used by permission from Cycling Sports Group*

a base bar and aerobars, optimizes aerodynamics and performance. Shift levers are located at the end of the aerobars right at your fingertips, allowing you to shift gears while maintaining an aerodynamic position. In a race format that does not permit drafting behind other riders, optimizing aerodynamics is extremely important.

Road bikes are commonly used to compete in triathlon. *Cannondale® is used by permission from Cycling Sports Group*

Road bikes are also a viable option. An entry-level road bike costs less than a dedicated triathlon bike. Many beginning triathletes spend their first few seasons on a road bike before finally purchasing a dedicated triathlon bike. Road bikes are similar to triathlon bikes with a few exceptions. The first is that the typical road bike will possess a frame and fork that is much less aerodynamic than a triathlon bike. The second major difference is the cockpit. Modern road bikes possess drop bars (road-style handlebars) with integrated brake and shift levers located on the bar. Road bars effectively limit the degree to which you can minimize your frontal area in an aerodynamic position. Adding aerobars to the road bike allows you to comfortably assume and maintain an aerodynamic position that reduces the frontal area and therefore drag. Placing aerobars on a road bike requires you to move out of the aero position to shift gears and brake.

Mountain bikes can be an inexpensive option to compete in your first triathlon. *Cannondale® is used by permission from Cycling Sports Group*

You can also use a mountain bike for your first triathlon. Mountain bikes are relatively prevalent and easy to borrow if you do not have your own. Be aware that your bike time will be slower in relation to riding a road or triathlon bike, since mountain bikes are heavier, typically have wider knobby tires, and possess a lower gear ratio. Some triathlons actually have a mountain bike category that allows those on mountain bikes to compete against each other as opposed to everyone else on road or triathlon bikes.

Frames

Frame choice is of primary significance when choosing which bike to purchase. There are three main factors to consider when choosing a frame: frame tube shape, frame material, and frame geometry. All three will affect comfort, weight, and performance. The following section will provide insight that will help you to make a decision based on comfort, performance, and budget.

Aero versus Traditional

To simplify frame tube choices, I will categorize frames as either aero or traditional tubing. Traditional tubing is typically round and provides the least aerodynamic advantages between the two types of frames. However, road bike frames are easier to produce and lighter at any given performance level. Aero frames are typically bladed to optimize aerodynamics by reducing turbulence at the trail edge. The extra material needed to create the bladed shape, also known as a foil shape, increases the weight of the frame at any given performance level. However, the aerodynamic advantages far outweigh the increased weight. Unless you are participating in a triathlon that requires a lot of climbing, an aerodynamic frame wins out.

Aero frame sets are constructed from bladed tubing to improve aerodynamics.
Cannondale® is used by permission from Cycling Sports Group

Traditional frame sets are constructed from rounded tube and are less aerodynamic.
Cannondale® is used by permission from Cycling Sports Group

Geometry

The frame geometry deals with the interaction of the lengths and angles of the frame tubing. On all bikes you will make contact at three primary locations: pedals, seat, and aerobars. The location of the three contact points in relation to each other is strongly influenced by geometry and will affect both bike fit and handling. Find the correct geometry that optimizes the fit and handling for your specific anthropometrics (size and proportions of your body) and skill level.

The typical head tube angle on most triathlon bikes is around 73 degrees. At any given frame size and fork rake, a shallower angle will increase stability, whereas a steeper angle will increase responsiveness. When comparing triathlon and road bikes there is greater variation when it comes to seat tube angle as opposed to head tube angle. Seat tube angles typically range from 74 to 78 degrees on most triathlon bikes. Road bikes commonly have seat tube angles of 73 to 74 degrees, placing the rider farther back on the bike. A triathlon bike with a set tube angle of 78 degrees would place the rider in a much greater forward aggressive position. While the current research is equivocal, it is generally accepted that a more forward position will create optimal neuromuscular alterations that will lead to a more favorable run. The bottom line is to purchase a bike that possesses geometry that will provide optimal aerodynamics, comfort, and handling.

There has been some concern and confusion as to whether triathlon bikes with certain frame geometry are legal to race during cycling time trials. There are three main regulating bodies that you need to be concerned with when considering regulations on frame geometry: USA Triathlon (USAT), USA Cycling (USAC), and Union Cycliste Internationale (UCI). The UCI is the most demanding of the three—if a bike meets UCI regulations it will meet USAT and USAC regulations. However, the reverse is not true, as USAT and USAC have minimum requirements.

Two main bike regulations differentiate USAT and USAC regulations from UCI regulations. The first requirement by UCI is a traditional double diamond configuration. This means that the bike will have rear chain stays and seat stays, a seat tube, top tube, head tube, and down tube. Bikes such as the Kestrel Airfoil would not be permitted under UCI regulations but would under USAT. For time trial bikes UCI also requires that the nose of the saddle must be 5 cm behind the center of the bottom bracket, which limits the seat tube angle to approximately 76 degrees. However, UCI regulations only affect those who wish to race at cycling nationals, set a national time trial record, or road race internationally under UCI.

Frame Material

Another concern when purchasing a triathlon bike is frame material. The most common materials used for bike frame production are carbon fiber, aluminum, steel, and titanium. However, the vast majority of triathlon bikes are constructed from either carbon fiber or aluminum and, because of this, the following discussion will focus on these two materials only.

The most popular frame material used today is carbon fiber. Carbon fiber can be manipulated to produce an extremely light frame that is stiff yet comfortable. The carbon fibers can be arranged to limit horizontal movement while allowing small vertical displacement to occur. The carbon fiber arrangement allows the frame to be stiff during a sprint and provides vibration dampening so that road vibrations are lessened, making for a more comfortable ride. These properties produce a frame that has little flex when power is applied to the pedals. Carbon fiber also allows manufacturers to produce tube shapes, which improves aerodynamics. Carbon fiber has a

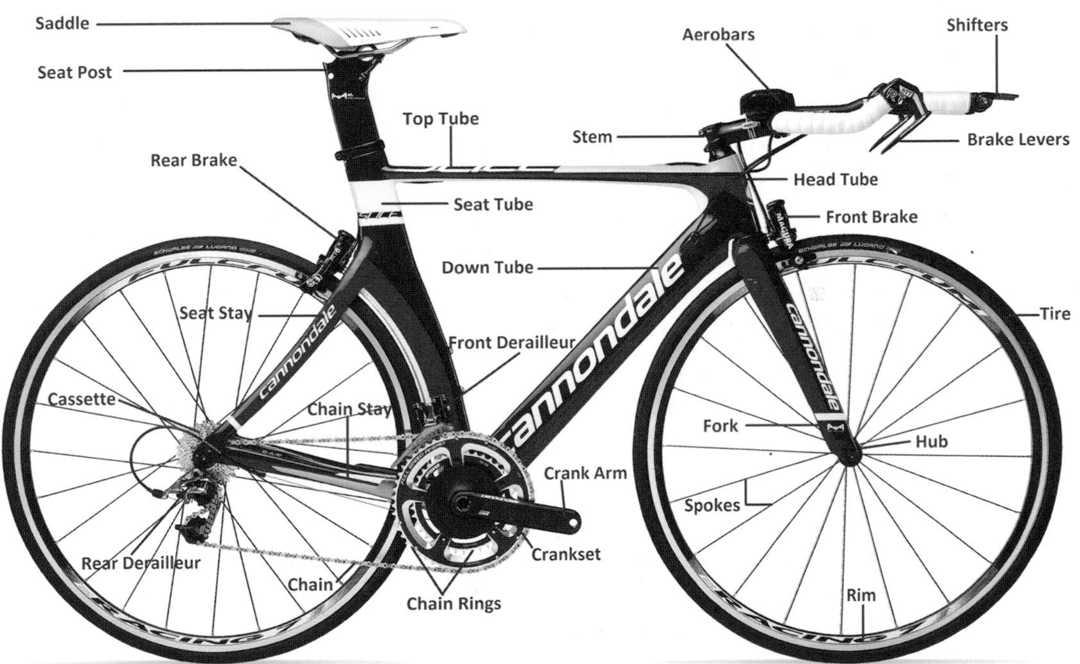

Anatomy of the bike *Cannondale® is used by permission from Cycling Sports Group*

longer fatigue life in relation to any other frame material. The downside to carbon fiber is that the price of the frame is more expensive to cover the higher manufacturing costs.

Aluminum bikes are a great choice for those on a budget. If worked correctly, aluminum is light and provides a fast stiff ride. The stiffness of the aluminum frame will easily transfer road vibrations and can make for a bone-jarring ride. However, with the addition of a carbon seat post, handlebar, and fork, an aluminum frame can ride as smoothly as a carbon frame. A well-made aluminum frame can outperform a cheaply made carbon frame and may be a better choice.

Aerobars

Aerobars are designed to place the triathlete in an aerodynamic position, reducing drag and increasing performance. When looking at the triathlete and bike as a unit, the triathlete makes up the largest percentage of the frontal area. Aerobars lower the triathlete from a more upright position and bring the arms in, both of which improve aerodynamics. Placing a triathlete into aerobars greatly decreases drag and significantly increases performance. Obtaining a proper aerodynamic position with the use of aerobars will be discussed in Chapter 8.

Aerobars come either as clip-ons or as a one-piece unit. *Profile Design*

Aerobars come in two main categories: clip-on and one-piece. Clip-on aerobars are designed to attach to either a road-style drop bar or a triathlon/time trial–specific bar, commonly referred to as a base bar, cow horn bar, bull horn bar, or wing bar.

If you are racing on a road bike, consider purchasing a set of clip-on aerobars to improve aerodynamics and performance. One-piece aerobars reduce weight, but slightly decrease your ability to adjust the aerobars for optimal

Base bars can be purchased in a traditional or wing design. *Profile Design*

comfort. They also are typically more expensive than clip-on aerobars and a separate base bar.

Component Groups

A component group consists of the derailleurs, brakes, brake levers, shift levers, crankset, bottom bracket, and rear cassette. There are three main manufacturers that currently provide bicycle components: Shimano, SRAM, and Campagnolo.

Each manufacturer produces different levels of component groups, starting with an entry-level group and ending with a professional-level group. As the performance level increases the reliability increases, weight decreases, and price increases. Typically the mid-tier group provides the best compromise on weight, performance, and price. Before buying research the current

Component groups come in different performance levels. *Cannondale® is used by permission from Cycling Sports Group*

reviews on each tier to determine the brand and level of component group right for you. Many budget-conscious triathletes will purchase a nicer frame with lower-level components. This allows them to upgrade components as they progress in the sport and as their individual budget allows.

Wheel Sets

There are two basic categories of wheel sets used by triathletes: training wheel sets and race wheel sets. Most people train and race on the wheel sets that came with their bike. However, some individuals will have two wheel sets, one designated for racing and the other for training.

Training Wheel Sets

Training wheel sets tend to be heavier, more durable, and less expensive in relation to race wheel sets. These wheel sets are used for everyday training and typically have a solid strong rim and a high spoke count that adds to the longevity of the wheel. While the weight of training wheels is typically considered in a negative manner (the lighter the better), it could also be considered in a positive light. If your wheel is heavier during training rides, then it will require a greater amount of energy compared to riding the same route with a lighter wheel set. Naturally, the added weight would not be beneficial for race day. While optimizing aerodynamics in triathlon is important, it is not a requirement for training wheels.

Training wheel sets are used in your everyday training. *Profile Design*

Race Wheel Sets

The point of having a separate set of race wheels is to improve performance on race day. Due to the cost, many people choose to have a training wheel set to decrease the risk of damaging their race wheels on a training day. Race wheels should be aerodynamic and lightweight—the rim will be light and there will be a lower spoke count in relation to a training wheel set. While the weight reduction is ideal for race day performance, it negatively impacts durability. This does not mean that race wheels are flimsy, but that they cannot handle the everyday abuse that training wheels can.

For triathlon bikes, race wheels with carbon fiber rims are common. A deep rim wheel is typically chosen for the front. The rear wheel can either be a deep rim wheel or a disc wheel. While a rear disc wheel optimizes aerodynamics, there are a couple of drawbacks. The first is that a rear disc wheel is heavier than a similar-level deep rim wheel. The other is that on windy days crosswinds will negatively impact handling. This is doubly true for lighter triathletes.

Race wheels are lightweight and aerodynamic. *Profile Design*

Disc wheels optimize aerodynamics by reducing drag. *Profile Design*

Tires: Tubular versus Clincher

One of the considerations when purchasing a wheel set is whether to go with tubular or clincher tires. The decision will be based on intended use, budget, and personal preference, but the type of rim on the wheel set will determine the type of tire used with the wheel set (they are not interchangeable).

The most commonly used wheel sets have clincher tires. A clincher tire has a separate tire and inner tube. The tire will have a bead that sits under the lip on the clincher rim, and the inner tube sits inside the tire. There are various benefits to using a clincher tire. First, at any given performance level, the tire is relatively inexpensive compared to a tubular tire. Second, it is much easier to change a tire or fix a flat on clinchers. Third, you will have a large and more readily available selection of clincher tires. The drawback to clinchers is that, at any given performance level, the wheel rim of a clincher will be slightly heavier than a tubular wheel rim and the inflation pressure of the tire will also be much lower.

A tubular tire, also referred to as a glue-on tire, sew up tire, or traditional tubeless tire (even though there is a tube sewn into the casing), consists of a tire casing with a tube sewn into the casing. Because tubular tires do not have beads to interlock with the rim, they must be glued on. This process, while not difficult, can be a pain and time consuming, although the recent introduction of glue tape has made this process much easier and less messy. Tubular tires are typically only used on race wheel sets due to the difficulty of changing and repairing the tires as well as the expense. There are various advantages to tubeless tires: There is no risk of a pinch flat, which can occur with clincher tires. And tubeless tires can be inflated to higher pressures, yet run at lower pressures when conditions require it.

A third option, tubeless tires, was introduced recently, but has yet to really take off. Just as the name indicates, there is no tube. The tire bead interlocks with the specialized rim and then inflates to lock in place. One of the problems with tubeless tires is that it takes high PSI to lock the bead to the rim.

Bike Fit

Once you purchase a bike, you will need to have it fit to your specific body type. Proper bike fit is vital for injury prevention, performance, and comfort. In this section I will discuss basic bike fit for triathlon. Keep in mind that it is extremely difficult to fit yourself on a bike; you will need assistance. An improper fitting session will result in an improper fit, so it is important to either know how to fit or seek out an expert. The guidelines provided offer a good basic fit.

Most good shops provide a bike fit at no charge when you purchase your bike. If a shop will not take the time or make the effort to fit you on your bike, then you should consider visiting another shop.

Through this process the fit expert may need to swap out parts, typically the stem or seat post, to optimize fit. Many triathlon / time trial bikes have specific shaped seat posts that come in different lengths. Most shops keep extra stems and seat posts on hand so that alterations can be made during the fitting process. They should change the parts out at no cost to you, unless you request an upgrade.

Performance versus Comfort

In an attempt to improve performance, triathletes will adjust their bike fit to assume the most aerodynamic position possible. On the surface this makes sense due to the fact that aerodynamics has such a large impact on energy requirement at any given speed. Many professional triathletes and cyclists spend a lot of money and time in a wind tunnel to optimize their aerodynamic position to gain seconds over their competitors.

However, an optimal aerodynamic position does not always lead to increased performance, especially for new triathletes. An optimal aerodynamic position places the triathlete low and forward. As a beginner you may not possess the flexibility, strength, and bike-handling skills necessary to assume this position, and you may actually see a decrease in your bike performance when an aggressive aerodynamic position is adopted. Work on assuming a cycling position that improves aerodynamics yet is still relatively comfortable. Consider starting with a more upright aero position and slowly work your way into a lower position as your strength and flexibility increases.

Handling a bike from aerobars has a completely different feel than riding on road handlebars and takes a while to become accustomed to. So even if you have the flexibility to assume a more aggressive aerodynamic position, you may not be comfortable riding in that position until you increase your bike-handling skills.

The bottom line? Choose a cycling position that allows optimal aerodynamics and comfort for your current level of fitness and flexibility.

Frame Size

One of the most important aspects of bike fit is fitting the correct frame size. The anthropometrics of the triathlete cannot be altered to fit the bike, so therefore the bike must be altered to fit the triathlete. However, the bike can only be altered within a limited range, which is predetermined by frame size and geometry. If the frame is too small or too large, you will be unable to achieve a proper fit.

There are various generic formulas for estimating frame size. Most of these formulas will get you in the ballpark, but are not overly accurate. The best way to determine frame size is to have the bike properly fit to you. Or, have a manufacturer take detailed measurements for a custom fit frame (which does not negate the detailed bike fit).

Crank Arm Length

Crank arm length (see photo on page 21) is measured in millimeters and is engraved on the back of most crank arms. If the crank arm is not marked, simply measure from the center of the bottom bracket to the center of the pedal axle to determine length. The length is dependent on bike frame. The most common crank arm lengths are 170, 172.5, and 175 mm.

Because crank arm lengths on stock bikes are proportional to frame size, for most triathletes there is no need to alter the crank arm length. Consult with a professional bike fitter prior to altering length. An improper crank arm length can lead to injury and decreased performance.

Cleat Position

Clipless pedal systems consist of the pedal and a shoe cleat that allows you to lock into the pedal while cycling. When using clipless pedal systems, you must properly position the cleat in order to prevent injury and optimize performance. The first step is to determine the fore and aft alignment of the cleat. Cleats should be positioned so that the metatarsophalangeal joint (MTP), commonly referred to as the ball of the foot, is centered over the pedal axle when the clip is engaged with the shoe. Most cleats have a mark on the side to easily line up the cleat with the MTP joint. It has recently become popular

The ball of the foot should be centered on the pedal axle. *Milay Galvez/Kestrel Bicycles*

to move the cleat back as far as possible and sometimes even drill holes in the shoes to move the cleat even farther back. There is currently no research to support this practice and I do not recommend it. However, if you have larger than average feet you may want to consider moving the cleat back slightly, placing the MTP joint just in front of the pedal axle. This will relieve stress on the Achilles tendon and ligaments on the bottom of the foot.

The next step is to adjust the medial and lateral alignment of the cleat. The cleat should be centered on the shoe. Clipless pedal systems possess enough float (amount of rotation allowed by the pedal without the cleat disengaging from the pedal) so that there is typically no need to alter medial and lateral alignment away from center. However, in extreme cases of internal or external rotation, alteration to cleat alignment should be considered.

Triathletes with severe inversion or eversion of the feet should consider visiting a fit specialist to determine if cleat wedges are needed. Cleat wedges adjust for inversion or eversion, bringing the feet closer to a neutral position on the pedal. Keep in mind that improperly placed cleat wedges can cause more harm than good.

Saddle Adjustment

Now that the foot is properly positioned on the pedal, it is time to adjust the saddle. Adjustment of the saddle should focus on saddle tilt, saddle height, and saddle fore and aft positions.

First, adjust saddle tilt. On a road bike you will want to keep the saddle tilt level. However, when riding in an aerodynamic position on a triathlon bike, a level saddle may be somewhat uncomfortable and may need to be tilted slightly, nose down. If the saddle is tilted too far down, you will continually slide down to the nose of the saddle and then push back along the seat, which can lead to chafing and saddle sores. If the saddle is tilted too far up, then the nose of the saddle may apply unnecessary pressure to the groin area. Begin the fit with a level saddle and then make adjustments as needed to obtain a comfortable fit. Use a bubble level to determine if the saddle is level.

Next, set saddle height. While there are various methods suggested for determining saddle height in the lay literature, use of a 25- to 35-degree knee angle has been supported in the scientific literature. While that is the recommended safe range for the knee angle, stay between 25 to 30 degrees to optimize performance and injury prevention. This knee angle can also be referred to as "25 to 30 degrees of knee flexion."

To measure knee angle you will need a goniometer (a device used to measure joint angles in degrees), which can be purchased from a medical supply store for approximately $15. Begin by placing the bike in a stationary trainer. Mount the bike and pedal until you are comfortable on the saddle. Once you are comfortable stop pedaling, with the crank arm perpendicular to the floor in the six o'clock position and the pedal parallel to the ground. Center the goniometer over the lateral femoral condyle (located at the knee) with the stationary end of the goniometer pointing down and centered on the lateral malleolus (the ankle bone). Rotate the other end of the goniometer until is pointing up and centered on the greater trochanter of the femur (at the hip joint). It is important to correctly locate these bony landmarks to properly measure joint angle. After measuring joint angle with the goniometer, adjust seat height up or down until the appropriate knee angle is obtained. Take two to three measurements to ensure accuracy.

A 25-degree knee angle is considered optimal for performance and injury prevention.
Gary Eippert

Plumb line should fall about 1 centimeter in front of the pedal axle. *Gary Eippert*

Finally, adjust the saddle fore and aft. For this step you will need a plumb line, which can be purchased from your local hardware store for about $2. Pedal until you feel comfortable and then stop, with the crank arms parallel to the ground and the right leg in the three o'clock position. From the right leg drop the plumb line from the tibial tuberosity (just below the kneecap). The plumb line should be centered over the pedal axle for road bike setup. However, for triathlon setup, the plumb line should fall 1 to 2 centimeters in front of the pedal axle. Adjust saddle fore and aft position until the plumb line falls between the recommended 1 to 2 centimeters. Moving the seat forward will effectively lower the saddle and moving the seat back effectively raises the saddle—if the saddle was adjusted significantly during this step go back and measure saddle height and adjust accordingly.

Aerobars

Placement of the aerobars is crucial for determining comfort, handling, and aerodynamics. The four areas of adjustment that must be addressed are: height of aerobars, arm pad placement fore and aft, width of arm pad placement, and bar extension. There are two key factors to consider when adjusting your aerobars. The first is bike handling. If the recommended position compromises bike handling, make alterations to the position that increase your ability to properly control the bike. The second factor is comfort. If the position makes you too uncomfortable, then make alterations until a compromise is reached between aerodynamics, comfort, and performance.

Your aero position should not only improve aerodynamics but be comfortable as well.
Gary Eippert

Aerobar height is adjusted by altering stack height (headset spacers) and arm pad height (if adjustable on your model). The drop from your saddle to your aerobars should allow you to assume a comfortable aerodynamic position, with your back somewhat flat, not rounded.

The stem length should be adjusted so that the arm pads of the aerobar begin approximately 8 centimeters from the elbow. If the arm pads are too far back, you will hit your knees on the pads when pealing out of the saddle while climbing or sprinting. There should be approximately an 80 to 95 degree bend in the elbow when in this position. Next, adjust the aerobar extension bars. If the extensions can be shortened or lengthened, adjust them so that shifters are located at the hands while riding in the aerobars. This will allow you to shift in the aerobars without having to reach forward. Finally, adjust the extension bars so that they run parallel to the ground.

Video Analysis

In recent years use of video analysis systems, such as MaxTRAQ, for bike fit has become more prevalent. Video analysis systems use high speed cameras to record the triathlete while in motion on the bike. The bike fitter then analyzes specific joint angles and adjusts fit accordingly. The recommended angles for stationary measurements will have to be altered during a dynamic bike fit with a video analysis system.

MaxTRAQ software allows you to use 2D video analysis during a bike fit session.
Gary Eippert

Record Fit

Once you have your bike appropriately adjusted to your body and riding style, record your fit. This will allow you to keep track of your bike measurements for future reference, and to make adjustments to your bike if the saddle slips down or you purchase a new bike.

Keep a copy of the geometry chart for your specific bike. This will allow you to compare the geometry of your current bike and a new bike. Next, record the key measurements of your bike fit:

Saddle height: Most commonly measured from the center of the pedal axle to the top of the saddle with the crank arm in the six o'clock position. However it can also be measured from the center of the bottom bracket to the top of the saddle.

Saddle fore and aft: Distance measured from the tibial tuberosity of the forward knee to the center of the pedal axle with the crank arms parallel to the ground.

Cockpit length: Measured from the front of the saddle to the center of the aerobars.

Drop: Measure the drop in height from the top of the saddle to the top of the aero pads using a level and tape measure.

Aerobar setup: Measure aero pad placement and extension length.

Other Gear

Helmet

One of the most important pieces of equipment that you can purchase is your helmet. Eventually you will crash your bike. Helmets are required at all USAT-sanctioned events and some events even require a helmet inspection at race check-in. You can even be penalized for riding your bike from your car to the start of the race without wearing a helmet.

Aerodynamic helmets are foil shaped in order to reduce drag and increase performance. *Gary Eippert Rudy Project*

Helmets are categorized as aerodynamic and non-aerodynamic. Aerodynamic helmets are foil shaped to optimize aerodynamics, allowing the air to flow smoothly over the shape and reduce turbulence at the trail edge. In order to optimize air flow over the helmet, there are very few vent holes, making the helmet hot on warm days. Most triathletes who have an aerodynamic helmet also possess a non-aero helmet for training, which has more vents for cooling and is typically more comfortable and less expensive.

Shoes and Pedals

Clipless pedals are used to lock your shoe in place while pedaling. A cleat, which is specific to the model of cycling pedal, is attached to the bottom of a rigid cycling shoe using screws. This cleat locks into place when force is applied downward into the pedal and prevents you from pulling the foot straight up and out during the pedal cycle. To disengage from the pedal, you must twist your heel away from the bike.

The shoe and pedal combination provides an interlocking platform that will increase overall performance. Economy increases—requiring less energy per pedal stroke—due to the ability of the leg to unweight during the upstroke of the pedal cycle and improved overall pedal technique. The increased interaction of the cycling shoe and pedal provides a more stable platform for power production and transfer to the pedal, and the solid connection to the bike increases road feel and bike-handling skills.

Most new bikes don't come with pedals because there is such a large selection of pedal styles from which to choose. There are a few things to consider when purchasing pedals: engagement, disengagement, and float. While some will argue that engagement and disengagement with the shoe are better with one style as opposed to another, ease of engagement and disengagement is more a function of practice. You will become accustomed to the style you choose. To engage (clip into) the pedal, place the front of the cleat into the front of the pedal and push your heel down. To disengage (unclip), twist your heel away from the bike. Prior to riding in clipless pedals for the first time practice clipping in and out of the pedals by placing your bike in a trainer.

Float refers to the distance traveled prior to the cleat disengaging from the pedal, measured in degrees. This allows your foot to naturally rotate during the pedal cycle. Too much or too little float can lead to the development of overuse injuries. Float varies by brand and model. Choose a model that provides the right amount of float for your individual biomechanics. Most pedals allow for adjustment to float.

Pedals cost from $60 to $600 and vary by brand and model. You will need to purchase clipless pedals that best fit your budget, needs, and comfort.

Once you have determined the pedal and cleat system that you would like to use, you will need to choose a pair of cycling shoes. Be sure to pick a shoe that provides not only a stiff sole and secure closure straps, but is also comfortable. The cost of cycling shoes ranges from about $70 to over $400.

Clothing

While triathlon suits are ideal for racing, you may wish to consider purchasing cycling jerseys and shorts for training. Cycling tops differ from triathlon tops. Cycling jerseys have three large pockets in the back of the jersey, used for carrying food and extra supplies. This is ideal especially for longer rides. Cycling jerseys also have sleeves whereas most triathlon tops are sleeveless. In the event of a crash, the material of the cycling jersey will offer some form of protection against road rash. Cycling jerseys also tend to be more breathable and provide greater cooling potential during a ride on a hot day.

A good pair of cycling shorts can make the difference between a nice, enjoyable ride and a pain-filled torture test. The chamois in a cycling short is thicker and more comfortable than the one found in a triathlon short. However, chamois that is too thick will feel uncomfortable. A good chamois is designed so that it is thicker in the parts that contact the saddle and thinner in other areas so that it does not bunch up between your legs.

Also consider some all-weather gear for year-round training. Some items to consider purchasing are: rain jacket, wind vest, cold weather jacket, winter cycling tights, arm and leg warmers, cap, gloves, and shoe covers. There is nothing worse than being miserably cold and wet on a ride.

Cycle Computers

It is vital that you use a cycle computer to assist in your bike training. They range from $20 to over $500, depending on the functions of the system. The basic $20 systems provide current/average/maximum speed, odometer, and trip distance, whereas the top-end systems also provide additional functions, such as power, heart rate, training zones, cadence, GPS data, and the ability to download this information to a home computer for evaluation. When purchasing a cycle computer, get at least the minimum of

A cycling computer is a very valuable training tool.

the basic functions plus cadence ($30–$40). Compare the costs of purchasing a cycle computer and heart monitor separately or within the same device. Polar produces a GPS and heart rate system that you can use both cycling and running and later download the data for evaluation of your training session. Heart rate monitors will be discussed in more detail in the following chapter.

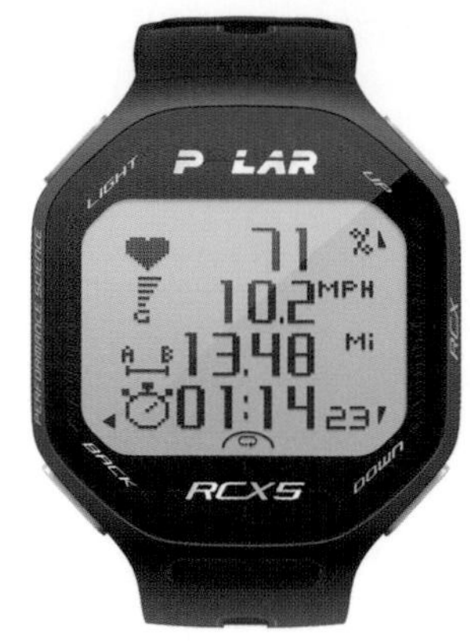

Polar provides a cycle computer that can also read heart rate. *Polar*

Power Meters

One of the best measurements of training intensity in cycling is power (discussed in greater detail in Chapter 8). There are four basic methods of measuring power: at the bottom bracket (Ergomo Sport), at the crank set (SRM & Quarq), at the rear hub (Power Tap), and at the pedals (Polar Keo Power Pedals). Each one of these systems has benefits and drawbacks. The Polar Keo Power Pedals, for example, measure power output at the pedal, which allows the users to more easily change measurement systems from one bike to the next.

While expensive, power meters are ideal for determining training intensity. *Polar*

While power meters are an excellent tool for determining training intensity, they are expensive ($1,500 to over $3,000). They also require more understanding and effort to properly incorporate into training. Prior to purchasing a power meter, look into what is required to incorporate the tool into your training program and how to use the system. While it does take a little effort to properly use, it can pay off tremendously for those who want to be competitive.

Bike Maintenance

It is extremely important to keep your bike maintained in order to increase its longevity, ensure optimal performance, and save money on repairs. Of all the equipment that you purchase, the bike is the most expensive and often the most neglected. Something as simple as cleaning the bike will add years to the components. This section is not designed to offer an in-depth guide to bike maintenance; instead it focuses on basic maintenance and cleaning of the bike. Purchase an in-depth bike maintenance book to learn more.

Cleaning

Cleaning is one of the most overlooked bike maintenance procedures. While it is not necessary to completely break down and wash your bike after every ride, it is important to at least wipe it down. Sweat is very corrosive to metal. Wiping the bike with a wet cloth will remove the sweat and protect your bike. Periodically and after wet, grimy rides, the bike should be completely washed.

To conduct a complete wash you will need the following: bucket of soapy water, soft sponge, soft bristle brush, water hose, and chain cleaning brush. Do not use a high-powered setting on the hose to wash your bike. This could lead to water being forced into areas that are greased to reduce friction. If water is forced into these areas grease will be removed, friction will increase, and parts will wear prematurely. Avoid spraying directly into the bottom bracket area, headset area, and wheel hubs.

First, clean the drive train, as this will be the dirtiest area. Start by cleaning the chain. You can use an old toothbrush or a tool specifically designed for chain cleaning. While soapy water will work, consider using a degreaser for this portion of the cleaning. Use a soft, bristled brush to clean the front chain rings and rear derailleur pulleys and a long, bristled brush to clean the rear cassette. After washing the rest of the bike, remember to dry the chain by running it through a dry cloth and then lubricate with an appropriate bicycle chain lube. Cleaning and lubing the chain will greatly prolong the life of your drive train. A dirty drive train prematurely wears down the rear cassette teeth, front chain ring teeth, and the chain itself.

Once the drive train has been cleaned, wash and rinse the rest of the bike. Upon completion dry the bike thoroughly. Though it may seem tedious, try to remove any water standing inside the bolt heads as they tend to rust over time.

Maintenance Procedures

Listed below are some simple procedures that will help you complete basic maintenance on your bike. You can also use the Internet to find instructional videos on maintenance. Park Tools' website provides very good instructional videos on basic bicycle repair (www.parktool.com).

Removing and Replacing Wheels

To remove the front wheel, first extend the brake calipers by raising the brake quick-release lever in order to allow the tire to slip between the brake pads. Next, push down on the skewer to release tension on the wheel axle. On the opposite side of the skewer, loosen the tension-adjusting nut located on the opposite end of the skewer. You do not have to remove the tension-adjusting nut, only loosen the nut until there is enough space for the skewer to clear the tabs located on the fork.

The quick release lever allows you to remove the tire from the bike.

To remove the rear wheel, shift the chain to the smallest cog on the rear cassette. This lines the rear derailleur up with the smallest cog and aids in removing the wheel. Next, open the brake calipers and loosen the skewer as described with the front wheel. For bikes with vertical drop-outs, the wheel will lower once the skewer is loosened. Remove the chain from around the cassette and the wheel is free. For bikes with horizontal drop-outs, pull the chain toward the rear and clear of the cassette, and pull the wheel to the rear until it is free of the drop-out and the chain.

Brakes

Brakes are typically low maintenance and require only slight adjustment from time to time. The brake calipers should be centered so that there is equal spacing between the rim and brake shoe on both sides of the wheel. When the brake caliper is off center, the simplest thing to do is to center the caliper with your hand. Once centered tighten the bolt on the opposite side of the fork or seat stay while holding the caliper centered. This is easier if you

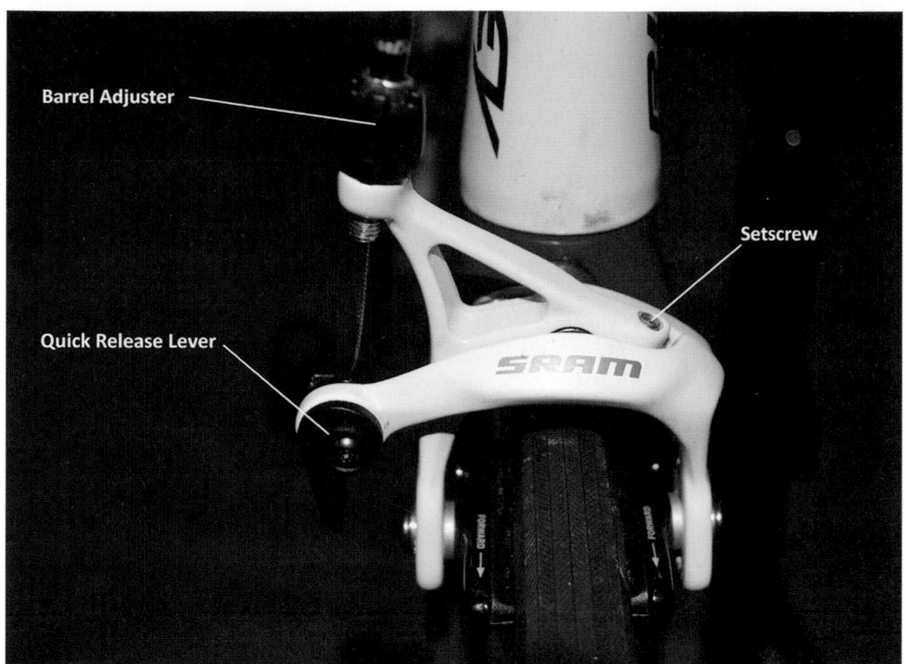

Brake caliper anatomy

have a thin cone wrench to hold the caliper centered. The brake calipers can also be centered by using the set screw located on the caliper.

Now that the brakes are centered, check to ensure that there is about 3 mm of clearance between the brake pad and the rim on both sides. To make small adjustments use the barrel adjuster located on the caliper. To make larger adjustments loosen the cable anchor bolt holding the cable in place. Next, adjust the calipers until there is about 3 mm of clearance on both sides, pull the cable tight, and tighten the cable anchor bolt.

Over time brake pads wear out and need to be replaced. There are two basic types of brake pads. The first type is a one-piece brake pad and shoe that unbolts from the calipers. The second type of brake pad fits into a metal brake shoe that bolts to the caliper.

To change the pads, unbolt the brake pad from the caliper. With the first type throw the entire pad away. After removing the second type loosen the retaining bolt on the brake shoe and slide the brake pad out. Replace the old pad with a new one and tighten the retaining bolt. From this point on installing is the same regardless of the type of brake pad.

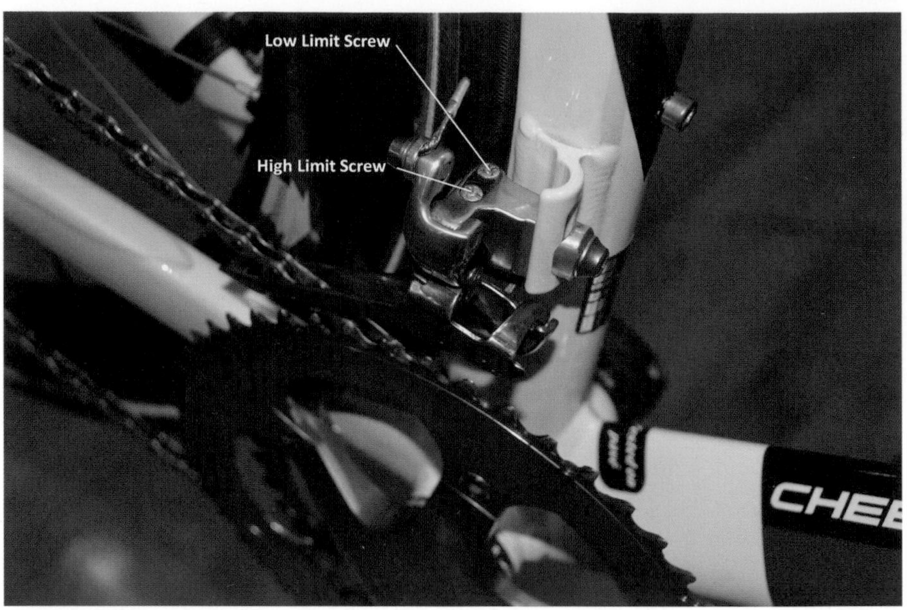

Front derailleur limit screws

Rear derailleur limit screws

Derailleurs

One of the more common issues that you will run across is misaligned derailleurs leading to poor shifting. There is nothing more annoying than being unable to smoothly shift from one gear to another, especially during a race. Most people are intimidated when it comes to derailleur adjustments. However, if you know the basics, adjustment is really easy.

Once the front derailleur is properly set, you probably will not have any problems with it. First, be sure your low- and high-gear limit screws are correctly set. The low- and high-gear limit screws are not used to adjust shifting. Instead, they are used to set the inner and outer limits of derailleur movement. If the low-gear limit screw is not set correctly, then you will drop the chain toward the frame when shifting to the small ring from the large. If the high-gear limit screw is not set correctly, then the chain can move past the large ring and off when shifting from the small to large ring.

Place the bike in a stand so that you can turn the crank arms and shift gears as you work. First, shift the chain to the small chain ring on the front and the largest cog on the rear cassette. Release the shift cable by loosening the cable retention bolt so that there will be no tension on the front derailleur during this process. In this position there should be about a 1 mm gap between the inner derailleur plate and the chain. If there is too much or too little of a gap, you will need to adjust the low-gear limit screw. Locate the low-gear limit screw (typically marked with an "L") on the front derailleur. Using a screwdriver, loosen or tighten the low-gear limit screw until a gap of 1 mm is obtained. Only use small turns of the screwdriver as it does not take much to move the derailleur. Attach the derailleur cable to the derailleur by sliding the cable behind the cable retention bolt, pulling out slack and tightening the bolt.

Next, set the outer limit with the high-gear limit screw. Shift the chain to the largest gear on the front and the smallest gear in the back. Again, you should have about a 1 mm gap between the outer derailleur plate and the chain. Locate the high-gear limit screw (typically labeled with an "H") and adjust until a 1 mm gap is obtained. Now shift back and forth between the chain rings on the crank set. The chain should move quickly and smoothly.

Problems more frequently occur with the rear derailleur adjustment and shifting. As with the front derailleur, start by setting the limit screws. First, shift the chain onto the large chain ring in the front and the smallest cog on the rear cassette. Loosen the cable retention bolt and remove the cable. The guide pulley of the rear derailleur should line up perfectly with the rear cog. The high-gear limit screw on the rear derailleur prevents the chain from being thrown off the smallest cog and into the frame. Adjust the high-gear limit screw until the guide pulley is correctly aligned. Pull the slack out of the rear derailleur cable, place it behind the retaining bolt and tighten. Next, shift the chain to the small ring on the front and the large on the back. With your hand push the derailleur toward the spokes of the wheel to ensure that it is up against the limit screw. The guide pulley should now line up perfectly with the largest cog. If it does not, adjust the low-gear limit screw until it does. The low-gear limit screw is used to prevent the chain and derailleur from going into the spokes.

After the limit screws are set, shift up and down the cogs on the rear cassette and ensure that the chain transfers smoothly from one cog to the next. If the chain does not shift smoothly, then adjust cable tension by turning the barrel adjuster located on the rear derailleur until the chain moves smoothly up and down the cogs. If you are still having problems shifting, check to make sure that the rear derailleur bolt that holds the derailleur to the frame is tight.

Chain

Over time chains wear and need to be replaced. Depending on the quality of the chain, how well the chain is cared for, and riding conditions, a typical chain will need to be replaced every 1,000 to 2,000 miles. Regularly cleaning and lubing increases the longevity of the chain and the rest of the drive train. Use a chain gauge to determine wear on your chain and replace once the chain has lengthened due to wear.

Use a chain tool to remove or replace a chain pin.

To remove a worn chain from your bike, remove the link pin using a chain tool. Center the chain tool over the link pin and then tighten the handle until the pin is pushed out the other side of the link. Next, back off the chain tool, separate the link, and remove the old chain. If the chain has a removable master link, then just remove this link. When purchasing a new chain, be sure you purchase the correct size.

A reusable master link can be used to connect the chain.

The new chain will have to be sized for your specific bike. There are various methods for determining chain length. The first is to line the old and new chain up side by side and count links to ensure you replace the old chain with a correctly sized chain.

In the second method, run the chain over the big ring in the front and the small ring in the back and through both derailleurs. Pull the chain together applying tension to the rear derailleur until the two pulleys are aligned in a vertical line underneath the small cog. Align the chain and mark it to remove the excess links. If the new chain is connected with a pin and chain tool, make sure that you have a roller end and a plate end. If the new chain uses a master link, then ensure that you have two roller ends and a gap for the master link. Use the chain tool to break the chain where it was marked and then connect the two ends of the chain. The new chain will come with either a new pin or master link to connect the chain. If you are using a pin, you will need to place the pin into the pin hole and use the chain tool to push the pin all the way through. Once you feel the pin seat into position, then carefully break off the excess pin. The pin is scored and designed to be broken off. If your chain came with a master link, then connect the two roller ends using the master link.

Tires and Tubes

One of the unfortunate facts about cycling is that tubes puncture and tires become worn and need to be replaced. Tires should be replaced when they become worn and lose traction, when any type of bulge or deformation appears, and when gashes occur. You should conduct a quick inspection of your tires prior to any ride. The tube should be replaced any time it does not properly hold air. Do not keep riding on a tube that has a slow leak, because at some point it will become a large leak. It is normal for tubes to lose some pressure overnight, so check pressure and pump up the tires prior to every ride. An improperly inflated tire can lead to a pinch flat.

The steps to replacing a tube or tire are virtually the same. First, deflate the tire. Next, use tire levers to separate one side of the tire from the rim. Place the tire lever between the tire and wheel rim and pry the tire bead up and over the rim. Place the hook on the end of the tire lever around a spoke. Move around the rim about 2 inches and use another tire lever in the same manner. From this point on the tire should easily roll up and over the rim. If not then use a third tire lever. Next, remove the tube from the tire. If you are replacing the tube due to a flat, then discard it. If you are not replacing it, set it to the side. At this point you will have the tube out and the tire half on and off the rim. If you are replacing a punctured tube, carefully run your fingers along the inside of the tire looking for any sharp protruding objects, removing any that you find. If you are replacing the tire, remove it completely by pulling the remaining tire bead up and over the rim. Next place one bead of the new tire over the rim. At this point you will have a tire that is half on and half off the wheel regardless of whether or not you replaced the tire.

Tire levers are used to assist in removing the tire bead from the rim.

The next step is to place a small amount of air in the tube, giving it shape. Insert the valve stem through the hole located on the rim of the wheel and then place the tube inside the tire. Once the tube has been fully placed inside the tire, begin pushing the tire bead back over the wheel rim. Start at the valve and work your way around the tire in both directions at the same time. Throughout this process make sure the tube does not get caught between the tire bead and the rim. Once your hands meet on the opposite side, push the last section up and over the rim, which can be somewhat difficult. Resist the urge to use the tire levers to force the bead over the rim as this will typically damage the tube and you will have to start all over with a new tube. Instead just keep working the bead up and over. Once the tire is fully on the rim, check that the tube is up inside the tire. If any of the tube is caught between the tire and the rim, it will rupture when you add air. The last step is to inflate to the desired PSI. The maximal PSI varies from tire to tire, but is typically around 110. The maximal pressure will be stamped on the side wall of the tire.

Replacement of tubular tires requires more time, patience, and skill and is beyond the scope of this entry-level book. If a tubular tire is not correctly glued to the rim, it can roll off in a curve, especially at high speeds. Ask a mechanic or other reliable source to teach you this technique prior to attempting it yourself.

Wheels

From time to time wheels will move out of true (rim becomes warped), often due to spokes loosening over many miles of riding or due to direct impact, such as riding through a pothole or over railroad tracks. When a wheel comes out of true, it will wobble from side to side as it spins and may rub against the brake, which makes it more difficult to ride or, in severe cases, impossible to ride. Learning to true your wheels will save you time and money in the long run. While not difficult, truing a wheel does require a truing stand and spoke wrench, which can be purchased at your local bike shop.

Remove the wheel from the bike and place it in a truing stand. Spin the wheel and slowly tighten the calipers of the truing stand until you hear the caliper scrape. At this point there should be sections of the wheel that move freely past the calipers and others that touch as it passes. It is also possible that one section of the wheel will make contact with the caliper on one side and another section of the wheel will make contact with the opposite caliper as it comes around. Stop the wheel at the point the caliper touches, loosen the spoke on the side of the wheel that touches, and then tighten the spoke opposite the side of the rim that touches. Only turn the spoke wrench one-quarter to one-half turn each time.

A truing stand is used to straighten (true) a wheel.

Spin the wheel to see if it clears. If it does not clear, repeat the first step. Once the rim clears tighten the caliper again until they touch and repeat the process. In most cases, it will not be possible to perfectly true a wheel, and a 1–2 mm gap between the rim and the caliper is normal.

Seat Posts

While seat posts do not require a lot of maintenance, there are a few key points to remember. Over time the seat post will slide down. So either mark your seat post or take a measurement from the center of the bottom bracket to the top of the saddle. After adjusting the seat post, always remember to tighten the seat collar bolt to the manufacturer's suggested torque. This will ensure that you do not damage the seat post or frame while minimizing the chances of the seat post slipping.

Always lubricate the seat post prior to placing in the frame. For metal seat posts that will be inserted into a metal frame, use normal bike grease. The lubrication helps prevent the seat post from becoming seized into the frame and helps keep water from entering the frame. If the frame or the seat post is composed of carbon fiber, then use a special carbon fiber grease. Never use normal bike grease on carbon.

When adjusting the seat post, make sure that the minimum insertion limit mark never shows. If it shows then purchase a longer seat post and replace the old one. Some of the newer bikes require that the seat tube of the frame be cut in order to adjust saddle height. I would highly advise visiting a specialist for a bike fit and having the specialist cut the seat tube to the proper length. If the seat tube is cut too short, the frame will be useless. Also, cutting carbon fiber requires a special blade and you will need a cutting guide to ensure a straight line.

Changing Pedals

From time to time you will need to remove your pedals. You will need either a pedal wrench, a thin wrench designed to fit between the crank arm and pedal, or a hex wrench, depending on the model of pedal on your bike. The drive side pedal is threaded normal, but the non-drive side, the left side, is reverse threaded. Always remember that turning the wrench toward the back of the bike will loosen the pedal and turning the wrench to the front of the bike will tighten the pedal, regardless of the side you are on. While it might require some torque to break a pedal free, the pedals should go on and off smoothly.

Repairs on the Road

Inevitably you will run into mechanical issues while on the road. In most cases you will be far enough from the finish line that walking back in cycling shoes will be undesirable if not close to impossible, so knowledge of some basic road repair will be helpful.

You'll need an adequate repair kit to cover all of the basic repairs you will encounter on the road. Most people choose to carry their repair kit in a saddle bag that attaches under the seat. The saddle bag should contain the following:

- Spare tube and patch kit. The patch kit is for those occasions when you have more than one flat.
- Small tire pump or CO_2 inflator. I prefer a mini-pump over a CO_2 inflator. While the pump takes longer and requires work, it is reliable and can be used more than once.
- One to three tire levers to assist in removing the tire to change a flat.
- Small multi-tool. Choose a lightweight multi-tool that contains a wide assortment of tools you will need on the road. An ideal multi-tool will have the hex wrenches you will need, chain tool, and spoke wrench.
- Master link for the chain.
- Spoke wrench.
- Cash and cell phone for emergencies.

It is a good idea to carry a basic repair kit with you on the road.

When conducting a repair on the side of the road, move as far off the road as possible. This may require you to move up or down the road from where you stopped originally. Conduct all repairs facing oncoming traffic. This allows you to observe all traffic closest to your side of the road and may give you time to get out of the way if a car swerves off the road. Conduct repairs quickly and then continue on with your training.

HAMMER
NUTRITION
HAMMER

CHAPTER THREE

Running Gear

Of the three modes of exercise that make up triathlon, running is probably the most familiar to the majority of people reading this book. While most people are familiar and comfortable with the concept of running, few have in-depth knowledge about the necessary equipment. This chapter will help you make educated decisions when purchasing running gear.

Shoes

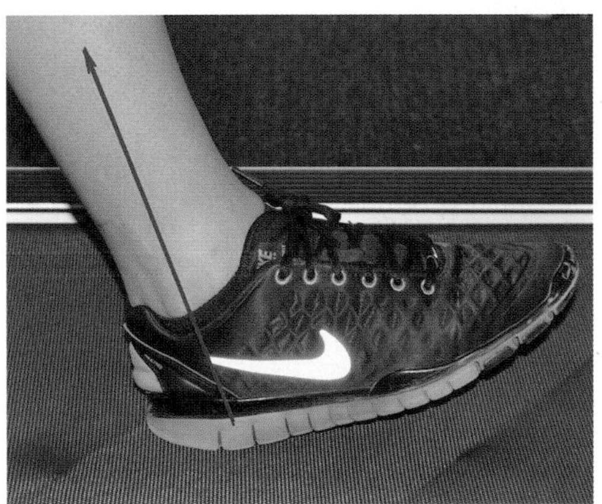

Ground reaction forces propel the body forward.

Before we go into shoe selection, it is important to discuss ground reaction forces. It is critical that you understand these forces to appreciate the importance of choosing appropriate running shoes. Ground reaction forces occur when the foot makes contact with the ground while running. Ground reaction force is equal and opposite in direction to the force applied to the ground and is based on your mass, the acceleration of gravity, and running speed.

In running, the ground reaction forces are typically two to three times your body weight, but can reach up to five times your body weight at high speeds. While this force is necessary to propel the body forward, it also must be absorbed up the kinetic chain, which is the main reason why running-related injuries occur.

The average runner runs at about 150 steps per minute and an elite runner may run at about 180 steps per minute. A 1-hour run would result

Involving kids in the sport of triathlon can be a great method for developing positive physical activity habits.

in 9,000 to 10,800 steps. These repetitive forces lead to a large amount of stress placed on the bones and joints of the body. Running shoes can assist in absorbing the impact.

The most vital piece of equipment that you will purchase for running is your shoes. A good pair of shoes can make all the difference in the world. Running in improper shoes can not only be uncomfortable, but can lead to overuse injuries that can negatively impact training. I receive a lot of training questions from beginner runners about leg pain. The typical complaint concerns lower leg pain (ankle, shin, and knee). These complaints tend to come from athletes who increase their intensity or duration too quickly, or from individuals with improper shoes.

Some common issues with shoes include:

- Using running shoes that are not designed for running, such as court shoes. Court shoes, such as basketball shoes, are designed to make quick lateral movements on a court surface whereas running shoes are designed primarily for forward movement only.
- Training in running shoes that are old and well past their usefulness.
- New running shoes that are not designed for your particular biomechanics, which can lead to overuse injuries.
- Shoes that do not fit correctly.

Choosing the Correct Shoes

When purchasing new shoes, choose shoes that best fit your needs, budget, and, most importantly, your individual anthropometrics and biomechanics. There are two key factors when choosing the right type of shoe. The first deals with the manner in which you run and the second concerns your weight.

There are three basic types of runners: neutral (also known as in line), overpronators, and supinators. In line or neutral runners follow normal running biomechanics with little variation. They typically have a normal arch and do not excessively pronate. A neutral cushion shoe is recommended for these runners. Overpronators deviate from the norm through excessive pronation (rolling in) during the midstance phase. A motion control shoe that provides medial support and is built on a straight sole is designed to best address overpronation. Individuals who supinate (run on the outside of the foot) will typically have a high arch, which forces the foot to the outside as they run. A cushioned shoe built on a curved sole is ideal for supinators.

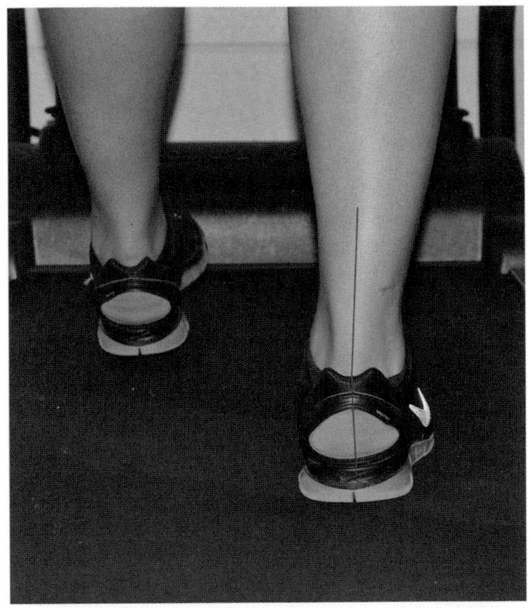

Normal pronation

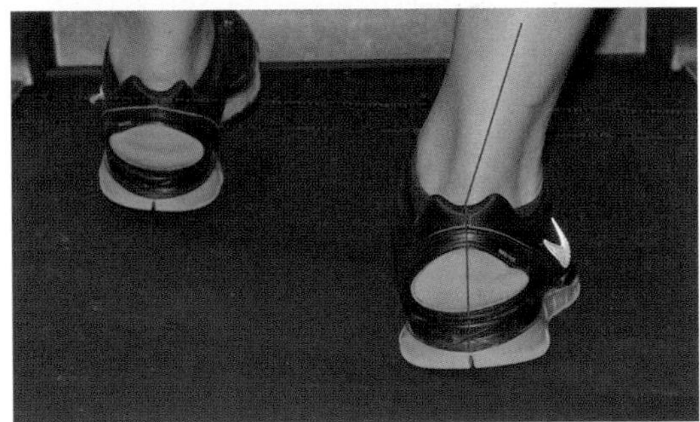

Overpronation

Barefoot or minimalist running has become popular recently. Barefoot or, more correctly termed, minimalist shoes are designed to have very little protection between the sole of your foot and the ground in order to promote "natural" running. The idea behind the theory is that the human foot was naturally designed to absorb ground reaction forces by running mid to front foot and that wearing a minimalist shoe encourages this type of running. A minimalist shoe provides greater proprioceptive feedback in order to adjust to the terrain and allows the foot more freedom of movement through the stance phase. A traditional running shoe is designed to protect against impact when the heel strikes the ground. However, because the heel is built up in the shoe it also encourages the heel to strike the ground first. A traditional shoe also has less freedom of movement during the stance phase and prevents meaningful proprioceptive feedback from ground contact. However, with a traditional shoe, you can worry less about injury due to the terrain and can concentrate more on running the race.

Although it is unclear whether the barefoot/minimalist shoes improve performance, there is an increased risk of injury when switching to these shoes. Greater stabilization will be required to run in minimalist shoes, and it will take a while for the body to adapt. I would recommend staying away from the trend, at least until enough research has been conducted to make an educated decision. If you do choose to make the switch to a minimalist shoe, make the change slowly and pay attention to how your body responds to the change.

This section was designed to give you the basic knowledge concerning the biomechanical rationale for shoe selection. Detailed running biomechanics are covered in Chapter 9. Unless you have extensive experience in this area, see a running shoe specialist, orthopedic specialist, or biomechanist to determine the shoe that will work with your biomechanics.

Fit

There are key points to look for in a proper fit. First, you should have a thumb's width between your big toe and the end of the shoe. This measurement will need to be conducted while standing. Second, with the shoes tied, the shoe should fit comfortably snug across the top of your foot (not tight). Finally, walk around to determine if the back of the shoe slips up and down on the heel of your foot. If the heel slides up and down, the shoe is too large. Also keep in mind that shoes from different brands may fit differently.

Prior to running in your new shoes, wear the shoes around the house for a few hours to determine if they are truly comfortable. This way you can return the shoes for another size or brand. Some running stores have treadmills set up and allow you to walk or run in the store prior to purchasing the shoes.

Replacing Shoes

Unfortunately running shoes wear down and must be replaced somewhat frequently. Not only does the sole wear thin and lose traction but the EVA material (the white cushioning material) becomes compressed and loses the ability to absorb ground reaction forces. The typical recommendations are to replace running shoes every 300 to 500 miles. The actual miles will vary due to the quality of the shoe, mass of the individual, intensity of the miles put on the shoes, and the conditions that the individual runs in. However, as long as the shoe is safe and comfortable there is no reason to purchase new shoes.

Where to Buy

Where you buy running shoes depends a lot on your knowledge and ability to choose the correct running shoe. If you currently know your running biomechanics (in line, overpronation, or supination) and the brand, style, and size of your shoe, then you can save a substantial amount of money by ordering online. I typically try and find closeout deals on models that are a year or two old and spend about half the money I would retail. The vast majority of the time the only difference between a model that is 1 to 2 years older and the brand new model is the color.

However, if you currently do not know the brand, style, and size of the shoe you need and possess minimal knowledge on choosing the correct running shoe, visiting a specialized running store may save you money in the long run.

A true running store will analyze your gait while you walk and run, choose a group of shoes for you to try on, ensure proper fit and comfort, reanalyze again in the chosen shoes, and then make final recommendations, often with the help of video analysis software, which can slow down the video and observe the kinematics of your run frame by frame. Local triathletes and runners should be able to tell you which stores to visit and which to stay away from.

Purchasing shoes in a specialized running store also allows you to immerse yourself in the community. Getting to know the running and triathlon community will provide you with a wealth of knowledge concerning the sport of triathlon, running, training, and local races.

Quick Laces

Taking the time to tie your shoe during transition can cost seconds, especially when fatigued. Using quick laces on your running shoes saves both time and effort. There are two basic types of quick lace systems. The first consists of a lace lock that fits onto your normal shoelaces. When using this type you will need to either cut your shoelaces shorter or attach the end of your shoelaces to the shoe in order to prevent tripping. The second type consists of an elastic shoelace and lace lock. The elastic shoelace

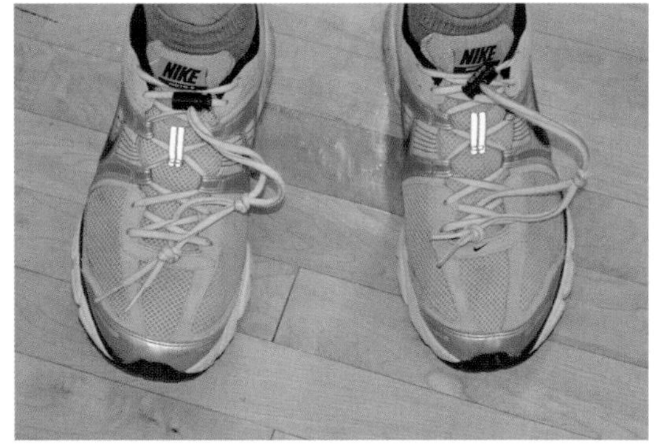

Quick laces allow you to put on and remove your running shoes quickly.

allows the lace and shoe to expand as you place the shoe on the foot. Prior to the race you pre-adjust the elastic laces and lace locks so that all you have to do is slide your feet into the shoes and start running. I prefer to use normal shoelaces and a lace lock in order to minimize movement of my foot within the shoe. Note that, with off-road running events, due to the unevenness of the terrain, normal shoelaces provide greater support in relation to elastic laces.

Clothing

The most important aspects to consider concerning clothing and running are comfort (material and fit) and environment. Avoid running in cotton shirts and shorts. Cotton is not breathable, retains water, negatively impacts heat dissipation, and can chafe. Instead, choose material made from synthetic fibers (primarily polyester) that are specifically woven in a manner that allows moisture to transfer from the skin and evaporation of sweat to occur. Nylon is another synthetic fiber commonly used in athletic attire, but does not wick moisture away in the same manner as polyester and therefore does not have the same cooling effect.

Clothing should fit comfortably and not chafe during the run. The most common places for chafing are inner thighs, under arms, nipples, and the bra area for females. Common causes of chafing are large or rough seams, rough material, and wet material repeatedly moving across the skin. Keep in mind that chafing can occur on long runs even when wearing the best clothing. To prevent chafing during long runs, use Band-Aids or an anti-chafing gel in the affected areas. Detailed information concerning chafing treatment and prevention can be found in Chapter 14.

In general clothing for running in the summer should be breathable so that heat can be easily dissipated to prevent overheating. Clothing should also be light so that it does not easily absorb heat. During the winter, clothing should be layered to wick moisture away from the skin and insulate against the cold. A common mistake is to overdress during the winter, which can cause overheating. Detailed information concerning clothing choices for training in the heat and cold is in Chapter 16.

Heart Rate Monitor

It is essential to monitor and control workout intensity during training (covered in Chapter 6), and heart rate is an excellent tool for monitoring intensity. While you can measure pulse rate with your fingers and a watch, it is not as accurate and convenient as using a heart rate monitor.

Heart rate monitors are excellent tools for monitoring and controlling intensity.

A heart rate monitor consists of a transmitter and a receiver. The transmitter fits around the thoracic region just below the pectoralis major. When placing the transmitter below the chest, make sure to center the transmitter midline. The transmitter should be tight enough to not move around, but not so tight as to be uncomfortable. The transmitter should be wetted first and placed against the skin in order to pick up the electrical impulse of the heart contractions. The receiver, typically worn on the wrist as a watch, acquires the signal from the transmitter and displays heart rate.

Heart rate monitors possess various functions that are useful for maintaining intensity and evaluating performance. They vary in price based on available functions (from $40 to over $300). An entry-level monitor that provides heart rate and time only will start at around $40. Purchase a heart rate monitor that at least has zone alarms. This will allow you to set alarms that sound when you go below (typically not a problem) or above (usually the problem) your training zone for the day. If you train in a group, you need a monitor that is coded so that you do not pick up another triathlete's heart rate as you train.

For those who are serious about training, I recommend purchasing an entry-level Garmin GPS / heart rate monitor, which provides heart rate and GPS data, which can then be downloaded after training. This monitor is less expensive than other heart rate monitors that download heart rate data only, priced currently at about $200, but it is an extremely valuable training tool. The multisport Garmin can be worn on the wrist for running and then mounted on the bike while cycling. The system is also waterproof for swimming. This allows you to not only know heart rate but also map distance during open water swims. As a coach I find the ability to download heart rate and GPS data invaluable. I can examine my athlete's heart rate in relation to alterations in grade, speed, and distance.

Details on how to use your heart rate monitor for training will be covered in Chapter 6.

Part II
TRAINING

STOP
AHEAD

CHAPTER FOUR

Basic Training Principles

This chapter covers the basic training principles that determine how you will plan and implement your training program. The body responds to stress in very predictable ways. If you understand these principles, you will make better training choices.

Training Adaptations

Training adaptations are how the body responds to the applied training stimulus over time. These adaptations can either be positive or negative depending on the type, volume, and intensity of the training stimulus. The goal of proper training is to manipulate these three factors in order to elicit a physiological response that will lead to positive training adaptations and increased performance. Incorrectly manipulating these factors can lead to improper physiological adaptations and, therefore, no alterations to performance. Alternately, it can lead to negative adaptations and subsequent decreases in performance.

Individual Differences

The principle of *individual differences* states that not every individual responds to the same training stimulus in the same manner. For example, some individuals recover quicker and can handle a higher training volume or intensity. Others may require longer recovery periods and therefore cannot handle higher volumes or frequent high-intensity bouts. There is a strong genetic component to training adaptation and performance. Current training status is also an obvious factor. Those that have been training longer will be able to handle greater volume and intensity than beginners.

Athletes and coaches will often overlook individual differences and use a generic boxed training program that does not vary based on individual progression and can often hinder progress by delaying it. Conversely, if the training program is too strenuous, it can lead to overtraining and burnout. That said, it is okay to use a boxed training program to begin with,

Understanding the basic training principles can help increase triathlon performance.

but adjustments to volume and intensity need to be made based on your response to that program.

Progressive Overload

The *progressive overload* principle states that the training stimulus needs to be continuously increased, allowing for adequate recovery between bouts, so that—ultimately—performance increases. You can increase stimulus by either increasing volume or intensity. For triathlon training, volume is increased by either increasing duration (distance or time) of training sessions or frequency (number of training sessions). Intensity is increased by increasing how hard the workout session is conducted. Volume should always be increased prior to increasing intensity. Make sure you can complete the distance before worrying about how fast you are going. Increasing intensity prior to increasing volume also increases the risk of injury.

Recovery

Too often athletes focus so much on training that they forget one of the most important components of training: recovery. Training is catabolic (molecules are broken down into smaller constituents) in nature, ultimately resulting in protein synthesis after the training bout. To optimize the body's response to the training stimuli, you must make sure that adequate recovery occurs between bouts.

Alternate hard and easy days to optimize recovery (discussed below). Monitor intensity to ensure that you don't go too hard too often. This is a common mistake made by most beginning triathletes. Focus on recovery nutrition in order to refuel and optimize protein synthesis, and make sure you get a minimum of 8 hours of good sleep every night.

Overtraining

One of the most common threats to performance is overtraining. An athlete will compete better 10 percent undertrained as opposed to 1 percent overtrained. To optimize performance, athletes continually walk the line of overtraining. Overtraining occurs when adequate recovery is not allowed between bouts and is often the result of a sudden increase in volume and/or intensity, or an accumulation of a small imbalance of recovery and training.

As an athlete, you need to be aware of how your body responds to training and know the signs and symptoms of overtraining. The common signs include:

- Multiple sessions of decreased performance. One bad day does not necessarily indicate overtraining. However, multiple days of decreased performance does indicate overtraining.
- Feeling constant fatigue.
- Bad attitude.
- A feeling of dread about training.
- Abnormal sleeping patterns.
- An increase in resting heart rate measured on multiple days. An increase on 1 day may indicate that you have not recovered from the previous day's workout or that you may be dehydrated. However, if the increase in resting heart rate persists over multiple days, it is a strong indicator of overtraining.
- Consistent overuse injuries.
- Chronic illness due to a lowered immune response.
- Abrupt changes in body composition.

Specificity of Training

Training adaptations are specific to the training stimulus applied. In simpler terms, train the body in the manner in which you would like for it to adapt. For example, as a triathlete it would not make sense for you to lift heavy weights year-round and never spend much time swimming, biking, or running. Triathlon is also an aerobic sport; therefore, the majority of training will be designed to enhance your aerobic capacity in all three of the sport's disciplines. At this level specificity of training seems fairly obvious. However, specificity of training can also apply to the not so obvious.

Specificity of training can even apply to your cycling position. You should conduct your training on the bike that you plan to race on, and if you have two bikes make sure that the setup is exactly the same for both.

Detraining

Detraining occurs when you decrease or remove the training stimulus, which leads to a decrease in performance and loss of training adaptations. Put quite simply, if you do not use it you lose it. Common reasons for detraining include injury, illness, and improper off-season training. Typically detraining occurs after 2 weeks of inactivity. This does not mean that you lose all adaptations after 2 weeks of detraining. It just means that there is a measurable difference after 2 weeks of no training.

Detraining is one of the biggest fears of most athletes, which often leads to overtraining. Many athletes believe that taking a few days off from training will detrain them. However, taking a couple of days off on occasion will not hurt your performance. As a matter of fact, if you are overtrained, a couple of days off to recover could be beneficial. Do not use this as an excuse to take multiple days off on a regular basis though.

If you have to take a break due to illness or injury, it will not take too long to get back to where you left off. When returning do not try to start at the same volume and intensity where you left off. Instead, start back up slowly and work your way back to where you left off. Start with volume first and then increase intensity. Coming back too quickly can lead to injury. This is especially true if the break from training occurred because of injury.

Consistency

Your training plan should be well laid out and consistent in terms of frequency of training. You still want to apply the progressive overload principle; you just want to apply it consistently.

One of the common mistakes that beginners make is to train haphazardly—4 days a week for a couple of weeks, then 2 days the following week, and then 1 day a week for the next couple of weeks. Increases in performance will be minimal at best.

Inconsistent training may also lead to injury. Trying to automatically pick up where you left off places too much stress on the body. For the best gains and to reduce the risk of injury, follow your training program. If life gets in the way—which it does—then alter your training program to minimize the impact.

Frequency

Frequency is defined as how often you train. This can be measured in days or the number of training sessions. Because of the need to adequately train in all three disciplines, there will be days when you will conduct two different training sessions, but two-a-days are typically only implemented 2 to 3 days per week.

Beginning triathletes should train a minimum of 3 days per week, with a day off between workouts. This method allows you to train harder on workout days and then recover prior to your next workout. Training only 3 days per week will be just enough to get you across the finish line; however, it will not get you to the finish line quickly.

To determine frequency of your workouts, first consider your current fitness level. As a beginner, you should start on the lower end and work your way up. Also consider time management. Family, work, and school commitments have a way of interfering with training time. You need to find a way to balance all aspects of your life so that you are ultimately happy. For me, family will always come first, then work, then training. My two high-energy boys and career have altered my training priorities, and I now train only 1 to 3 hours per day. Be realistic in your training goals.

Duration

Duration is the length of your training session, which will be determined by the goal of that session. Most often it will be determined by the desired intensity for that session. Duration and intensity are inversely related, meaning as one goes up the other must go down. You cannot race a 5K at the same pace you would race a 400 m sprint. As the distance increases the intensity will decrease.

You can determine the length of your training sessions by specifying a time limit or a specific distance. I usually prefer distance over time because it allows for a more precise measure. If the goal for the day is a mid-distance ride at an easy pace, it makes more sense to state that you will ride for 30 miles at a heart rate that is equal to your easy training zone and then mark the time when you are finished. This will give you more precise measures as opposed to riding at an easy pace for 1 hour and 30 minutes. With the exception of an ultra-endurance event, such as an ironman distance race, you should be able to complete the distance of the race prior to race day to ensure that you have an enjoyable race.

Intensity / Hard-Easy Principle

Intensity is the "how hard" of training and it is extremely important to properly manipulate in order for appropriate training adaptations to occur. The hard-easy principle is one method of manipulating training intensity. The hard-easy principle states that you cannot train hard every day and instead must alternate hard and easy days to optimize training adaptations. While this principle does oversimplify the problem, it does work, especially in the development of a training program for you, the beginning triathlete.

Intensity levels can be categorized into three basic levels: below anaerobic threshold, at anaerobic threshold, and above anaerobic threshold. When training or racing, you will be at one of these three physiological intensities. Intensities below threshold involve workouts that are below race pace—active recovery training, easy mid-distance training, and long slow distance. At threshold training consists of race pace and tempo work (short tempo work may actually be above threshold). Above threshold training is your interval training. Knowing and understanding intensity levels allows you to better plan a training regimen to ensure that you do not overtrain.

Now that you understand the different intensity levels, you need to know how to determine intensity level. There are various methods used to determine intensity level during training. The following section discusses each method and the practical application of that method.

Determining Intensity Using Speed

Speed is often used to control intensity in swimming, cycling, and running. In swim training, time per a specific distance is used to determine intensity. For example, you may conduct the 100 m at a 2-minute pace during warmup, but compete at an average 1:30 per 100 m at race pace during a 600 m race. While this method may not be the most accurate way to determine intensity, it is an inexpensive and easy method to use.

Running intensity can be determined using time per given distance, most commonly minutes per mile. One problem with this method is that until you reach the end of each mile, you will not know your time for that mile, and you will also need to know each mile mark. As you become accustomed to running pace, you will be able to somewhat accurately guess your minute per mile pace. The Garmin system (see page 55) will be able to give your minute per mile pace somewhat accurately as you run. Another problem is that the course grade and strong winds can play a factor in your minute-per-mile pace. If your normal race pace is 7 minutes per mile on a flat course, it will be higher on a hilly course or if you are running into a heavy headwind. Even though your pace per mile will be slower in both situations, your intensity will probably be higher.

Speed is commonly used to measure intensity in cycling. However, it is a poor overall measure. As speed increases, so too does drag and, therefore, wind has a much stronger impact on cycling. This concept will be covered in greater detail in Chapter 8. When winds are calm and you are time trialing the same distance on the same course, then speed is a good measure of intensity. However, on a windy day you may be fighting to hold 15 mph when normally you can hold 18 mph on your easy day. Also, you cannot compare average speed of a 20-mile flat course to speeds obtained on a 20-mile hilly course.

While using speed has its drawbacks, it is still an easy and practical tool. But do not fall into the trap of trying to obtain a personal best every time you train. You should stick with the specific goal of that training session and make adjustments only based on the environmental conditions (wind, hills, etc.).

I use time as a marker set for improved performance and you can do the same periodically (no more than once or twice a month). You should time trial on the same course in similar environmental conditions to determine if your training is working and whether or not positive adaptations are occurring. If times are faster, then you know the program is working. However, if times have declined or have not improved, you need to look at your training and recovery to determine if changes need to be made.

Determining Intensity by Using Heart Rate

Using your heart rate is a very good method for setting training intensity. Heart rate shares a linear relationship with intensity from rest to maximal effort, meaning that as intensity increases, so, too, does heart rate in equal measure.

Recently, there has been a trend toward not relying on heart rate for determining intensity levels, due to day-to-day variability in heart rate. While it is true that heart rate varies from day to day, it does not invalidate heart rate as a useful tool. Being aware of normal heart rate variability allows you to better understand heart rate and better implement the method in your training program.

Hydration levels and recovery have a strong impact on heart rate. As you become dehydrated, blood plasma volumes decrease, which in turn leads to a decrease in stroke volume (volume of blood ejected from the heart with each beat). A decrease in stroke volume results in an increase in heart rate at any resting or submaximal (also known as submax) intensity level. Endurance athletes who are training in the summer have a tendency to stay chronically dehydrated. Heart rate also remains elevated during recovery from training due to replenishing energy systems, cooling the body, and anabolic (tissue building) processes. During easy days, heart rate returns to resting levels fairly quickly. However, after a hard day of training, resting and sub-max heart rates can remain elevated.

You must also be aware that heart rate and perceived exertion will vary across the three disciplines. Your race pace heart rate will be highest for the run and lowest for the swim, with the bike in between. For example, my max heart rate (HR) is 201 bpm (beats per minute), I can hold a decent conversation running at 175 bpm, and my 5K average race HR is 190 bpm. If I am at 175 bpm on the bike, not only can I not hold a conversation, but the finish line had better be close.

There are three key physiological factors involved that result in this phenomenon: body position, heat dissipation, and weight bearing. First, consider body position. While running you are upright and blood must be moved upward against the acceleration of gravity (9.81 meters per second). This requires a greater heart rate compared to a prone (lying face down) or semi-prone position. Swimming is conducted in a prone position and, therefore, blood return to the heart does not fight against gravity. There will be a greater blood return to the heart, which increases stroke volume. Due to the increase in stroke volume, heart rate will decrease at any given submaximal level. While riding the bike in an aero position, the upper portion of the body is prone and therefore assists in blood return to the heart and increases stroke volume. It is also thought that the high cadence (RPM) assists with the muscle pump and increases blood return to the heart.

Next, consider heat dissipation. During exercise heat is produced through metabolic processes and must be dissipated to prevent the body's core temperature from increasing too much. Blood is redirected to the skin for cooling, and the higher the core temperature becomes the more blood is redirected to the skin for cooling. Swimming provides the greatest opportunity to dissipate heat, because water transfers heat roughly twenty-five times faster than air. Therefore, there is less work needed for cooling, which ultimately results in a lower heart rate. Due to the speeds obtained on the bike, air passes over the body (the body passes through the air) leading to large heat loss through convection, which greatly assists in heat transfer. While convection assists with heat transfer in running, it does not have as large an impact on cooling due to the lower speeds.

Finally, consider weight bearing. Running is a weight-bearing activity and therefore requires greater effort than the other two disciplines. Not only does the runner have to provide a concentric (muscle shortens during the contraction) contraction when pushing off from the ground, but he also has a heavy eccentric (muscle lengthens during the contraction) contraction to prevent the body from just collapsing to the ground on contact. Remember that ground reaction forces are typically two to three times an individual's body weight. This effort requires greater work. Neither cycling nor swimming is a weight-bearing activity.

If you are going to use heart rate to measure intensity, you need to develop heart rate training zones for each of the three disciplines. Using one set of training zones for all three will leave you overtrained in one area and undertrained in another.

One last factor to keep in mind is cardiovascular drift, which is an increase in heart rate without an increase in intensity during prolonged steady state exercise, particularly in a hot environment. Cardiovascular drift is typically a result of dehydration. During prolonged exercise, plasma volume decreases due to sweating, which leads to a decrease in blood volume resulting in a decrease in blood return to the heart and a subsequent decrease in stroke volume. To dissipate heat, more blood will be sent to the skin for cooling, which also decreases venous return and stroke volume. Cardiac output (volume of blood ejected from the heart each minute) is the product of heart rate and stroke volume. Because cardiac output must be maintained in order to maintain intensity, heart rate must increase in order to compensate for the decrease in stroke volume. Do not be surprised if your heart rate begins to creep up on a long run or ride, especially if it is hot outside.

How to Measure Heart Rate

A monitor is the best method for measuring heart rate, because it detects the electrical impulse of the contractions. You can also count pulse rate, but this method is not as accurate. Pulse rate is measured by feeling the blood as

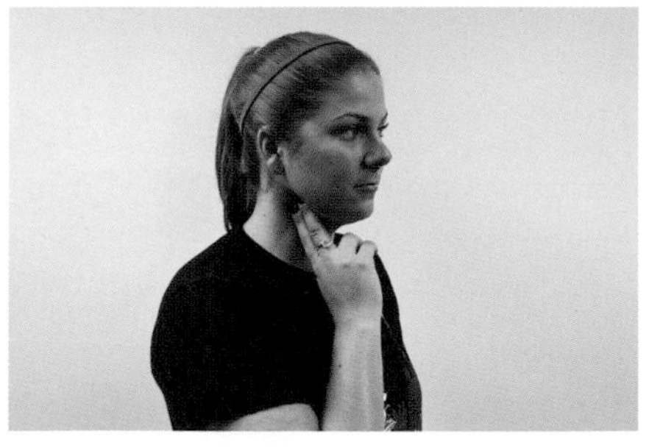

Measuring pulse rate at the carotid artery

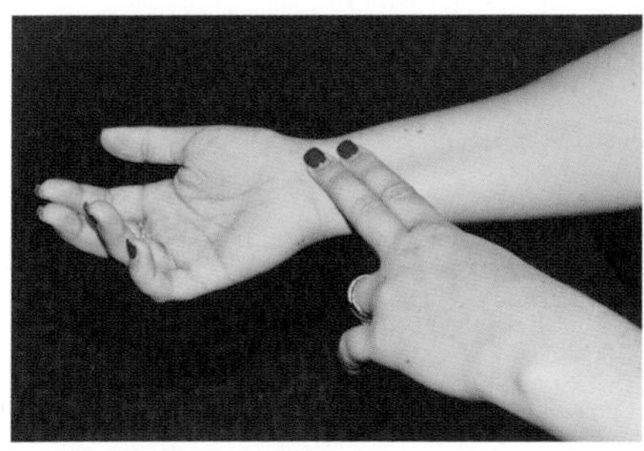

Measuring pulse rate at the radial artery

it pulses through the arteries. Pulse rate is typically measured at either the carotid artery (located at the neck) or radial artery (located at the wrist). This method requires you to quickly locate the point of measure, count the pulses over a given time (6, 10, 15, or 30 seconds), and then multiply the number of pulses to equate 1 minute. If you conducted a 6-second count and you counted 15 pulses, then your pulse rate would be 150.

How to Use Heart Rate

To use heart rate as a training tool, the first thing that you need is an anchor point. The most common anchor point used is heart rate max. Heart rate max is the highest heart rate measured at maximal intensity. In order to determine max heart rate, you will need to either conduct hill repeats at maximal effort or conduct a VO_{2max} test.

You do not need a laboratory or sophisticated equipment to determine max heart rate. Below are field tests that you can use to determine max heart rate for all three disciplines.

Cycling

Find a hill that is about half a mile to a mile long. Warm up for about 15 to 30 minutes and then climb the hill as fast as possible. If you are not completely exhausted at the top of the climb, you did not climb hard enough. The idea here is to achieve your max heart rate. Repeat the climb two to four times and record the highest heart rate achieved. Upon completion cool down by riding 10 to 20 minutes.

Running

Find a hill that is about 400 to 800 meters long. Begin by warming up for about 10 minutes and then run the hill as quickly as possible. Repeat the hill climbs three to five times and record the highest heart rate achieved. Finish by cooling down for at least 10 minutes.

Swimming

Conduct 100-meter repeats. Begin by warming up for about 5 to 10 minutes. If you are an experienced swimmer you may want to warm up for a longer period. Beginners may be fatigued if they warm up longer than 10 minutes. Conduct five 100-meter swims, swimming each as fast as possible and record the highest heart rate achieved. Upon completion cool down for approximately 5 to 10 minutes.

The problem with using intervals to determine max heart rate is that it requires you to repeatedly engage in maximal effort bouts. This is not typically recommended for beginners; you may want to consider estimating max heart rate instead. There are various formulas that allow you to estimate your max heart rate. These formulas are not overly accurate, but will provide an anchor point that will be relatively accurate for most individuals:

220 - age = HR_{max}
Example: 220 - 41 years of age = 179 bpm
210 - (age x .5) - (body weight in pounds x .05) + correction factor = HR_{max}
Correction factor = + 4 for males and + 0 for females
210 - (41 x .5) - (180 X .05) + 4 = 184.5 bpm

I used my numbers in the examples to demonstrate a point. I am currently 41. According to the first formula my max heart rate is 179 bpm, and according to the second formula my max heart rate is 184.5 bpm. However, my real max heart rate is 201 bpm. I know this because I have seen it there on more than one occasion. If I were to calculate my intensity based off estimated max heart rate, then I would not be training to my full potential. These prediction equations are okay to use for you, the beginner, until you are ready to conduct intervals to truly measure max heart rate.

Now that you have established max heart rate, you will next need to determine intensity based on heart rate. Training zone heart rates will set the parameters of your training session for that day by providing an upper and lower heart rate limit. This is where the training zone alarm becomes beneficial on your heart rate monitor, which allows you to train without constantly checking your heart rate monitor to determine if you are in or out of your training zone.

Here are four basic heart rate training zones:

Zone 1—Active Recovery

50 to 65 percent of heart rate max.

Beginners will typically stay closer to 50 percent.

Training below 70 percent ensures that it is an active recovery day.

Zone 2—Aerobic

70 to 80 percent of heart rate max.

For beginners 80 percent may be too high and you may want to consider staying closer to 70 percent.

This is where the majority of your training will occur.

Zone 3—Threshold

80 to 90 percent of heart rate max.

This will be your race pace or tempo training.

Zone 4—Interval

90 to 100 percent of max heart rate.

This will be your high-intensity training above threshold.

When calculating training zone heart rates you have two options: take the direct percentage or use the Karvonen method to calculate. The Karvonen is a commonly recommended method that takes into account your resting heart rate. The formula for the Karvonen method is: $[(HR_{max} - HR_{rest}) \times \% \text{ intensity}] + HR_{rest} = THR$ (target heart rate). The Karvonen method tends to overestimate.

Here is an example using both methods for a trained individual who has a max heart rate of 200 bpm during the run and a resting heart rate of 40 bpm and an untrained individual who has a max heart rate of 200 bpm on the run and a resting heart rate of 70 bpm.

ZONE	INTENSITY	% HR max	KARVONEN TRAINED	KARVONEN UNTRAINED
1	50 - 65%	100 – 130 bpm	120 – 144 bpm	135 – 154 bpm
2	70 - 80%	140 – 160 bpm	152 – 168 bpm	161 – 174 bpm
3	80 - 90%	160 – 180 bpm	168 – 184 bpm	174 – 187 bpm
4	90 - 100%	180 – 200 bpm	184 – 200 bpm	187 – 200 bpm

Notice that training zones are higher using the Karvonen method. The beginner has higher heart rate zones than the trained individual and this difference decreases as the percent of max heart rate increases. The untrained individual has higher heart rate training zones because his resting heart rate is higher. An aerobically untrained individual will have an average resting heart rate of 70 bpm. An elite triathlete can have a resting heart rate in the low 30s and can get as low as mid 20s in some individuals. A lower resting heart rate is an adaptation to endurance training (covered in chapter 5). I typically do not recommend using the Karvonen method for setting heart rate training zones, especially with beginning triathletes.

You can also set heart rate training zones using heart rate at anaerobic threshold (defined in Chapter 5). If you know the heart rate that corresponds to your current anaerobic threshold, you can set training zones based off that anchor point. The common four zones when using threshold heart rate are:

Zone 1—Active Recovery

25 percent or more below threshold heart rate.

Zone 2—Aerobic

25 to 10 percent below threshold heart rate.

Zone 3—Threshold

± 10 percent of threshold heart rate.

Zone 4—Interval

> 110 percent of heart rate threshold.

The reason that an upper and lower heart rate is given with each training zone is due to day-to-day heart rate variability, which makes it somewhat impossible to stay at a single fixed heart rate for each given zone. I typically have my athletes focus on heart rate when training in zones one and two to ensure that they do not train too hard on those days. Naturally, if you are climbing a steep hill on those days you may have to go out of your zone in order to climb the hill. However, it's best if you can slow down and take the hill easier to stay within your zone.

Heart rate training in zone three (race pace) becomes a little more complicated. Here, I want my athletes to learn to pace themselves off of feel and known distance in a race situation. As triathlon is a self-paced event, you will need to develop pacing strategies. Do not use a heart rate monitor to control intensity during a race. You may end up limiting your race performance. Instead learn to pace based off of how you feel at race pace. One benefit of training zones during race simulation is when climbing hills. Setting the upper limit helps prevent you from climbing too hard and negatively impacting performance for the rest of the session.

I never worry about heart rate during interval training and typically will use time or power to conduct intervals. Intervals are conducted at high intensities and heart rate can even continue to climb briefly after a high-intensity interval. However, you can look at heart rate recovery between intervals to ensure adequate recovery.

Determining Intensity Using Power

Cycling power meters are considered the optimal method for determining intensity during cycling. However, due to the expense and knowledge level required to correctly integrate a power meter into your training, the use of power meters is beyond the scope of this book. Prior to purchasing a power meter do some reading to make an educated decision based on your ability and willingness to apply power to training. *Training and Racing with Power* by Allen and Coggan is a good place to start; it explains the principles behind the use of power as well as how to integrate power into your training.

Determining Intensity by Feel

Determining intensity based on feel is a valuable tool that is often applied incorrectly or overlooked altogether. Triathletes who have been racing for years are able to pace correctly for different training zones based on known distance and how they feel (peripheral feedback). For them to correctly control intensity through peripheral feedback has taken years of training. Beginners typically have a difficult time correctly gauging intensity, especially during a race. Beginners will typically go out too fast, experience fatigue, and slow down leading to a poor performance time. Research has demonstrated that an even-paced race strategy is ideal for endurance sports such as triathlon. The key is that you must be able to maintain an even pace throughout the race.

There are a couple of simple methods that allow you to control intensity through feel, the first of which being the talk test, which is extremely simple to use and, yet, very effective. The talk test allows you to determine if you are below, at, or above threshold. If you are training below threshold, you should be able to hold a decent conversation. The closer that you get to threshold the harder it will be to hold a conversation. At threshold you should only be able to get out a short sentence at most. Above threshold you may get out one or two words at most.

The next method, a bit more complicated, uses a rating of perceived exertion (RPE) scale to determine intensity (numbered scale indicating level of fatigue). You can use the Borg scale, one of the most common RPE scales used in exercise science, which runs from a rating of 6 (no exertion) to 20 (maximal exertion), to correlate to an average resting heart rate of 60 bpm and max heart rate of 200 bpm. Or, use the OMNI scale (rating of 0 [extremely easy] to 10 [extremely hard]), which has become the preferred RPE scale because it's a simpler rating span.

You'll need to anchor the scale prior to using it to determine intensity. What does this mean? To make the numbers meaningful you need to anchor them during a graded exercise protocol. A graded exercise protocol starts off at an easy level and increases intensity every 2 to 3 minutes (depending on the protocol). Every minute during the protocol establish an RPE by determining how you feel at that point and time. This allows you to anchor all numbers from first to last.

Flexibility

Flexibility is the ability of a joint to move through a full range of motion. While flexibility is not considered one of the basic training principles, it is extremely important for all triathletes. Lack of proper flexibility leads to improper motion, resulting in a decrease in performance and possible injury. Triathletes should be as diligent with maintaining or improving flexibility as they are with the rest of their training.

This section covers the basic stretches needed to maintain flexibility for triathlon. Keep in mind that these are the basic stretches and can be replaced with other stretches that work similarly.

Slowly move into the stretch until you feel the stretch. Hold the stretch for up to 30 seconds and then relax. Conduct each stretch two to four times. Do not stretch to the point of pain, as this is counterproductive. Instead, just stretch to the point that you feel the muscle stretch. A feeling of mild discomfort is okay; pain is not.

Dynamic stretching (actively moving the joint through a full range of motion) prior to competition promotes increased performance. But this should not be a reason to eliminate static stretching (stretching and then holding that stretch for a period of 15–30 seconds) from your training.

While dynamic stretching should be implemented as a part of the warmup routine for the race, static stretching should be incorporated into your training program to increase or maintain flexibility.

Upper Body

Neck Stretch

It is very important that you spend the time to stretch the muscles of your neck. Both swimming and cycling, especially in an aero position, place a great amount of stress on the neck. You want to cover rotation, flexion, extension, and lateral flexion.

Neck stretch

Rotate your head to the left as far as it will move and hold for 15–30 seconds. Then repeat this process to the right.

Take the neck into flexion by trying to touch your chin to your chest; hold the stretch for 15–30 seconds. Then move the head into extension by rotating your chin toward the ceiling and hold for 15–30 seconds.

Take your head into lateral flexion to the right by moving your right ear toward your shoulder. Hold that position for 15–30 seconds and then repeat this process to the left.

When stretching the neck it is very important not to apply too great a force or to conduct these movements in a fast or bouncing movement.

Anterior Shoulder Stretch

This stretches the anterior deltoid and pectoralis major. The corner stretch is a great way to conduct this stretch. Face into a corner and place your hands on the walls. Keep your hands in place and walk toward the corner to stretch. You can also conduct this stretch by doing one arm at a time by placing your arm against an object and

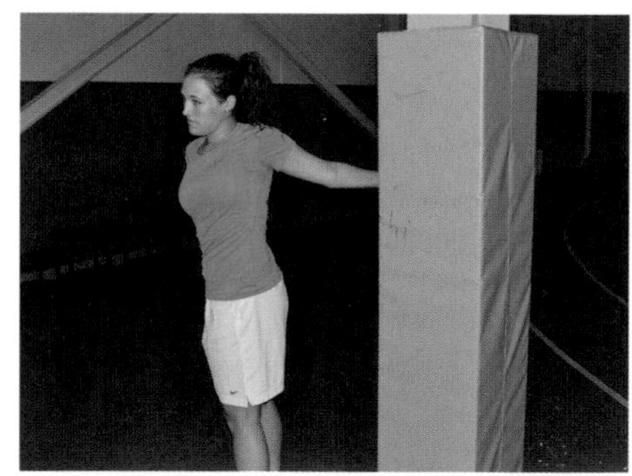

Anterior shoulder and pectoral stretch

rotating away from the point of contact (as seen in photo).

Posterior shoulder stretch

Posterior Shoulder Stretch

The posterior shoulder stretch focuses on the posterior deltoid and muscles of the back. Horizontally adduct your right arm across your chest, place your left hand on your right elbow, and apply pressure to stretch. Then switch.

Behind the neck stretch

Behind the Head Stretch

The behind the head stretch focuses on the triceps and latissimus dorsi. Raise your right arm above your head and then flex at the elbow until your hand is behind your head. Reach up with your left hand, grab your elbow, and apply pressure to the left. Repeat this process with the left arm.

Abdominal stretch

Abdominal Stretch

Lie prone and place your hands palm down on the floor. Push upward with your arms, leaving your lower body flat on the floor.

Lower Body

Calf Stretch

The calf muscle (triceps surae) is made up of the gastrocnemius and soleus muscles. To stretch the calf muscle, stand on a raised surface with the fore part of the foot on the surface and the heel hanging off the surface. Allow the heel to go down by placing the foot in dorsiflexion (heel down). To concentrate on the gastrocnemius, keep the leg straight during this process. To focus more on the soleus, slightly flex at the knee and repeat the process. Placing the knee into flexion places slack on the gastrocnemius and allows a greater focus on the soleus.

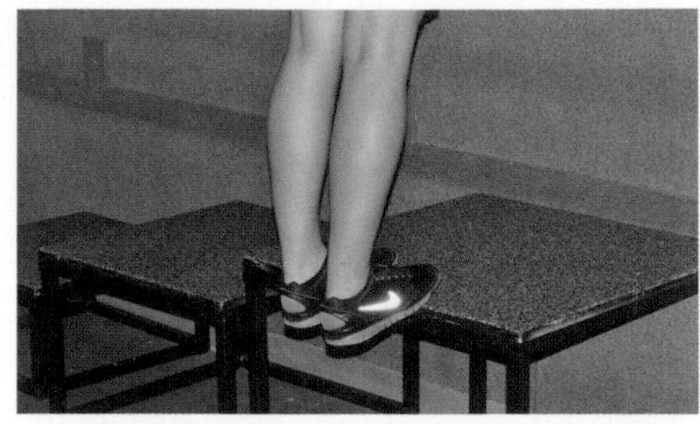
Calf stretch

Hamstring Stretch

The basic hamstring stretch does much more than just stretch the hamstrings. This stretch also is great for the muscles of the lower back. If you can reach your toes and pull the foot into dorsiflexion, it will also stretch the calf. While this stretch can be conducted standing, I advise conducting the stretch seated. Sit with your legs together and straight out in front of you. Bend forward at the waist, going as far forward and down as possible. Grab your toes and pull the foot into dorsiflexion. If you cannot reach your toes, grab as far down the leg as you can. During this process keep your legs straight and do not allow a lot of bend at the knee.

Hamstring stretch

Quadriceps stretch

Quadriceps Stretch

The quadriceps stretch is typically conducted incorrectly by trying to push the heel into the gluteus maximus while in flexion. Instead, reach behind the body and grab the right foot or ankle with the left hand, place the knee into flexion, and pull rearward. Repeat this process with the other leg. If you have trouble balancing on one leg during this process, move to a wall and place your free hand on the wall for balance.

Adductor Stretch

This stretch focuses on the adductor muscles. Sit on the floor and place the knees into flexion with the soles of the feet touching. Grab your feet and place your elbows on your legs. Push down on your legs with your elbows and bend forward at the waist.

Adductor stretch

Hip Stretch

This stretch focusses on the gluteus maximus and hamstrings. Lie supine with both legs straight out. Bring your right leg up by flexing at the hip. As you bring the leg up allow the knee to go into flexion. Place your hands below the knee and pull. Repeat this process with the left leg.

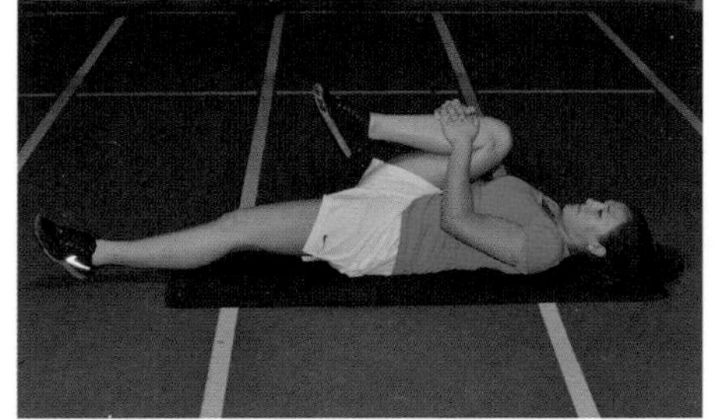

Hip stretch

Tensor Fascia Latae and Iliotibial Band Stretch

Tensor fascia latae and iliotibial band problems are common in both cyclists and runners. They are located laterally on the leg and are responsible for promoting proper biomechanics. They ensure that the leg is not rotated externally as the leg drives forward at the hip. To stretch this muscle stand with your right side toward the wall, place your right hand against the wall, and cross your right leg behind the left. Push your hips toward the wall until you feel a stretch across the outside of your right leg. Repeat this process with the left side.

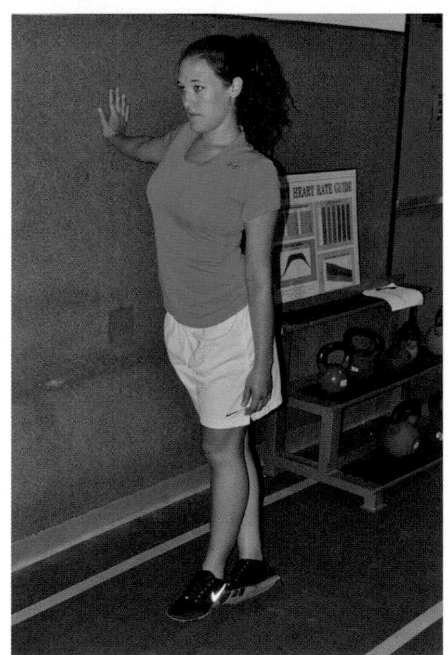

Iliotibial band stretch

CHAPTER FIVE

Triathlon Physiology

Before you can optimize performance by correctly applying training principles, you will need a basic understanding of physiology as it applies to sport. This understanding will allow you to make educated decisions about your training methods. It will also help you determine if your body is correctly adapting to the applied training stimulus. If you understand the physiological adaptations that should occur, then you can better gauge the degree to which your training program elicits these changes.

The key to understanding physiology is to know *form* and *function*. Every element of the body is formed to perform a specific function. Adaptations through training may slightly alter form in order to improve function. Understanding the function of a system, organ, hormone, substrate, or enzyme allows you to determine the effect of each on human performance. This chapter explains basic physiology, which provides a foundation that will allow you to grasp the physiological adaptations that occur with endurance training.

Cardiorespiratory Endurance

The cardiorespiratory system is comprised of the cardiovascular system and the respiratory system. The cardiovascular system encompasses the heart and blood vessels and is responsible for the movement of blood through the body, which is vital for transporting oxygen, glucose, free fatty acids, hormones, and other key substrates to the working muscle. Equally important are the byproducts that blood carries away from the working tissue (carbon dioxide and lactate).

The respiratory system includes the air passages and lungs and is responsible for the transport and diffusion of gasses. Air moves through the air passageways, bringing in vital oxygen to the lungs, where it is diffused across the respiratory membrane and into the lungs. Carbon dioxide crosses the respiratory membrane into the lungs and is then exhaled into the atmosphere.

Understanding physiology as it applies to exercise will greatly increase your understanding of training and racing.

The cardiorespiratory system is key during endurance performance and many times will limit performance based on the individual's current fitness level. During endurance training adaptations occur that greatly improve the body's ability to transport blood and oxygen. These adaptations will be discussed at the end of this chapter.

Heart

The heart is a specialized muscle (myocardium) that pumps blood through the body. The heart differs from other muscles in that it is the most oxidative (utilizes oxygen for energy processes) muscle in the body; it conducts the electrical impulse rapidly, and the signal for contraction originates in the muscle (sinoatrial node). The heart consists of four chambers (left and right atria and left and right ventricles). Pulmonary circulation (right atrium and ventricle) pumps "oxygen-poor" blood returning from the body into the lungs. Systemic circulation (left atrium and ventricle) pumps "oxygen-rich" blood to the body.

Here, I will make a long, complicated story short: Oxygen-poor blood returns to the right side of the heart and then is pumped to the lungs, where carbon dioxide is released from the blood and oxygen is picked up. The oxygen-rich blood then travels to the left side of the heart where it is pumped out to the body. The blood then travels through smaller and smaller arteries until it reaches arterioles and then capillaries at the tissue. This is where oxygen, nutrients, water, carbon dioxide, and other byproducts are transported to and from the tissue. As the capillaries leave the tissue, they connect to venules and then veins before returning to the heart.

The heart is not strong enough to pump blood down through the body and then back up toward the heart against gravity from the lower extremities. So there are mechanisms in place that assist with blood return to the heart. The first is called the muscle pump. Muscles in the leg contract rhythmically, causing blood to be pushed upward during the contraction phase. When the muscles relax one way, valves in the veins prevent the blood from flowing back down. The second method is the respiratory pump. Changes in thoracic pressure due to breathing aids in blood return to the heart.

Cardiac Output

Cardiac output is the volume of blood pumped per minute and is a product of stroke volume and heart rate. Stroke volume is the volume of blood pumped from the left ventricle each beat and heart rate is defined as the number of times the heart beats each minute. Cardiac output responds to exercise by increasing linearly with increases in intensity until max intensity is reached. Heart rate also increases linearly with an increase in intensity. Stroke volume can nearly double from resting but only increase to about 50 percent of maximal intensity before leveling off. So after about 50 percent of max intensity, all increases in cardiac output come primarily from heart rate only.

Autoregulation of Blood Flow

Autoregulation of blood flow concerns the redirection of blood flow based on tissue need. Blood flow is redirected by altering blood vessel diameter through vasoconstriction and vasodilatation. As we move from a resting state to an exercising state, metabolism substantially increases. Going for an easy run can increase metabolism by six to nine times above resting levels. Because the metabolic demand of the working muscles has increased substantially, a greater amount of blood flow must be sent to the working muscle to increase the delivery of oxygen and nutrients. During exercise, blood flow is redirected to the working muscles, skin (for cooling), heart, and brain and reduced in areas where it is less needed, such as the digestive system and kidneys. During rest, approximately 20 percent of blood flow travels to the muscles. During exercise, as much as 80 percent of blood flow can be redirected to muscle.

This concept is vital for a complete understanding of the body's response to exercise. For example, autoregulation of blood flow explains the body's response to exercise after eating. You have probably eaten a meal and then exercised at some point in your life. The experience is never as comfortable as you would like it to be and your performance is subpar; this is because your digestive system is in direct competition with the working muscles for blood flow. Due to the body's "fight or flight" instinct, the sympathetic response will win out over the parasympathetic response and greater blood flow will go to the muscles. However, a greater amount of blood will be redirected to the digestive system because you just ate, as opposed to if exercising without prior food consumption. Because of this redirection, your performance will decrease and your stomach may become upset.

When exercising in the heat, a greater amount of blood flow will be redirected to the skin for cooling. Dissipating heat is vital for survival and will take priority over blood flow to muscles. Due to this, performance decreases in a hot environment.

Blood

Blood is made up of around 55 percent plasma, 45 percent red blood cells (erythrocytes), and less than 1 percent white blood cells (leukocytes) and platelets. *Hematocrit,* the percent of red blood cells in relation to whole blood, is used to measure the makeup of your specific blood. The average hematocrit for a male is around 45 and for a female it is around 42.

Blood plays five major roles: transportation, heat transfer, acid/base balance, coagulation, and immune response. While all five are important, we typically concentrate on the first three in exercise physiology, as they have the greatest impact on performance. Each red blood cell contains a large number of hemoglobin molecules, which are responsible for the transportation of oxygen.

Blood is extremely important when it comes to heat dissipation. Water makes up about 90 percent of plasma, which is why plasma is an excellent mechanism for heat transfer. Heat is transferred from the core and working muscles to the blood, where it is dissipated at the skin surface. Plasma is also important for cooling, as it provides sweat for evaporation at the skin.

Gas Exchange

As a triathlete, you are concerned with gas exchange in the lungs and tissue (primarily muscle). Gas dissolves in liquids based on three factors: partial pressure of the individual gas, solubility of a specific gas in a specific fluid, and temperature. While all three affect how gases dissolve in liquid, partial pressure is the main driving force behind gas exchange in the body. Gasses will flow from high to low pressure.

Muscle

Skeletal muscle originates (point of muscle attachment that is the least moveable) and inserts (point of muscle attachment that is the least moveable) on bone and crosses at least one joint. Therefore the primary purpose of skeletal muscle is human movement. There are more than 600 muscles in the human body, and you need to learn the primary muscles used in triathlon in order to properly strengthen and stretch those muscles (covered in Chapters 4 & 11).

Skeletal muscles are composed of numerous muscle fibers. Muscle fibers are classified by type: Type I (slow-twitch), Type IIa (intermediate/fast-twitch), Type IIx (fast-twitch), and Type IIb (truly fast-twitch). Muscle fiber types are categorized by characteristics. To simplify matters fibers are often classified as slow-twitch (I), and fast-twitch (IIa, IIx and IIb).

Fast-twitch fibers—larger than slow-twitch fibers—are made for power and strength. They are larger than slow-twitch fibers and are highly glycolytic-relying on anaerobic energetics for metabolic processes. These fibers contract and relax very quickly, but fatigue easily; they are great for initiating a sprint for the finish line.

Slow-twitch fibers are of the utmost importance for triathletes as they are primarily oxidative muscle fibers. Slow-twitch fibers do not activate as quickly or produce as much force as fast-twitch and do not produce as much force as fast twitch fibers; however, they are slow to fatigue and ideal for endurance activities.

Distribution of muscle fiber type is genetic—most people are born 50 percent slow-twitch and 50 percent fast-twitch, but some individuals are born with a greater amount of one type of fiber or another. Elite-level endurance athletes typically possess up to around 80 percent slow-twitch fibers, whereas an elite-level Olympic lifter can have around 65 percent fast-twitch fibers. The predominant theory is that muscle fiber types cannot change from one type to another through training.

Energy Systems

Energy is required for movement. Swimming, cycling, and running all require repetitive muscle contractions because, during a sprint distance triathlon, the average individual produces around 432 swim strokes, 4,410 pedal strokes, and 3,000 steps.

We derive energy from the ingestion of food. There are three primary sources for energy: lipids (fatty acids), carbohydrates, and proteins. The two main sources used for energy in the human body are lipids (fats) and carbohydrates. Carbohydrates are stored as glycogen (around 2000 kCals—a kCal is the amount of heat necessary to raise one liter of water 1 degree Celsius and is commonly referred to as "Calories," with a big "C.") in the muscles and liver and are transported in the blood as glucose. Lipids are stored as triacylglycerol (commonly referred to as triglycerides—averaging between 60–80,000 kCals) in muscle and adipose tissue (under the skin and around organs). Naturally the volume of stored lipids can vary greatly among individuals. Excess protein is not stored in the body. Regardless of the source, all ingested food must be converted to adenosine triphosphate (ATP) in order for it to be utilized as fuel in the human body.

Energy systems are frequently categorized into aerobic and anaerobic systems. Aerobic systems are those systems that require oxygen for the metabolic processes to occur, and anaerobic systems are those that do not require oxygen for metabolic processes to occur. While you will use all energy systems, the aerobic systems are the primary energy source for triathlon.

VO_{2max}

Triathlon is an endurance sport; your ability to perform is highly dependent on your ability to transport and utilize oxygen. It is common practice to test your VO_{2max} in order to determine your current fitness level. VO_{2max} is the body's maximal ability to deliver oxygen to the working muscles and the muscle's ability to use that oxygen to produce energy for movement. As VO_{2max} increases with training, so too does endurance performance.

The extent to which VO_{2max} can be increased through training is highly dependent on genetics. While everyone can increase VO_{2max}, improvements are limited by a predetermined genetic ceiling.

As there is a strong linear relationship between VO_{2max} measures and endurance performance, it is often used to predict performance. Below is a chart representing what measures would be expected by gender and training status.

	SEDENTARY	MODERATELY TRAINED	ELITE
Male	45–50 ml/kg/min	55–65 ml/kg/min	≥ 70ml/kg/min
Female	35–40 ml/kg/min	45–55 ml/kg/min	≥ 60 ml/kg/min

VO_{2max} is measured during a graded exercise protocol conducted in a laboratory setting. Testing is typically conducted on either a treadmill or cycle ergometer (stationary bike). The test can also be conducted swimming, but requires specialized equipment. The graded exercise protocol starts easy and

VO_{2max} provides a great scientific measure of endurance performance.

intensity increases at regular time intervals until complete exhaustion. Most protocols consist of 2- or 3-minute stages. Intensity increases during the treadmill protocol by increasing both speed and grade. Intensity increases during the cycle protocol by increasing resistance on the cycle ergometer. During the graded exercise protocol, gas exchange of O_2 and CO_2 is measured using an automated metabolic cart. This requires the participant to wear an airtight mask that allows him to breathe in room air and breathe out into a gas mixing chamber. From the gas mixing chamber the air is analyzed for O_2 and CO_2.

Measurement of VO_{2max} requires expensive specialized equipment and trained personnel to run the test and evaluate the data, so testing is typically expensive, between \$100 and \$300 depending on the facilities, testing personnel, and other services offered. Testing can be conducted at local

VO_{2max} protocol on a cycle ergometer

performance centers or universities. If you are interested in these tests, the best option is to contact the Exercise Physiology (sometimes called Kinesiology, Physical Education, or Exercise Science) Department at your local university. Most researchers are always looking for subjects and will offer low-cost or free testing.

Anaerobic Threshold / Lactate Threshold

Anaerobic threshold (also known as lactate threshold) is the point at which lactic acid production exceeds removal. Knowing your anaerobic threshold is just as important as knowing your VO_{2max}. The higher your anaerobic threshold, the faster your race pace will be. Focus your training both on increasing your VO_{2max} and on increasing your anaerobic threshold. Changes in anaerobic threshold occur quicker and have a greater impact on performance than changes in VO_{2max}.

Threshold terminology is used a lot in sports performance but few actually understand or know how to correctly apply the concept. The two most common terms that are used are *anaerobic threshold* and *lactate threshold.* Anaerobic threshold is defined as the point at which metabolic processes begin to switch from aerobic energetics (energy processes requiring oxygen) to anaerobic energetics (energy processes which do not require oxygen). Lactate threshold is defined as the point at which lactate production exceeds the body's ability to remove it. As intensity increases lactate production increases, and reliance on glycogen as a fuel source increases to the point that hydrogen is being produced at such a rate that it builds up, leading to a decrease in pH. To offset this decrease in pH, two hydrogen molecules will bind with pyruvate to form lactic acid. This is unstable and hydrogen is released, forming lactate. Although typically viewed in a negative light, lactic acid itself is not the problem; instead it is the buildup of hydrogen. The formation of lactic acid offsets the increase in acidity due to a buildup of hydrogen. While lactic acid is an acid, it is much less acidic than free hydrogen in the cell and, therefore, the formation offsets the increase in acidity. Upon completion of exercise lactic acid will be converted back into fuel through specific pathways and therefore should not be considered a waste product.

Lastly, lactic acid is not responsible for delayed onset of muscle soreness (DOMS). DOMS is the soreness felt the day after a workout that can last 1 or more days, depending on the damage done during exercise. DOMS is not caused by lactic acid but instead by tiny tears in muscle tissue that occur during eccentric contractions.

There are two common methods for measuring threshold. Lactate threshold is measured by taking blood samples every minute during a graded exercise protocol where intensity increases every three minutes until maximal effort is reached. Blood samples are then measured for blood lactate and then blood lactate is plotted in order to determine the inflection point (point where blood lactate concentrations increase exponentially). The second method, referred to as *Ventilatory* threshold, is also used to determine threshold and is measured during a VO_{2max} test. It is the point at which ventilation deviates from linearity with oxygen consumption. Both methods are considered reliable and valid.

Regardless of the method used to determine anaerobic threshold, it will be expressed as either a percentage of max or relative to heart rate. An untrained individual can have an anaerobic threshold of about 70 percent of max whereas an elite triathlete will have a threshold of around 90 percent of max. In order to use anaerobic threshold to monitor training intensity, you will need to know your heart rate at threshold.

Adaptations to Endurance Training

Almost every adaptation that occurs due to endurance training is designed to increase the delivery of oxygen to the working muscles and increase the oxidative processes that occur within the working muscles. The entire point of your training program is to elicit these adaptations in order to improve performance. The purpose of this section is to identify the primary adaptations and explain the importance of each.

With endurance training there will be an increase in overall blood volume. Red blood cells will increase in order to boost the oxygen-carrying capacity of the blood. Plasma volume will also increase, both in response to the increase in red blood cell volume and in response to the heavy sweating and plasma loss that occurs during exercise. The increased plasma volume assists in heat dissipation and thermoregulation.

Increased blood volume would do no good if delivery at the muscles was not also increased. In response to the greater demand, capillary density increases at the tissue, primarily the working muscles. The increased capillary density supplies more blood to the working muscles, allowing greater gas, nutrient, and metabolic byproduct exchange.

Improved cardiac function also occurs with endurance training. As mentioned earlier cardiac output equals stroke volume multiplied by heart rate. Endurance training increases stroke volume, which affects both cardiac output and heart rate. Stroke volume increases because there is a healthy enlargement of the left ventricle, allowing a greater volume of blood to enter; because the increased blood volume results in a larger volume of blood returning to the heart and therefore greater filling; and because the cardiac muscle produces a more forceful contraction. When stroke volume increases there will be a corresponding decrease in heart rate at any submaximal intensity because cardiac output for that given submaximal intensity will not be greatly altered. This is why endurance athletes have low resting heart rates. Max heart rate does not alter with training and remains relatively constant. There will be an increase in cardiac output with endurance training.

Alterations to muscle fiber will also occur with endurance training. Type I muscle hypertrophy occurs, leading to improved performance. Slow-twitch muscle hypertrophy is often overlooked because it is not as visibly noticed compared to type II muscle hypertrophy, which occurs during strength and power training. Type I muscle fibers will greatly increase their oxidative capacity. Type IIa (intermediate fibers) will shift toward oxidative properties. There will also be an increase in myoglobin to increase oxygen-carrying capacity within the muscle. Mitochondria (the oxidative powerhouses of the cell) will increase, leading to an increase in oxidative processes. There will be an overall increase in all oxidative enzymes as well.

Changes to energy sources also occur due to endurance training, including an increase in glycogen stores. Glycogen stores for the average individual are around 2,000 kCals. An elite endurance athlete will store around 2,500 kCals. Lipid stores will decrease in adipose tissue and increase in muscle. This will provide greater stores in the muscles readily available for production of ATP. As your training continues, you will begin to utilize fat at a higher percentage earlier during prolonged exercise in order to spare glycogen.

The last adaptation is an increase in lactate threshold, due to a decrease in lactic acid production and an increase in lactate clearance. While endurance training, especially tempo work, increases lactate threshold, anaerobic training is key to increasing lactate threshold.

CHAPTER SIX

Training Programs

You can have all the best triathlon gear in the world, but it will mean nothing without a sound training plan. The importance of a well-made training program is often overlooked. A haphazard approach to training is insufficient for making marked performance gains, and in many cases it is counterproductive. To avoid you making those mistakes, this chapter discusses using an appropriate training plan, developing a training plan, and monitoring your training.

The two most common mistakes beginners make are to (a) train at or near race pace every time that they train and to (b) train too often, not allowing time for recovery. Make sure you allow adequate time for recovery so you do not end up overtrained and injured.

A good training program will bring together all of the key training principles discussed during Chapter 4 and optimize your race performance. There are three common approaches to developing an optimal training program. The first approach involves hiring a coach to help you develop and implement a training program. The second is to use a boxed training plan from a book. The last approach involves making your own training program.

Coaching

The main benefit of working with a coach is that the coach has the ability to tailor a training program that is specific to your current fitness level, goals, and schedule. As you progress in triathlon, a coach will also be able to alter the program as needed based on how you are adapting to training. There will be times when volume or intensity can increase beyond what was scheduled and times when volume or intensity may need to be reduced due to overtraining. A good coach will be able to evaluate performance and adaptations in order to make educated decisions concerning the training program.

The trick to hiring a coach is to find a good one. Since your goal is to optimize triathlon performance, you will need to do a little homework first. How much does the coach know about triathlon and training

Developing a sound training program is the key to success.

principles? The two main credentials to look for are certifications and formal education.

USA Triathlon has a coaching certification program, with three different coaching levels (levels 1–3). As the coaching levels move up, the requirements and experience of the coach increases as well. USA Triathlon is not the only organization to provide triathlon coaching certifications. The International Triathlon Coaching Association (ITCA) also provides an excellent, well-respected coaching certification. There are other certifications besides triathlon coaching to consider as well. The most widely respected strength and conditioning certification is the National Strength and Conditioning Associations Certified Strength and Conditioning Specialists (CSCS). This certification requires the coach to possess a 4-year degree, pass a rigorous certification exam, and supply continuing education credits after obtaining the certification. The CSCS is not specific to triathlon and does not ensure that the individual can coach triathlon.

Look for a coach who possesses a 4-year degree in Exercise Science or a related field. You should also consider the coach's experience as both a racer and a coach. Coaches with race experience truly understand what it is like to be out on the course, and remember that the extent of the coach's experience is more important than how fast or slow he is on the course. One of the best ways to gauge a coach's experience is by talking with others who he has coached. Ask for a reference list of current and past athletes and talk to more than one person to get a fair assessment.

Online coaching has become very popular recently. Due to technological advances a coach can work with you and never even meet with you face to face. Tools such as Garmin GPS systems, downloadable heart rate monitors, and power meters allow coaches to evaluate your performance, mark adaptations, and prescribe training based on those adaptations. While this method may not be equivalent to the one-on-one sessions a local coach can give you, it is a valid coaching method. Here is a list of a few online coaching sites:

www.trainright.com

www.t2coaching.com

www.markallenonline.com

Do your homework prior to making a commitment to an online coach. Find out what options are available and at what price. The price will vary with the level of coaching you receive. Just like with a local coach, it would be a good idea to check references.

How much a coach charges for his services is highly variable, but typically as the qualifications and experience level of the coach increases so too does the fee. With coaching, just like with most things in life, you get what you pay for. You should expect to pay adequately for the services provided. Do your homework on what coaching costs in your area to get an idea on what you should spend.

Boxed Training Plans

Another training option is to use boxed training plans. These are training plans that you find in magazines, in books, or online. These boxed plans lay out a day-to-day training program designed to provide adequate training stimulus to get you to race day. Most of these programs work fine and allow you to complete your race. However, they typically will not allow you to reach peak performance. You cannot use a "one size fits all" approach to training programs if you want to reach your full potential.

These rigid programs are designed to elicit training adaptations for increased performance while ensuring overtraining does not occur. To

A boxed training plan provides a place for you to start.

accomplish this goal most programs have lower volume and intensity than if you were working with a coach who monitors your progress and can adapt the program accordingly. Keep in mind, though, that it is better to be 10 percent undertrained as opposed to 1 percent overtrained. These programs are typically very useful for beginners who wish to simply complete the course and are not overly concerned with optimizing time. If you have a strong background in strength and conditioning, you could take a boxed program and modify it to fit to your specific needs and make alterations as training adaptations occur.

Developing Your Own Training Program

Another option is to develop your own plan that accommodates your work schedule, family schedule, experience, and fitness level. Choosing to develop your own workout program can be challenging, especially for beginners. Do your research first; the more information that you have the better you will be able to design your program. Below are some simple steps to program development. Keep in mind the information below is designed to create a simple program for beginning triathletes. As you become more advanced, you will need to apply a program with more depth.

Determine Goals

When developing a training program, the first thing to do is set goals. Be realistic. If you have never competed in a triathlon, you should probably not choose an ultra-distance race for your first one. Your goals should be challenging but achievable. Here are some specific questions that you should ask yourself:

- What do I want to accomplish with this adventure overall?
- What is my current fitness level?
- What is my current skill level in each event?
- What distance do I want to race?
- Do I have enough time to adequately train for the race?
- Am I more concerned with just finishing or speed?
- What are my time constraints?
- What are my logistical challenges?

You should set both short- and long-term goals. Look at it like a ladder. If you only had the bottom and top rung of the ladder, you would be unable to climb to the top (your ultimate goal). By adding rungs to the ladder between the bottom and top, you can climb, ultimately reaching your goal. The rungs are the short-term goals that allow you to reach your ultimate goal; they give you something to strive for. If you have just started swimming and your goal is to swim 800 meters comfortably, then break it down into shorter distances to help you stay motivated. If you can only swim 50 meters without stopping, then your next goal is to be able to complete 75 meters without stopping. Keep adding distance until the full 800 meters is met. Do not set too many short-term goals.

Write down your goals so you have them for future reference. The act of writing down your goals makes it much more likely that you will stick to those goals. Placing your goals where you can see them can also act as motivation.

Establish Baseline Measures

When beginning a training program, you should establish baseline measures. The importance of these measures is twofold. First, they provide a mark of where you started, which allows you to look back and determine if there have been improvements in performance. The markers give you a goal to strive for improvement. Second, baseline measures also give you an unbiased look at your current fitness and skill level that you would not have received otherwise. Numbers do not lie.

Baseline measures can be either lab- or field-based. Lab-based measures, such as VO_{2max}, threshold testing, and body composition, are excellent for providing baseline measures and for marking progression. However, lab-based methods may not be readily available in your area or may not be cost-effective. Another method is to use field-based markers to determine current fitness level and to monitor progress along the way. Field-based markers do not require special training or expensive equipment and are extremely easy to conduct and analyze.

Time trials are the most common markers used in sport performance. The concept is quite simple. If you travel the same distance under the same conditions and times are faster, then the training program is working. If the times are slower or unchanged, then you need to examine the program. When conducting a marker set, the conditions between trials need to be identical.

To conduct a marker set, choose a fixed distance, typically based on the distance you wish to race (600 m swim, 16-mile bike, 5K run). The swim can be conducted in a pool or open water. The pool will provide a more accurate and consistent measurement of distance while open water swims are more true to the race. The optimal measure would be to set up a fixed course in an open water setting. However, the distance swam needs to be consistent between trials.

Cycling and running time trials can be easily set up to measure performance. Running can be conducted on a track, trail, or road. A track is nice because it provides an accurate measurement of distance. Setting up a cycling time trial course requires a little more effort as the trial will most likely be located on an open road. Try to find a stretch of road with low traffic and minimum stops along the distance you want to travel. It will be difficult to determine the differences between trials if you continually have to stop at stoplights. Ensure that you conduct the trials on relatively non-windy days so that times can be compared between trials.

Determine Volume

When determining training volume you have to determine training frequency and duration. The combination of the two gives you your overall training volume. Training volume is typically evaluated as daily volume and then as weekly volume and is planned out to elicit adaptation for optimal performance.

The first thing to determine is the frequency of your training. How many days per week do you wish to train and how many of those days will be two-a-day training sessions? Very few people have unlimited free time to train. Family, work, and other responsibilities will limit your ability to schedule training sessions.

Write out your daily schedule to find openings that will allow you to insert training. The time slot allotted to training should be large enough to accommodate setup, training, cleanup, and any other logistics that may need to be handled. Many times, especially when conducting two-a-days, you may want to consider training early in the morning prior to the start of your daily routine. Ideally you want to develop a program that allows you to train 5 to 7 days per week, with easy recovery days incorporated in. Consider starting with just 3 days per week, allowing a day of rest between, and then progressively work your way up to 5 to 7 days a week.

The duration of each training session must be determined as well. This is vital for first-timers. *You must be able to complete the distance prior to race day to ensure a safe and enjoyable race.* There are three things you need to know in order to determine duration: the distance of the race, the distance that you can currently complete, and the time between the first day of training and race day. Mark a calendar with the start of training and the current distances you can complete in swimming, cycling, and running. Next, mark the calendar with the race date and the distances of all three modes during that race. You should be able to reach your goal by increasing weekly training volume by roughly 10 percent. If, by your calculations, you cannot theoretically complete the distance by the race date, then you may want to consider choosing a race later in the season.

Determine Intensity

Once frequency has been determined, you need to assign training intensity for each day. Keep in mind the hard/easy principle and training zones from Chapter 4 in order to optimize adaptations to training. Choose your training zone based on the training goal for that day (recovery, aerobic, threshold, or interval). As a beginner, you should only have one to two high-intensity days (threshold, interval) per week. You can do more if you are in a specific periodization program that permits a higher level of volume and intensity followed by recovery. Low-intensity days (recovery, aerobic) should be monitored and controlled using a heart rate monitor and defined training zones.

Periodization

Triathlon lends itself well to the traditional periodization plan. The goal of a periodization plan is to break training up into specific phases so that intensity and volume can be manipulated in order to optimize performance. You cannot train at the same level throughout the year, as this will lead to staleness at best and overtraining at worst.

Macro-Cycle

The macro-cycle breaks the year up into phases centered on the competitive season. There are four distinct phases to the macro-cycle: preparation, competition, transition, and off-season. To plan the macro-cycle first mark the start and stop dates of the triathlon season. These dates are determined by the first and last race that you would like to participate in. If you only do one or two early-season races, then those can be put into the preparation phase as preseason races. After determining season then you can schedule the remaining phases:

Preparation. The preparation phase, also known as preseason, is designed to increase volume and intensity as the upcoming race season approaches. Begin by building a base through increased volume and then move into increasing intensity. This phase will last approximately 9 to 12 weeks. This is a good point to begin your marker sets to determine baseline performance. As you repeat these measures throughout the preparation phase and into the race season, you can evaluate your training methodology to ensure that you are improving appropriately.

Competition. The competition phase is also known as in-season or race season. You need to establish the races you wish to participate in and then prioritize those races so that you can optimally plan your meso-cycle (explained below). Typically you will not be in top race shape for the early-season races. If you have an early-season race that is important, then you will need to alter your preseason training.

Transition. The transition phase is a short 1- to 2-week period of recovery from the race season prior to going into the off-season. The transition allows you down time for recovery and relaxation before going back to work.

Off-season. The off-season provides time for physical and mental recovery from the race season and will last from transition phase to preparation phase. Remember that the off-season is not only designed for recovery, but also for training that will help you in the upcoming season. Depending on where you live, off-season will last about 6 to 10 weeks before moving into the preparation phase.

Meso-Cycle

The meso-cycle is designed to break the macro-cycle into meaningful phases. Once you have the year broken down into the macro-cycle phases, then the competition phase will need to be broken down into meso-cycles. The meso-cycle is designed to undulate the training stimulus in order to optimize results. Keep in mind that off-season and preparation training also needs to be undulated, but will follow a different pattern than the competition phase as there is no completion meso-cycle within those phases. You have to provide increased stimulus, followed by recovery, and then followed by increased stimulus again. This process will allow you to greatly increase performance. The meso-cycle is divided into five distinct phases: preparation, build, tapering, competition, and recovery.

Preparation. During the preparation phase more focus is placed on increasing volume as opposed to increasing intensity.

Build. The build phase is designed to increase intensity, which will in turn increase anaerobic threshold and improve race performance.

Tapering. Tapering allows for recovery from training in order to optimize performance in an upcoming race or series of races. Depending on the event tapering can last 1 to 2 weeks. Many individuals conduct tapering incorrectly. If volume and intensity are decreased too much, performance can decrease. Slightly decrease volume and reduce the intensity and the number of high-intensity days leading up to competition. Do not train hard (high intensity or overly long distance) 2 days prior to the race. You still need to train but in recovery phase only.

Competition. The competition phase, also known as the peaking phase, may be for the period of one race weekend or for multiple races in succession. Do not try to peak for more than 2 to 3 weeks before moving to recovery. The length of the race (sprint to ultra-distance) determines how many times you can peak in a race season. Typically you will peak two to three times.

Recovery. A 1- to 2-week recovery period after a competition phase allows your body to heal and prepare for the next phase, leading to another peak. If you have another peak, you will move into the next preparation phase. If it is the end of the season, you will move into transition and then off-season.

Micro-Cycle

The micro-cycle is the daily and weekly training plan. Once you have determined the macro-cycle and the meso-cycle, design your program so that you reach the goals of each phase. Use your knowledge of altering hard and easy days as well as scheduling type of training and two-a-days to fill in the schedule.

Put Your Plan into Writing

Using the periodization theory above puts your training plan into writing. This allows you to better organize and lay out your training plan and prevent training haphazardly. Choose the races that you wish to participate in and record them on a calendar so that you can determine your competition phase. Then plan out the rest of the macro-cycle. Mark the beginning and end of the preparation, transition, and off-season on the calendar.

Once the macro-cycle is planned out, the next step involves scheduling the meso-cycle for the competition phase. Label the chosen races by priority. The most common method for prioritizing races is to label them as A, B, or C races with "A" level races being of the highest priority. This helps you determine when you need to peak in order to optimize performance. After

Once you have developed your plan put it into writing.

you determine where you want to peak, you can fill in the rest of the meso-cycle. Then, implement the micro-cycle. The micro-cycle involves the day-to-day training sessions that are the nuts and bolts of your program. Ensure that each day has a specific goal and that the training session is designed to best meet that goal.

The program that you develop will be a road map that takes you from the beginning of your training to race day. Be sure to develop a strong training program and then stick with it. Monitor your performance improvements, or lack thereof, and make adjustments to the training program as needed.

Monitor Training

Monitoring your training is essential to ensure that you are on track to reach your goals. Adaptations to training do not occur overnight and will take a while to significantly manifest. By monitoring training you can collect meaningful data that allows you to determine if you are improving or not. A training log will help you monitor training. Changes occur subtly over time and are sometimes difficult to notice. A log provides concrete numbers that allow you to determine if your training is going as planned. It also allows you to analyze your training and performances throughout the season so that you can make the necessary adjustments to training the following season. A training log should contain the following:

Body weight. Tracking body weight serves two main purposes. The first is so that you can monitor alterations to body weight over time. The second is so that you can track fluid loss when training in the heat in order to optimize rehydration. To accurately measure water loss, you must weigh yourself both before and after training.

Morning heart rate. Morning heart rate is typically used for two main purposes. The first is to monitor a decrease in morning heart rate over a long period of time as a marker of increased fitness. This is of limited use as there are other more accurate measures of increased aerobic capacity. Second, morning heart rate determines if you are recovered enough for the next training day. An increased morning heart rate over consecutive days could indicate overtraining or dehydration.

Type of training. State the type of training conducted: swim, bike, run, etc. If you are conducting two training sessions in one day, record both.

Distance and time. Record the distance and time for each training session. If you are conducting a brick workout, write down the time for each leg as well as the overall time.

Intensity. Record the intensity of the training session. Record all measures used to determine intensity during the training session (HR, RPE, Power). Also record time in and out of the desired training zone.

General comments on the training session. General comments provide an opportunity to include other pertinent information (weather, fatigue, injury, sleep, stress levels, etc.).

You can create your own training log with the information provided above, purchase a training log, or use a digital log. Digital logs can be found online for free or at a minimal cost. These training logs allow you to input data and compare workouts across time. Here are a couple of sites that provide online training logs:

www.beginnertriathlete.com
www.training.slowtwitch.com

It is very important that training sessions are logged on a regular basis. Attempt to log each training session upon completion so that it is still fresh in your memory.

HAMMER
HAMMER

CHAPTER SEVEN

Swim Training

When it comes to swimming, learning the proper technique is vital for both safety and performance. If you get tired running, you can stop and walk. If you become tired while cycling, you can pull the bike to the side of the road and get off. However, if you fatigue or panic during the swim, you must get to a point where you can touch or hold onto an object. I have worked with very fast cyclists and runners who wanted to become triathletes, yet had no swimming background. Getting a runner on a bike or getting a cyclist running requires very little effort as a coach. However, taking either and making a swimmer out of them is a completely different story. This chapter focuses on swim training techniques.

Swimming Technique

Many people who master the other disciplines and are otherwise in great shape need extra attention on swim technique. I strongly recommend you find a local swim coach to help you learn technique. Most areas will have a masters swim program that you can join for a minimal cost and receive excellent coaching.

Often beginning swimmers must overcome psychological issues before they can improve. We were not designed as aquatic animals and therefore we often have a healthy fear of the water (notice I said healthy and not irrational). As a beginner, you need to get comfortable with placing your head underwater. Until you become comfortable with this, you will be unable to learn proper swim technique, which is what is needed to ultimately improve performance.

Biomechanics of the Front Crawl

There are many more swim techniques than the front crawl, and they should be implemented into a well-balanced swim program. However, they are not overly efficient for triathlon and, for the purposes of this book, I will only cover the biomechanics of the front crawl. The front crawl is often referred

Learning proper swim techniques is crucial for improving performance on the swim.

to as freestyle because it is the fastest stroke and therefore the most common stroke used during freestyle competition.

Head and Body Position

The body should be horizontal in the water, not slanted. This allows you to glide through the water with less resistance. A slanted, feet-down position increases drag forces and buoyancy is negatively impacted, which results in greater effort and slower times. The main factor that affects body position is head position. It is actually quite simple: If the head goes up then the feet go down, and if the head goes down the feet come up. Place your head down into the water to where a small portion of the back of the head is the only part above the water line. Your head should be in a natural position looking at the lane line as you swim. The higher your head is positioned in the water the farther your legs and feet will drop. This is a common mistake for beginners.

The body should be positioned horizontally in the water. The body naturally rotates from side to side as you move through the water. When the hand enters the water and moves into a forward position, called reaching, it causes the opposing side to rotate upward. As you begin the pull and the other hand moves forward, you begin to rotate to the other side.

You want to use this natural side-to-side movement when developing your breathing pattern. There are three recommendations for breathing: every stroke, every other stroke, and every third stroke. The most common recommendation and the method that I suggest is breathing every third stroke. Breathing at this rate allows you to bring in enough oxygen, breathe out enough carbon dioxide, and breathe on both sides, which is beneficial when swimming in a group of people.

To breathe every third stroke, you want to count strokes (one, two, three, breathe, one, two, three, breathe, etc.). As you reach forward and rotate up on the opposite side, turn your head with the rotation, take a breath, and rotate back down into the water. While underwater, exhale through your nose until you rotate up for your next breath on the other side. With practice you will develop timing that allows exhalation to occur so that you come up for a breath without having to exhale prior to inhaling. There should be a natural rhythm to the breathing pattern. Do not hold your breath at any point. Once you become accustomed to the breathing pattern there is no longer a need to count.

Stroke

The hand should enter the water before the arm. *Gabe Sanders*

The stroke begins as the hand enters the water. The hand should enter the water first and just in front of the head. The elbow should be bent and high as the hand pierces the water. The most common mistake people make is to bring the arm down straight so that the arm enters the water prior to the hand. As the hand enters the water it shoots forward. The hand should move forward as opposed to downward. Pushing the hand straight down increases drag and eliminates a portion of the stroke. As you push your hand forward and reach out, the body will turn and the opposite side rotates upward.

From this position the pull begins. Throughout the pull ensure that the palm of the hand is always facing toward the feet until right before the hand leaves the water. Bring the hand down and back toward the feet.

The hand should be close to the body as it leaves the water. Keeping the elbow high will bring the hand up along the side and out of the water until it reaches the water entry point just in front of the head. Work on keeping the elbow high throughout the movement. *Gabe Sanders*

As the pull progresses the elbow bends and reaches close to 90 degrees as it passes under the body. The elbow straightens as the pull finishes. When the hand passes underneath the body, it roughly travels along the midline of the body. The hand moves toward the side as the elbow extends. The hand rotates toward the thigh as the pull finishes and the hand starts to exit the water. Pull the elbow high as the arm and hand leave the water.

Kick

The flutter kick is used during the front crawl. It serves two purposes. The first and foremost is to propel the body through the water and the second is to help keep the lower body elevated and stabilized in the water.

The flutter kick is executed primarily from the hips, with little movement at the knees. The legs will alternate movement.

As one leg begins the downstroke, the other begins the upstroke. The foot should be plantar flexed (foot pointed) and the knee slightly bent throughout most of the downstroke. At the last portion of the downstroke, the knee extends. From this position the upstroke begins, where the leg moves upward and back to the start of the next downstroke.

The flutter kick is conducted in a shallow, quick manner. The feet should not break the surface of the water or kick down too deep. Stroke rate will determine the number of kicks per stroke. There is no need to count out a six-beat kick count, as the natural rhythm will fall into place with practice.

Swim Drills

Swim training should not consist of countless laps swimming freestyle. In order to optimize performance, drills should be added to your training regimen. Each one of these drills provides specific training that allows you to work on improving technique.

Catch-Up

The catch-up drill is designed to work on stroke, body alignment in the water, and breathing. The goal is to get more glide out of each stroke. When conducting the catch-up drill, one arm will remain straight out in front at all times. Begin by pushing off the wall and placing both arms straight out in front of you as you glide through the water. Keeping your left arm out in front, complete a stroke with the right arm, finishing back in the start position. Glide forward and then take a stroke with the left arm.

Catch-up drill *Gabe Sanders*

When the arm comes forward, the hands will touch. Work on gliding as far as possible with each stroke.

Kick Drills

Kick drills allow you to work on technique and strengthen your legs for kicking. The drills can be conducted with and without a kickboard. When concentrating on kicking for the front crawl, you want to go up on your side with the lower arm reaching out in front in the same manner that you do when normally swimming the front crawl. The other arm should be along the side of the body with the hand resting on the hip. This position allows you to maintain proper body alignment for the front crawl and makes breathing easy. Maintain this position as you kick to the other side of the pool. Alternate sides each length.

Using a kickboard will help you focus on your kicking. *Gabe Sanders*

A kickboard is used to keep the upper body buoyant while working on kicking drills. Kickboards make kicking drills easier for beginning swimmers by allowing them to focus only on kicking. However, using a kickboard places the body in a position that differs from the normal position during the front crawl. The board adds buoyancy to the front of the swimmer and the swimmer's head is out of the water, which results in the hips dropping low in the water, and energy will be spent kicking to raise the lower body instead of propelling you forward through the water. There are a couple of techniques that you can use to place the body more in line with a normal position. The first is to use your arms to slightly push down on the kickboard, which results in the hips raising and the body going back in line. Or, place the head down in the water in order to raise the hips. As you kick down the lane, raise your head anytime that you would like to take a breath and then lower it back into the water.

Swim fins can be used in either method of kick drills. Fins serve two main purposes. The first is to propel the body through the water at a faster rate, and the second is to increase resistance for an improved workout. Do not use the fins during every kick drill as they do slightly alter the kick. Fins also increase the moment arm (lever length) and therefore can lead to the development of an overuse injury if used too much too soon.

Pull Buoy

Pull buoys are constructed of foam and are used to float the lower body, allowing you to concentrate on the upper body. Pull buoys are especially beneficial for new swimmers who need to spend a lot of time focusing on technique. The buoys allow the lower body to float effortlessly and the focus to remain on upper body motion. When using a pull buoy, place it between your legs as high up as possible and then swim normally with the upper body.

The pull buoy is used to help focus on arm stroke technique. *Gabe Sanders*

Hand Paddles

Hand paddles are primarily for adding resistance during the swim stroke, but they also help work on technique. The paddles are designed to grab more water by increasing the surface area of the hand and closing the gaps between the fingers. This greatly increases resistance and requires greater effort with each stroke. Using hand paddles provides feedback on hand placement throughout the stroke as well. As you exit the water and bring your hand up alongside the body, the elbow should be high and the hand should be clear of the water until reentry. If the hand contacts the water at any point prior to the reentry point, the paddle grabs the water. Work on getting your elbow higher until your hand no longer touches the water. If you enter the water at too steep of an angle, the water grabs the paddle and pulls it away from your hand. Work on entering the water at an angle that allows you to push your hand forward and not down.

Hand paddles are used to work on technique and for added resistance. *Gabe Sanders*

Hand paddles add a great deal of resistance to swimming and therefore should be used carefully. Improper use can lead to injury. Gradually work hand paddles into your program by starting with shorter distances and working your way up. Consider starting with smaller paddles. As you advance in your training, you can combine the use of hand paddles with a pull buoy.

Head Down

To maintain proper body alignment, it is very important to keep your head down during the swim. The higher your head is positioned in the water, the more the lower body drops, increasing drag and, therefore, energy requirements.

To maintain proper body position, focus on keeping your head down. *Gabe Sanders*

During the front crawl the cervical spine should be placed in a neutral position. You do not want the head up or too far down. One of the drills that helps with this is a ball drill. You can use either a tennis ball or a racquet ball for this drill. Place the ball under the chin and hold it in place as you swim. The act of holding the ball in place lowers the head into the correct position. This is a drill and should not be used throughout the entire training session. Once you hold your head in the correct position without the ball, there is no need to use the ball anymore.

Other Strokes

In an ideal world you should train using other strokes, for three main reasons. The first is that it will balance you out as a swimmer and prevent overuse injuries. Swimming is a repetitive motion and overuse injuries of the shoulder are common, especially during high-volume swim training. The second is that it breaks up the monotony of swim training. And, finally, the more strokes you can complete comfortably, the more comfortable and competent you will be in the water. However, due to limited training time, you may want to consider focusing only on the stroke that you intend to race.

Pool Etiquette

Learning pool etiquette is an important part of becoming a swimmer. I am a little spoiled, because where I swim now I rarely ever have to share a lane. However this is a very rare occurrence as most pools have more swimmers than the lanes can handle. In order to ensure that everyone has an opportunity to train and that everyone gets along, it is important to have established guidelines.

When the pool is crowded lanes are often identified by speed from slow to fast. Pick the lane that will best accommodate your speed. If the lanes are not designated by speed, attempt to join individuals who are swimming at about your speed. Enter the pool when there is a gap in the flow of traffic. If there is only one other swimmer in the lane, you can pick sides and stay on each side of the lane or circle swim counter-clockwise, always keeping the lane lines to your right. If there are three or more swimmers in a lane, you will always need to circle swim. When passing slower swimmers tap their foot to let them know you are there and pass on the left. Always be cautious when approaching and pushing off the wall.

Open Water Swimming

To optimize training and ensure safety, you need to be aware of the significant differences between swimming laps in a pool and swimming in open water. It is also important to obtain open water swimming experience prior to your first race. The more comfortable you are swimming in open water, the better experience you will have on race day.

Unlike a pool, you will rarely be able to touch the bottom when swimming in open water. This fact can have a very strong negative impact on beginning swimmers. First and foremost, it is of the utmost importance that you can comfortably and easily swim the race distance in a pool before attempting it in open water. If you fatigue while in the open water, there is no lane line or wall that you can grab to rest. Creating confidence in your ability in the pool goes a long way when you transfer to swimming in open water.

Visibility is another important difference between indoor and outdoor swimming. Unfortunately, you will very rarely be swimming in crystal clear water and there are never lane lines on the lake floor. When swimming laps in a pool, you can maintain a relatively straight line by following the lane line painted on the bottom of the pool. In open water you will need to learn to

It is important to become comfortable with open water swimming.

sight in order to stay on course. Never blindly follow the person in front of you, because he may not know where he is going. In every race it is inevitable that at least one competitor will become a little disoriented and swim in the wrong direction, taking a large group with him.

The swim course will be marked with floating buoys that require you to swim a specific route. In order to stay on route, it is important to frequently sight these buoys. Sighting requires you to pick your head up out of the water to see the buoy. When the head rotates to the side to take in a breath, pull the head up as you rotate back down so that the eyes are out of the water. Once the buoy is sighted, drop the head back into the water. You want to minimize the time your head is out of the water. The longer your head is out of the water, the slower you will go. Frequency of sighting is highly variable and depends on visibility and your ability to swim a somewhat straight line.

Unlike pools, it is very difficult to determine distances when swimming in open water. Use of time is a better marker of training volume. If it takes you 28 minutes to swim 1,600 meters in the pool and your goal for the day is to swim 1,600 meters, then swim for 28 minutes. Another option is to measure a distance with GPS. Garmin makes multisport GPS / heart rate monitors that allow you to measure distance.

Properly sighting swim buoys is an important skill to learn.

Not all open water swimming is the same. There are distinct differences between lakes, rivers, and oceans. A lake provides the calmest waters for swimming (assuming that there are no heavy winds or storms). When swimming in a river, you always have to be aware of the strength and direction of the current. Most river courses require you to swim out into the river to a buoy, around the buoy, swim down river, then swim back in to the exit. When swimming out into the river and then back to shore, the current will be roughly perpendicular to your path of travel. You want to angle upstream from the turn buoy. If you aim straight for the buoy, the current will take you downstream and you will have to swim directly against the current to make it around the buoy.

When swimming in the ocean, you will have to contend with the surf, swells, and rip currents. I was racing the Gulf Coast Triathlon in a year when the beaches were flagged and there were large swells coming in. As I was waiting to start my wave, I watched those in front of me start and noticed that many of the triathletes did not know how to get through the surf even to start the swim. When faced with a tough surf, the trick is to duck dive through the swells. As the swell comes toward you, dive deep into the swell, allowing it to pass over you as you come out the other side. Once you pass through that swell, advance toward the next swell and repeat until you reach the point that you can swim.

Rip currents pose a significant risk when swimming in the ocean. A rip current is a channel of water that is flowing away from the shore and out to sea. If you are caught in a rip current, remain calm and try not to fight it. Trying to swim against the current will only make you fatigue. Instead of fighting the rip current, conserve your energy and move out of the current by swimming parallel to the shore until you are free of the flow and then head straight back to shore.

Swim Safety

Whether you are an expert or a beginner, be cautious while swimming. While there is an inherent danger to swimming, it is minimized when swimming at a pool that employs lifeguards. Be sure to follow all of the posted rules and any direction from the lifeguards.

When conducting open water swims, the risk goes up exponentially. There are rarely lifeguards on duty and, when there are, it may take them a little time to reach you. You should be competent in your swimming abilities prior to attempting an open water swim. It is always a good idea to swim with a group or another individual in case of an emergency. I used to have someone kayak with me when I did my long swims. This was helpful in two ways. The kayaker could get to me quickly in the event of an emergency and haul me to shore if he had to, and a person in a boat is much more visible than a swimmer and could help ward off other boats.

Familiarize yourself with the area where you intend to swim prior to swimming there. Just because it is a body of water does not mean that it is a good place to swim. Here are some factors to consider:

- Boat traffic: Refrain from swimming in waters where there is heavy boat traffic.
- Currents: Be aware of any currents that you may encounter.
- Critters: Know and understand the wildlife that inhabits the area.
- Topography: Know the topography of the lake, ocean, or river. This allows you to know where you can touch bottom as well as locations of possible currents.
- Bacteria levels: It is good to know the bacteria levels of the area where you swim. Most public lakes will be able to provide the information. Avoid areas with unsafe levels of bacteria.

RUDY
FUJI
ZIPP

CHAPTER EIGHT

Bike Training

Many triathletes start with a limited cycling background, with the exception of those who were cyclists first. This chapter outlines the cycling skills required to successfully complete the bike leg of a triathlon.

Cycling Biomechanics

Aerodynamics

The bike leg of a triathlon is designed as a self-paced event where drafting behind other riders is not permitted. When drafting behind another rider, you will conduct approximately 30 percent less work than the cyclists in front of you. In order to ensure that each rider is advancing with no unfair advantage due to drafting, course marshals monitor drafting and assess penalties. Therefore, the aerodynamics of the triathlete and the bike becomes extremely important. On flat terrain up to 90 percent of your cycling power output is used to overcome drag force. In the last twenty years significant aerodynamic improvements have been made to both cycling equipment and rider position in order to optimize performance.

To understand how aerodynamics affects cycling, it is important to define drag and identify factors that affect drag. Drag is generated as an object passes through a fluid—in this case, air. As the object passes through the fluid the fluid flow is disrupted, beginning with the boundary layer right next to the object's surface and then moving outward to subsequent layers. The disruption of the fluid layers leads to the creation of turbulence at the trail edge of the object, which in turn creates an area of low pressure. Because you now have relatively low pressure at the trail edge and high pressure at the leading edge, drag occurs and adds resistance to forward momentum.

There are two main components of drag force that we can impact to improve aerodynamics. The first is *surface drag,* which is affected by the type of surface and the size of the surface area. If the surface material is rough, it will cause greater turbulence as the air passes over the surface, and the greater the surface area the greater the fluid flow disturbance. So tight-fitting

As a triathlete you should have a basic understanding of aerodynamics.
Nathan Kortuem

clothing that is smooth will greatly improve aerodynamics compared to baggy clothing that flops in the wind as you ride. Companies have developed skin suits that improve aerodynamics by having smooth patches of material in some areas and dimpled material in others. The dimples create a special type of turbulence that pulls the fluid close so that subsequent layers of fluid flow are not as disrupted, leading to less turbulence at the trail edge.

Triathlon bikes employ bladed tubing to improve aerodynamics. *Cannondale® is used by permission from Cycling Sports Group*

The second component that affects drag is known as *form drag,* which is affected by the shape and surface area of an object. By altering the shape of an object, you can improve aerodynamics. The most common alteration is to turn a sphere- or somewhat sphere-shaped object into a foil (bladed) shape.

A foil shape is rounded in the front and then trails to a point in the back. This design reduces turbulent flow and improves aerodynamics. For example, if you compare a triathlon bike to a traditional road bike, you can see the difference between a rounded tube and a bladed tube. Another example is comparing a road helmet to a triathlon helmet. While a lot of attention is focused on equipment, riding position can be altered to positively affect form drag. When examining the rider and bike as a unit, the rider accounts for 70 to 80 percent of total drag. Aerobars are designed to both reduce the frontal area of the rider and alter form to improve aerodynamics. Moving into an aerodynamic position using aerobars can reduce workload by up to 10 percent.

The speed of the object traveling through the fluid has a strong impact on drag. As you train you will notice that a windy day has a much greater impact during cycling as opposed to running. This phenomenon is explained by the theoretical square law, which states that drag increases with the square of velocity. If a cyclist doubles his speed from 12 to 24 miles per hour, drag will increase by four. This is also why drag has less of an impact on the individual when running at 10 mph compared to cycling at 24 mph.

Pedaling

While pedaling is relatively easy, proper pedaling mechanics take time to develop. Over time you will develop neuromuscular recruitment patterns that will allow you to pedal smoothly and efficiently.

When you first start cycling, your pedal cycle will not occur smoothly, and only through hours on the bike will it smooth out. The nature of cycling requires that each leg conducts the opposite movement throughout the pedal stroke. One leg applies a lot of force in a downward direction while the other leg pulls up with just enough force to unweight the pedal.

When examining the pedal stroke starting at the twelve o'clock position, the following is observed:

Twelve o'clock to Three o'clock

Force is applied down and forward

Primary muscles:

Hip: Gluteus Maximus

Hamstrings

Knee: Quadriceps

Ankle: Gastrocnemius

Soleus

Three o'clock to Six o'clock

Force is applied down and back

Primary muscles:

Hip: Hamstrings

Slight Gluteus Maximus

Knee: Slight Quadriceps

Ankle: Gastrocnemius

Soleus

When determining muscle activation, look at the pedal stroke as a clock face.
Gary Eippert

Six o'clock to Nine o'clock

Force is applied up and back

Primary Muscles:

Hip: Rectus Femoris

Knee: Hamstrings

Ankle: Slight Gastrocnemius

Nine o'clock to Twelve o'clock

Force is applied up and forward

Primary muscles:

Hip:	Rectus Femoris
Knee:	Hamstrings (flexion)
	Quadriceps (extension)
Ankle:	Tibialis Anterior

There are a couple of methods that you can use to determine if you are pedaling smoothly. If the high cost of computer-driven trainers does not deter you, the first is using the SpinScan feature on the CompuTrainer, which can calculate alterations to power output for both the left and right pedal strokes. The SpinScan graph and numbers will give instantaneous feedback on pedal stroke. Another method is to put your bike in a trainer and listen to the wheel on the roller. If the roller speeds up with every downstroke, then you are not pedaling smoothly. When you are pedaling smoothly, the wheel on the roller will sound smooth.

Cadence (how many times the pedal completes a full circle), which is measured in revolutions per minute (RPM), is an important component of both speed and efficiency. If possible purchase a cycle computer that allows you to measure cadence. To optimize efficiency, aim for a cadence of 90 to 100 RPM. A higher cadence reduces type II muscle fiber recruitment and increases blood return to the heart, though it also increases aerobic requirement. At lower cadences each pedal stroke will require a greater amount of power.

If you are not accustomed to cycling, you will typically start off pedaling at a lower cadence (70 to 90 RPM) and will take a little while to adjust to a higher cadence. Due to the increased aerobic demand, a higher cadence may even seem counterproductive in the beginning. However, after adaptations occur you will find a higher cadence much more efficient, and you will fatigue at a slower rate at any given speed.

An exception to the 90 to 100 RPM recommendation is when climbing. While it is a good idea to spin the climbs as much as possible, steep climbs require a reduction in cadence that corresponds to the steepness of the grade and your aerobic capacity and weight. The key to riding is to find the gear combination and cadence that will optimize the climb without being overtaxing.

Gear selection becomes an important consideration when cycling. The combination of cadence, the number of teeth on the front chain ring, and the number of teeth on the rear cog will determine speed. A typical crank set has a large chain ring consisting of fifty-three teeth and a small chain ring of thirty-nine teeth. A typical rear cassette for racing will have a range of eleven to twenty-one or twenty-three teeth for the rear cogs. Gear combinations are expressed as the product of the number of teeth on the front chain ring and the number of teeth on the rear cog (i.e., 53 times 16).

When looking at gear combinations, you will first need to understand the interaction of the front chain ring and rear cassette. The large chain ring requires more power per stroke, but propels the bike forward a greater distance per stroke. The opposite is true of the cogs located on the rear cassette. A small cog requires more power and propels the bike forward a greater distance per pedal stroke. Gear combination will be highly dependent upon your riding ability and terrain. A highly fit triathlete may choose a traditional two chain ring combination on the front and a smaller gear range on the rear cassette. A beginning triathlete may choose a triple chain ring on the front and larger cogs on the rear cassette. Rear cassettes are also commonly altered based on how much climbing is required.

Riding Skills

For both safety and performance reasons, you should spend time perfecting your cycling skills, especially if you are not accustomed to riding in an aerodynamic position. This section provides basic information on proper riding skills. However, there is no substitute for practice; the more you ride the more competent you will get, and the more you will be able to push the boundaries of your abilities. You do not want your speed on the bike to be limited by your riding skills.

Steering

Learning how to control and steer a triathlon bike from the aerobars takes practice, even for those who are accustomed to riding bikes. Riding in an aerodynamic position significantly alters bike handling compared to riding in an upright road position because the upper body weight is focused on the arm pads of the aerobar. When you ride a triathlon for the first time, it is normal to feel unstable. The degree of that instability is primarily dependent on your level of cycling experience.

The first step toward improving bike-handling skill is to ensure that the bike is fit correctly. If your current cycling position places too much weight toward the front of the bike, it will negatively impact bike handling. Another common fitting mistake is to place the forearms too close together, which makes it difficult to stabilize the upper body. You should obtain a professional bike fit prior to the beginning of training.

Work on relaxing your upper body while riding in an aero position. If you are too stiff, then handling becomes difficult and tiring. Most turns are made by shifting weight and not by significantly turning the front wheel. One of the common mistakes made by beginners is to try to turn the bike with the hands. Because the upper body weight is distributed on both forearm pads, the forearms are one of the key points used to shift weight during a turn.

When making a turn, look well into the turn in order to pick the most appropriate path of travel. You want to lift the inside pedal to the top of the stroke to give you ground clearance on the inside. I have seen more than one wreck because someone took a turn with the inside pedal down. Your weight should be placed on the outside pedal as you lean into the curve. The faster you take the curve the more you will need to lean the bike. Be sure to keep your center of gravity low throughout the turn. As you come out of the curve, start pedaling again in order to pick up momentum. With practice you will learn how to pick your path through the curve in order to successfully negotiate the curve without scrubbing off too much speed.

If you need to slow to negotiate a curve, make sure that you brake prior to the curve and not in it. Also, avoid panicking and braking during a curve. If you slam on the brakes during a curve, you will no longer follow the path of the curve. Instead at the point the wheels lock up the bike will move in a straight line. This could either put you into oncoming traffic or off the road.

Sharp turns are conducted at slower speeds and require the front wheel to be turned to a greater degree than in wider turns. If you are traveling slowly enough, you will need to turn the handlebars in the direction in which you are traveling. When approaching a sharp turn get out of the aerobars and slow down just before the turn. As soon as you are through the turn, begin pedaling to pick up speed and assume an aerodynamic position.

Remember that the bike will travel in the direction in which you look. Always focus your vision on the path you want to travel and the bike will follow. If you are on the edge of the pavement and about to go off, do not focus on the edge of the pavement, because that is where you will go. Instead

When taking turns there are times you will want to get out of the aero position in order to improve bike handling.

focus your vision on the road and the bike will follow. When looking over your shoulder, slightly shift the bike in the opposite direction to counter the natural drift occurring toward the direction in which you are looking. This skill takes practice, so try it in a large empty parking lot prior to attempting on the open road.

Braking

Braking looks easy, but it requires a little bit of knowledge and skill to do it correctly. On a triathlon bike the brake levers are located on the base bar with the left brake lever operating the front brake and the right brake lever operating the back brake. The front brake has considerably more stopping power than the rear brake. This occurs due to the inertial properties of the bike and rider. As you begin to stop, weight is shifted forward due to momentum and, therefore, the stopping power occurs at the front of the bike. Do not slam on the front brake or you may get thrown over the handlebars. When stopping you want to apply pressure to both brake levers. Through practice you will learn how to feather both the front and rear brake to maximize stopping. When breaking downhill or during an emergency situation, shift your weight toward the back of the bike as you stop.

Don't lock up the wheels when braking. If the wheels are not turning, then the bike becomes almost impossible to steer. In an emergency situation you will apply a lot of force to the front wheel while shifting your weight back in an attempt to keep the rear wheel on the ground. If the wheels lock up and you start to lose control, lift off the brakes a little and then reapply when you gain control. While allowing the wheels to turn will keep you upright, it also means that it will take longer to stop. So you may have a decision to make.

Never slam on your brakes going into or in a curve. Once the brakes lock up and the wheels stop turning, you will go into a straight line. Instead apply enough pressure to the brakes so that you slow down without losing control of the bike.

Shifting

The first step to proper shifting is to ensure that your shifters and derailleurs are working properly. Proper adjustment is covered in Chapter 2. There is nothing more annoying than not being able to shift quickly and cleanly from one gear to the next. The method of shifting will depend on the type of shift levers that you have on your bike. If you are on a road bike, you will most likely be using dual-purpose shift and brake levers. These levers allow you to brake and shift using the same mechanism. If you are riding a triathlon bike, then the brake and shift levers will be separate. Aerobars are set up so that the shift levers are located at the bar ends, allowing you to shift gears without coming out of an aero position. The brake levers are located on the end of the base bar separate from the shift levers.

One of the first rules of shifting is that you must be pedaling when shifting gears. If you attempt to shift without pedaling, it can place the chain in a bind. If the chain is in a bind and then you pedal, it can cause damage to the drive train, most often resulting in a broken chain or bent derailleur. The left shifter operates the front derailleur while the right shifter operates the rear derailleur. It is a good idea to spend time learning how the shifters function prior to your first long ride.

Learn to anticipate the need to shift gears. When you have to come to a complete stop, it is a good idea to shift to an easier gear prior to stopping. If you are in too large a gear when you stop, it will take some effort to get going again. This same concept applies when going into a sharp curve or turn that requires you to slow down.

When climbing adjust to easier gears as the climb progressively steepens. Do not try to force the climb without changing gears. When approaching a climb that is too steep to attempt in your big ring, shift gears just as the climb starts. In anticipation of the climb, shift down two to three smaller cogs in the back. Immediately after the final shift on the rear cassette, drop from the large chain ring to the small chain ring on the front. This will prevent you from losing too much momentum as you begin the climb. A common mistake is to just drop to the small ring on the front without altering the back, resulting in a significant drop in power output and sharp decrease in speed. Once over the climb and you begin to descend, shift up two to three gears on the rear cassette and then shift to the large ring on the front.

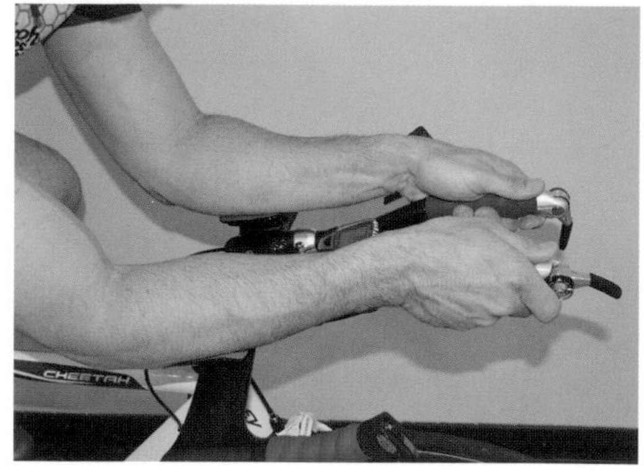

Aerobars place the shifters within easy reach of your hands.

Climbing and Descending Hills

No matter how fit you are climbing is always a challenge. And the only way to get better at climbing is to climb.

Body mass and aerobic capacity are two major factors that impact climbing. Triathletes with low body mass, especially those with a high power to body mass ratio and a high aerobic capacity, tend to be good climbers. Those who have difficulty climbing tend to have a deficiency in at least one of these areas, and most often they will have issues in both areas. Use the testing procedures discussed earlier in the book to determine your areas of weakness.

When climbing mild to moderate inclines, stay in the aerobars, and ride through the climb. As your speed slows there is greater benefit in climbing out of the aerobars as opposed to staying in them. Try to stay seated for as long as possible. When it gets to the point where you have to climb out of the saddle, do not exaggerate your movements. The bike will naturally move back and forth as you climb out of the saddle, which assists with climbing.

To safely descend at a specific speed, you will need both skill and confidence in your abilities. Learning to properly descend will give you the opportunity to gain time during the bike leg. Maintain a good aerodynamic position. When you travel at a speed that makes pedaling useless, place the crank arms parallel to the ground and bring your knees in toward the top tube. At high speeds the bike may develop what is called a high-speed wobble. Do not panic or make any sudden movements and do not slam on the brakes. Instead, maintain control of the bike and gently slow down until the wobble subsides. Most high-speed wobbles occur due to the rider being too tense. They can also be caused by equipment malfunction. Ensure that the headset is tight and that the wheels are sound (hub, rim, and spokes).

Road Conditions

As you ride always look down the road and be aware of your surroundings. When riding in aerobars there is a tendency to look straight down, which is exacerbated when you are fatigued. Always concentrate on looking down the road so that you can better negotiate obstacles (potholes, cracks, railroad tracks, cars, etc.). It is the pothole that you do not see coming that will get you.

Wet roads will alter how the bike handles, as the interaction between the asphalt and the wheel can change. During heavy rains oil on the asphalt moves to the surface, creating a slick area that limits tire traction. Tire traction also decreases when running water shifts dirt, sand, or debris onto the road. Any painted asphalt surface (lane lines, crosswalks, etc.) becomes slick when wet, so cross with caution. All of these conditions make turns and curves more hazardous, requiring slower speeds and greater caution.

When coming up on railroad tracks, always cross the tracks as close to perpendicular as you can manage. If the tire does not cross perpendicular to the tracks, the tire can fall into the crack, which will grab the front wheel and send you flying. When crossing the railroad tracks shift your weight to the rear as the front tire crosses and then toward the front as the bike tire crosses in order to prevent a pinch flat or damage to the wheel.

Riding Safely

Riding on the Road

When training it is inevitable that you are going to have to get out onto the roads and interact with traffic. By taking proper precautions, understanding the rules of the road, and using common sense, you can reduce the risk of an accident.

By law bicycles are road-legal vehicles and, therefore, have the same rights and restrictions other road-legal vehicles (such as cars) have. There are regulations that pertain specifically to cyclists and they do vary slightly from state to state. One regulation requires that cyclists stay to the right of the road unless making a left-hand turn. This allows cars to more easily pass on your left. However, this does not mean that you must ride on the side of the road outside the line. On the contrary it is a good idea to stay inside the line so that your path of travel is more predictable, there is less debris to worry about, and you are still considered a vehicle on the road. Under certain circumstances you will need to move out into the lane. When conducting a left-hand turn, you will need to move out into the lane, signal, and then turn. When approaching a stop sign or stoplight, move out into traffic and take your spot in line. It becomes very dangerous if you are still to the far right and you have cars squeezing past you at the stop sign. Laws vary from state to state so make sure that you learn the laws of your particular area.

Be aware of your surroundings. Always watch for cars crossing or entering the road. You are a small target and as such are often not seen by drivers. Watch when riding past cars parked along the road. Always assume that someone is about to open the car door into your path of travel; you may even want to move out into the lane a little until you are past the parked cars.

To turn, point your arm in the desired direction. To move into the lane, make eye contact with the car driver, point, and then move into the lane. At a four-way stop come to a complete stop and then go when it is your turn, just as you would in a car. Ride predictably and decisively when riding in traffic. Though you should ride like you belong on the road, always use common sense. It is called the law of gross tonnage; if it weighs significantly more than you do, then get out of the way. It is irrelevant who had the right of way when you have been flattened like a pancake.

Though there is no need to practice drafting, since it is illegal during triathlons, group riding during training is very common. Long hours out on the road alone can become boring and tedious. Riding in a group helps pass the time, breaks the monotony, and also can enhance your bike-handling skills.

Do not ride in your aerobars when riding in a group; this can be dangerous, as your hands are nowhere near the brakes. When riding in a group, you have to learn to hold a steady line and ride predictably. There should be no sudden changes in direction or speed. When drafting your front wheel will be 6 to 12 inches off the back wheel of the cyclist in front of you and there will be a cyclist 6 to 12 inches off your back wheel. You may also have riders on either side of you. Any sudden changes in speed or direction could be disastrous. Try not to use the brakes to slow if you get too close to the rider's back wheel. Instead of breaking slow your cadence, stop pedaling, or briefly move out into the wind in order to slow. If you are continually closing the gap on the person in front of you, consider shifting to an easier gear. Do not allow your front wheel to overlap the back wheel of the rider in front of you.

Learn how to properly ride within a group.

If that rider makes any sudden moves, his back wheel will make contact with your front wheel, causing you to crash. As the trail rider it is your responsibility to stay off the rider's back wheel.

When riding in a group, communication is very important. Communication can either be verbal or through the use of arm or hand signals. It is the lead cyclist's responsibility to initiate signals in the majority of situations and everyone's responsibility to relay the signal down the line of riders. Some of the following are common signals used for communicating while riding:

When approaching an obstacle (pothole, branch, etc.) that requires a change in direction, the lead rider needs to signal the rest of the pack to go around. The lead rider points to the obstacle as he veers around it and the signal is passed down the line. If the signal is not passed down the line, eventually someone will hit the obstacle.

The lead rider will signal turns by pointing in the desired direction. Signal well before the turn so that the signal has time to reach the back and riders have a chance to prepare for the turn.

When slowing or stopping signal by verbally yelling "slowing" or "stopping," or signal by lowering your arm with the palm of your hand facing rearward and repeatedly pushing your hand back.

One signal that is typically sent from the back to the front is when you are being overtaken by a car. As hand signals cannot be sent from the back to the front, a verbal command is used. The typical signal is "Car back."

Yell "Standing" whenever you get out of the saddle to climb so that others are aware of your movement. When you stand to climb, the bike decelerates slightly and then moves side to side as you apply pressure to the pedals. When passing always pass on the left-hand side and yell "On your left" as you pass other triathletes.

As mentioned earlier in this chapter, riding on the road is inherently dangerous. Be careful which roads you ride on. The ideal road is one that has little traffic, low speed limits, no blind curves, wide areas, and no dogs. When you find this place, let me know so I can ride there as well. When riding in areas of high traffic, pick a route that has designated bike lanes.

It is vital to remain aware of your surroundings. It is easy to get lost in thought, especially on long rides, and as a matter of fact it is one of the reasons I like riding. But don't let it detract your attention from the road. Do not wear earphones and listen to music while cycling. You need to be able to hear cars coming up from behind.

Carry a cell phone with you whenever you ride in case of emergency. The last thing you want is to have an accident or mechanical error 40 miles from home and have no way to call someone for assistance. If you need to use the phone for a non-emergency reason, pull over to the side of the road and make the call. Don't use it while riding.

No discussion of road safety is complete without mentioning the angry motorist. I have had everything from objects to insults thrown at me from moving vehicles. The best thing to do in these situations is to remain calm, record the make, model, and license plate (if possible) of the vehicle, and then report the attack to local authorities. Most of the time things happen so fast that it is difficult if not impossible to get all the necessary information. If possible avoid escalating the incident; there are too many crazy people out there.

Motorists are not always the problem—sometimes it's other cyclists. Always ride within the local laws and be as courteous as possible when riding. Do not run red lights or stop signs and interact with traffic appropriately. Where I live the law specifically states that cyclists shall not ride more than two abreast. The group I ride with rides two abreast and out of respect singles up whenever we are overtaken by a car. Cyclists who do not obey the local laws and are discourteous without reason make things rough on all cyclists.

Dogs are another common danger when riding on the road. The biggest concern with dogs is that they will run out in front of you and get under your wheel, which typically results in you flying over the handlebars. While most cities have leash laws that are strictly enforced, there are rarely leash laws in the country and when there are they typically are not enforced. As a result, there are a lot of unleashed dogs out along the roads. Lack of a leash law does not remove the owner's responsibility if damage to you or your bike occurs due to interaction with his dog on public roads. If you have a run-in with a dog, it is always good to report it, even if you got away without a scratch. This way there will be a record of the dog's aggressive behavior in the event something serious should occur. This also alerts the dog's owner to the animal's behavior and will typically provide a warning. If a dog comes at you, be sure not to swerve into oncoming traffic just to avoid being taken down by the dog. Carry dog spray with you when riding in order to fend off dogs. One spraying is usually enough to discourage dogs from attacking or chasing cyclists.

Wear sunglasses for protection. Sunglasses block UV rays and allow you to more comfortably look down the road on sunny days. They also protect you from wind irritation and help prevent debris (bugs, dust, etc.) from getting into your eyes. It is not uncommon to have debris thrown up from the asphalt by car tires. Consider purchasing a pair of glasses that allow you to change lenses. Using a rose-tinted lens increases visibility on an overcast day but may not provide adequate protection on a very bright day. In this case, you would simply switch to a darker lens.

Safety Checks

It is always good to perform a regular safety check on your equipment to ensure that it is functioning properly prior to riding. Over time bolts become loose due to road vibrations. Check the following components to ensure they are tight: pedals, crank set, stem, handlebars, headset, saddle, and seat post. Use a torque wrench to ensure that you do not over-tighten any part of the bike. Also, check the spokes of the wheels to ensure that they are not loose and that the wheel is still in true.

A lot of force is applied to the bike frame during races and strenuous training sessions, which can lead to fatigue cracks occurring in the frame. Bike wrecks can also result in fractures to the frame. Inspect the frame for any cracks that may have developed. Cracks may appear in the paint or clear coat without an actual crack occurring in the frame material. If in doubt have the bike inspected at your local bike shop.

CHAPTER NINE

Run Training

Of the three disciplines running comes most naturally. Running occurs as part of a natural progression, as we move from crawling to walking and then to running. However, just because you started running early in life does not mean that you are doing it correctly. Implementing the proper running biomechanics decreases the risk of injury while improving overall performance. Running biomechanics follow a basic pattern in all humans, but vary slightly based on your individual anthropometrics and joint architecture. Possessing a basic knowledge of biomechanics will not only provide a strong foundation for your own training, but allow you to better interact with the specialist at your local running store.

This section covers the basic biomechanics of running in order to provide an entry-level assessment. If you frequently experience injuries from running, it would be a good idea to be assessed by an experienced, knowledgeable professional who can adequately analyze your running biomechanics.

Lower Body Mechanics

Running is a natural extension of walking. However, during running there is the flight phase where neither foot is on the ground. There is also a much greater eccentric load and that causes alterations to muscle activation to occur. Because you have to propel the body up and forward while running, you must produce a larger amount of force. The hip muscles responsible for hip extension and the knee muscles responsible for knee extension must contract forcibly in order to propel the body forward in the air. The heavy eccentric load followed by the strong concentric contraction places a large amount of torque at each joint, especially the knee. When a runner uses incorrect biomechanics, the amount of force and direction of force alter slightly and can lead to overuse injuries. This is why it is very important to run correctly.

When running there are two very distinct lower body phases that occur: the stance phase and the flight phase. The stance phase can be divided into

The run is the third and final leg of the triathlon.

three distinct subphases. The first subphase is the heel strike, where the heel makes contact with the ground with the foot in a slightly supinated position (foot rolling away from the midline of your body). The goal of the heel strike is to absorb the ground reaction forces up the kinetic chain through a heavy eccentric contraction. In very fast runners it often appears that the heel strike does not occur. This is due to the extremely fast turnover rate and the minimum time that the foot is in contact with the ground. In some runners the heel strike may not be as emphasized and may be more of a heel mid strike in others. When observed with a high-speed camera, the heel strike can be seen in most runners.

Heel strike occurs when the foot first makes contact with the ground.

Midstance occurs as you move forward from the heel strike.

From the slightly supinated position of the heel strike, the foot moves toward pronation (foot rolling toward the midline of your body) as it transfers into the midstance subphase. During the midstance subphase the leg is perpendicular to the ground and body weight is distributed over the foot. During this phase the foot moves back to supination as it moves into the toe off phase.

Toe off occurs as you push off the ground, leading to the flight phase.

Neither foot is on the ground during flight phase.

The next subphase is the toe off. During the toe off the foot is pressing off the ground in order to propel the body forward as it moves into the flight phase. This is where the heavy concentric contraction occurs that propels the body up and forward. The key here is to propel the body forward more than up; exaggerated bouncing does not move you forward at a faster rate and is ultimately a waste of energy. During the flight phase neither foot is in contact with the ground. Next, the opposite foot hits the ground and the procedure is continued.

An important concept to understand concerning the stance phase is the stretch-shortening cycle. The stretch-shortening cycle consists of the muscle being placed on stretch followed by a forceful concentric contraction where the muscle shortens. When the heel strikes the ground, the muscles of the leg are placed on stretch during the eccentric contraction. This spring energy will then be transferred into a powerful concentric contraction in order to propel the body forward during the toe off subphase.

Improper biomechanics often lead to the development of overuse injuries. Biomechanical problems that occur at the foot are transferred up the kinetic chain and can apply significant stress at the foot, ankle, knee, and hip. One of the most commonly talked about biomechanical abnormalities is overpronation, which involves the foot collapsing too far inward to the point where it exceeds normal pronation, often resulting in shin splints or knee pain. Typically 8 degrees of pronation and higher is considered overpronation, while 15 degrees or higher would be considered severe overpronation.

It is very important to determine the cause of overpronation in order to adequately address the issue. If overpronation occurs as a result of either a low arch or an arch that is too high (collapses without medial support), a running shoe designed to correct for overpronation by providing medial support may help rectify the problem. If overpronation occurs due to reasons other than foot arch, a corrective running shoe may not help.

Overpronation can also occur due to lack of flexibility or muscular weakness. Ensuring that you maintain the proper range of motion in the lower body will go a long way in preventing most biomechanical abnormalities, and overpronation is no different. The gluteus maximus is one of the primary muscles that can affect overpronation, as it ties into the IT band and is responsible for the leg moving along the correct path during running. If the gluteus maximus is weak, then the leg does not track forward correctly, leading to overpronation and the possibility of developing an overuse injury.

Some experts believe that overpronation occurs in elite runners as a protective response to ground reaction forces. The large ground reaction forces and high turnover rates of these athletes results in greater pronation as a method to lessen the impact up the kinetic chain. In most cases the hips and knees of these runners are stable, and they have not developed injuries due to overpronation and therefore alterations are not needed.

If someone is overpronating or underpronating and everything else is okay, then leave it alone. If you are dealing with injury as a result, then it should be addressed. Any strength or inflexibility issues should be addressed immediately, as both situations are a ticking time bomb.

Gait

When examining lower extremity biomechanics, your gait must also be considered. Gait is a product of your stride length and stride frequency. The main determinant of stride length is leg length. Stride length is also dependent on speed, grade, fatigue, and injury. Stride frequency is based on desired speed and stride length. Gait can be altered by either adjusting stride length or stride frequency and is highly dependent on running speed. At lower speeds you will run faster by increasing stride length and at faster speeds gait is altered by increasing stride frequency. Keep in mind that you will have small alterations to both stride length and stride frequency throughout the range of speeds.

Grade and elevation changes require alterations to gait. When running downhill stride length will increase to compensate for the slightly increased drop in elevation. Be careful not to over-stride when running downhill, as this may lead to injury. If the downward grade becomes too steep, stride length and stride frequency will decrease in order to help maintain balance. When running uphill stride length decreases in order to compensate for the slight increase in elevation.

In most cases you will find the gait that is most economical at any given speed. Specific alterations to stride length or frequency are made without conscious thought. These adjustments occur as your neuromuscular recruitment patterns adapt over a period of time to become as economical as possible at any given speed. It is rare that gait will need to be directly altered in order to improve performance or decrease the risk of injury. Keep in mind that it will take you a while to properly develop gait. Most cases of incorrect gait are a function of muscle tightness or muscle weaknesses. Triathletes are notoriously inflexible. This inflexibility results in a limited range of motion resulting in a shortened stride length.

Over-striding is an example of an irregular gait pattern that would need to be directly addressed. Over-striding places the foot too far in front of the center of gravity and places a lot of force onto the lower extremities when making contact with the ground. Shin splint, knee, and hip pain are typical in those who significantly over-stride. Some athletes even learn to over-stride because they believe that it will make them faster runners. However, it does not increase performance and can actually lead to a decrease in performance as well as injury.

Upper Body

While it requires less technical explanation than lower-extremity position, upper body running position is also very important. Many novice runners place their head down and lean too far forward. Instead, the head should be in a neutral position with the eyes focused down the road. There should be a very slight lean forward in order to maintain proper balance. Your upper body should not be rigidly upright or leaning too far forward. The trick is to find that slight lean forward that allows you to maintain dynamic balance without strain. Keeping the core and neck muscles too tight is counterproductive.

The arms should be bent at roughly a 90-degree angle. Find a relaxed position that feels comfortable that is in the ballpark of 90 degrees. A common mistake is to hold the hands too high while running. Another common mistake is attempting to relax the arms too much to where they are almost straight. This position is biomechanically counterproductive and actually requires greater energy. The arms should swing front to back naturally and not across the midline of the body. Ensuring that the hands and fingers are relaxed is one method of relaxing the rest of the arm. If your hands are clenched into tight fists then the rest of the upper body will be as well.

Maintaining proper upper body position leads to greater economy.

The key with upper body mechanics is to maintain the recommended form in a relaxed state. The more relaxed you run, the less energy you will expend. Tense runners will fatigue at a much faster rate. Remind yourself to relax as you run and eventually as training progresses you will not consciously have to work on relaxing while running. To help gauge how tense you are, pay close attention to your jaw and hands. If your jaw or fist is clenched then so too are the rest of the muscles in the upper body.

Safety

There are some simple factors you should focus on to ensure a safe and enjoyable run. One is the location of your run. Before running in a specific location, it is always a good idea to gather information about the area. Get a runner's perspective, because non-runners may not have a good perspective on what is safe or not safe for running in an area. Local triathlon and running clubs can typically provide information on locations where it is safe and locations to avoid, such as secluded dark areas.

Running and cycling trails are a great place to run. When running on a trail, make sure that you follow the designated rules. Do not make sudden lateral movements on the trail as another runner or cyclists may be attempting to pass you. Always pass on the left side of the individual you are passing.

Yell, "On your left," as you pass so that the individual knows you are there.

While a running trail is a great place to run, you do need to be cautious. The factors that make running trails attractive are the same factors that can make them dangerous. Run with a partner, as there is strength in numbers. The more people in your running group the less chance of an incident occurring. Also, if an accident was to occur, you would have someone there to assist you until help arrived. Let someone know where you are running and when to expect you back. In case of emergency carry a cell phone and identification that includes your name, blood type, any special medical considerations, and emergency contact information. Identification tags can be worn on the shoe, around the wrist, or around the neck.

Carry protection with you on runs, if needed. The most common form of protection used by runners is pepper spray, which is small and can be easily clipped to your running shorts. If you choose other forms of protection, such as a stun gun or gun, it may be difficult to carry. It is very important to be familiar with your local state laws on carrying and using protection. The best way to handle provoking a situation is to avoid it all together. Situational awareness is critical when running. Remain aware of your surroundings and place everything into the context of safety. If you are running and you come across an area or an individual that make you nervous, keep moving, avoid the area, and do not stop moving for any reason. Do not wear headphones while running outdoors. If you have your headphones on, it will be impossible to pick up on audio clues of danger (i.e., someone running up behind you or a car engine).

When running outdoors it is inevitable that you will have to interact with traffic. Attempt to avoid traffic by running on sidewalks as much as possible. If you have to run in the road, you should run against traffic so that approaching cars are easily visible. Seeing oncoming traffic will give you more time to move out of the way in an emergency. If the vehicle comes up from behind, you may not notice it in time to avoid being hit. I also like to run against the flow of traffic even when I am on the sidewalk. I do not like unknown vehicles coming up from behind.

When crossing a street do not assume that the vehicle will stop at the stop sign or stoplight. Make eye contact to ensure the driver sees you, wait for him to stop, and then cross the street. Always look both ways before crossing the street, even if it is a one-way street. I was hit by a car driving the wrong way down a one-way street, and I did not see it because I only watched the correct way for traffic.

When possible, avoid running when it is dark and during times of poor visibility (e.g., fog). If you have to run when it is dark, wear reflective clothing. A blinking light also adds to visibility.

Be familiar with the local wildlife and how to handle an encounter. While dogs are the typical culprit, runners have also had encounters with snakes, bears, mountain lions, and alligators, just to name a few. These encounters are extremely rare and are more likely to occur when running trails. The appropriate response differs depending on the animal. For example, the vast majority of snake bites occur due to attempting to handle the snake or stepping on or too close to the snake. To avoid an encounter with a snake, simply pay attention and leave them alone.

With dog encounters, the first thing to keep in mind is that you cannot outrun a dog; in fact, running will trigger the dog's natural instinct to chase. As the dog approaches attempt to determine its demeanor. This may be more difficult for those who have not spent a lot of time with dogs. If the dog is wagging its tail, bouncing around, and barking chances are it just wants to play. If the dog is stiff from head to tail, growling and purposefully coming straight at you, then chances are it will attack. The playful ones are easy to deal with as they get bored and go home, so the biggest concern is them jumping on you or tripping you. On a long run I had a lab run next to me for about 4 miles before he got bored and started heading back the way he had come.

Aggressive dogs are of greater concern for a runner. An aggressive dog can cause serious bodily harm or death, regardless of size (okay, maybe not a teacup poodle), and an attack should be taken seriously. The following steps are recommended when attacked by an aggressive dog:

Do not run, as it gives the dog your back, conveys a sense of weakness, and you cannot defend yourself. The exception to this rule is if you have time to get to an object you can get behind or climb before the dog reaches you.

Stand calmly and slowly back away. The thought is that the dog will lose interest if you are not aggressive. Also, some dogs are aggressive because they are territorial and you are too close to their territory. Once you are at a safe distance, they will return to protect their territory.

Attempt to use common command words in a dominant voice (e.g., *stop, sit, no*). If the dog has been trained to respond to commands, it might listen. Naturally this will not work on wild dogs.

The opposite of using the commanding voice is to talk soothingly to the dog. Some dogs attack out of fear. If they are accustomed to humans and you talk softly to them, it will ease their fear and their aggression. This does not mean that you should pet the dog. Calm them and back away from the situation.

If you fall to the ground, curl up in a ball in order to protect your neck, head, and vital organs. Place your body weight full on the dog to subdue or to cause serious damage to the animal. Placing the full weight of your body on the dog will only work if you have a large enough weight differential between you and the dog. This is a desperation maneuver and should only be attempted if you are already on the ground and the dog is latched onto you. When using this maneuver you will be bitten and scratched, but you are attempting to limit the damage.

Defend yourself by any means available. Tasers, stun guns, and pepper spray will do the trick. Know and understand the laws of your state prior to using any of the above mentioned. A large stick can also be used to protect against an attack.

Whenever you encounter an aggressive dog you should always report it to the local authorities. Even if the dog did not attack you, it may attack the next person.

SPEEDY

CHAPTER TEN

Combining All Three Sports

If you come from a single sport background, you cannot take the volume you trained with in that sport and then add training for the other two sports on top of it. This is a common mistake made by many athletes moving from one sport into triathlon. The devotion to high training volume in one sport will need to be altered when training for triathlon in order to prevent overtraining syndrome. This chapter discusses specifically training for triathlon.

Optimal Training for all Three Sports

With triathlon training, the body will adapt specifically to the applied stimulus. Swimming requires a unique set of neuromuscular adaptations in order for you to become an efficient swimmer. The entire body is used to propel the swimmer through the water with a particular focus on the arms. Developing the proper neuromuscular recruitment patterns in order to perform the proper techniques is the key to success.

Cycling and running may appear to be more similar on the surface as they both require the legs for locomotion. However, the neuromuscular recruitment patterns differ. Cycling is considered a "closed chain kinetic activity" because the feet are attached to the pedals and the hips and upper body close the chain through contact with the bike. The crank arms form a perfect circle as they spin around the axis of rotation (at the bottom bracket). This requires that the legs move in a very specific, non-altering pattern. Running is considered an "open kinetic chain activity" because the feet make contact with the ground but the rest of the body has freedom of movement. The ground reaction forces differ between the run and the bike too. When the foot strikes the ground, the muscles of the legs have to contract eccentrically in order to handle the ground reaction forces, decelerate, and transfer the runner's momentum up and forward with a strong concentric contraction when pushing off. The heavy eccentric load that occurs during running places a large strain on the system and is where the damage that results in

Develop your training plan to include all three sports.

You will need to determine how many days per week you can run.

delayed onset of muscle soreness occurs. Cycling is non–weight bearing and muscle contractions are all concentric with no eccentric contractions.

When you combine sports, you have to realize that your overall training volume for each particular sport will decrease. Runners, cyclists, and triathletes have a tendency to obsess over the distance covered in training each week. Attempting to add training for the other two sports on top of your normal training volume for the one sport will result in overtraining. Typically runners who move to cycling find the transition relatively easy with one exception—the ability to produce high power output on the bike. Runners initially have difficulty generating power for climbing and sprinting. However, their endurance and ability to maintain speed on the flats is good. Cyclists switching to running will possess the necessary endurance, but will suffer with the ground reaction forces and the resulting eccentric contractions.

To excel at triathlon you have to look at it as a single sport and not three different sports. You have to complete all three between the start and the finish line. Any weakness in any of the three areas will result in poor overall performance, so focus on improving your weaknesses during training, while also maintaining focus on the areas where you do excel.

Frequency of Each Mode of Training

Scheduling training so that you can adequately train all three sports is difficult. You can train every day of the week in order to get all of your training in; however, I advise you take one day off per week, and you must have at least one easy day. Use the hard/easy principle to incorporate easy days into your program.

Consider training goals (performance-oriented or recreational) and volume when scheduling your training. A recreational triathlete will mainly be concerned with finishing the triathlon and accomplishing his individual goals. Therefore, training volume will be lower, allowing for an easier scheduling process, compared to a performance-oriented triathlete, who will have a higher training volume and intensity. There are two common methods for optimizing training for triathlon: two-a-day training sessions (where you conduct two different training sessions in one day with recovery time between sessions) and a brick workout (where you conduct two or more training modes in one session—bike followed by run, for example—without rest between modes).

Two-a-Days

Many triathletes implement two-a-day training into their programs in order to optimize training adaptations for triathlon. There are two basic theories on how to implement two-a-day training sessions. The first involves swimming in the mornings, followed by a recovery period, and then biking or running later that day. Swimming is low impact and does not overly stress the legs, so your performance while running or cycling later in the day will not be greatly affected. Ideally you should conduct the run on the same day as the swim and then cycle the following day. Also, there is nothing wrong with running in the morning and swimming later in the day.

A second approach is to conduct the bike and the run on the same day with recovery time between training bouts. Because training the run and the bike in the same day places strain on the system, I recommend you follow up the next day with a swim, which is less stressful. Less stressful does not mean that the swim workout will be an easy one, but swimming is a non–weight bearing activity and is less stressful on the lower extremities than running. While swimming will work the entire body, it truly taxes the upper body (especially the shoulders), whereas cycling and running do not.

When conducting two-a-day workouts, remember that you must recover between workouts in order to optimally perform during the second workout. One of the issues with training twice in one day is depleting energy stores. Lipid stores will not be an issue; however, glycogen stores will. Glycogen stores are limited to about 2,000 kCals and are heavily depleted during triathlon training, so you must replenish glycogen between training bouts. You must also recover from muscular fatigue between bouts. I recommend you conduct one session in the morning and then one session just prior to dinner. Two-a-day workouts should be conducted no more than 2 to 3 days per week. Elite athletes can conduct two-a-days more frequently, but must be cautious of overtraining.

Brick Workouts

Brick workouts are conducted by participating in multiple modes during one training bout with little to no recovery between modes. The most common brick workout used is a bike followed by a run. To conduct a bike-to-run brick workout, you need to have your running gear set up for an easy transition to the run upon completing the bike. Head out on your bike and immediately upon return switch to your running gear and take off on the run. This is a good way to practice your transition from the bike to the run. While a brick workout most commonly refers to a bike followed by a run, you can conduct different types of multiple-mode training bouts.

There are numerous benefits to conducting brick workouts. The first is that going from one mode of exercise to another will cause a shift in neuromuscular recruitment patterns. When you first start brick workouts, you will notice that your legs feel extremely uncoordinated when you move from the bike to the run. While this feeling will never completely disappear, it will lessen with training.

Another benefit to brick workouts is that they allow you to complete the distance to be done on race day. While there are obvious physiological reasons as to why being able to complete the entire distance prior to race day is ideal, there are also psychological reasons. If you know you can comfortably complete the distance, on race day you will have greater confidence.

A typical brick workout consists of full distance in each of the modes that you wish to focus on for that training session. However, you can conduct brick workouts with shorter sessions. For example, you can follow a long bike with a short easy run so that you can work on transitioning your legs from the bike to the run without overtaxing the legs on the run.

Brick workouts save time by covering two or more sports in one training bout. However, full brick workouts should be conducted sparingly as they are very stressful on the body. You should conduct no more than three full brick workouts per week, though short brick workouts can be conducted more often. You will need to listen to your body in order to determine if you are adapting appropriately to the training stimuli.

Basic Program

To develop a basic training program, you will want to apply the principles that were discussed in Chapter 4 and Chapter 6. Remember there is always more than one road to reach the same destination, and that while some roads are better than others, they all arrive at the same place. Here are a simple program outline and guidelines for altering the basic program to fit your current fitness level and goals. We will start with a basic outline for frequency and layout for all three sports:

	SWIM	BIKE	RUN
Monday	Recovery	Recovery	Recovery
Tuesday	Morning Swim	Off	Afternoon Run
Wednesday	Off	Bike	Off
Thursday	Morning Swim	Off	Afternoon Run
Friday	Off	Bike	Off
Saturday	Off	Brick	Brick
Sunday	Morning Swim	Bike	Off

The program is designed so that during a week period you swim 3 days, run 3 days, and bike 4 days. The brick workouts are held on Saturday for a couple of reasons. The first is that most races are held on Saturday and you become accustomed to long, hard days on that day. The second is that most people have more time to fit in a longer workout during the weekend. The brick workout can be the typical bike to run, or you could do all three as though it was a race. On the bike-only days you could follow the bike with a short easy run just to work on the transition from bike to run. Keep in mind that on those days the goal is to focus on the bike and the transition to run is secondary.

The next step is to determine the training intensity for each of your workouts so that you know the training goal for each day.

	SWIM	BIKE	RUN
Monday	Recovery	Recovery	Recovery
Tuesday	Morning Swim Moderate to hard: Intervals and technique	Off	Afternoon Run Hard: Intervals or race pace
Wednesday	Off	Bike Easy: Mid distance	Off
Thursday	Morning Swim Hard: Intervals and technique	Off	Afternoon Run Easy: Long slow distance
Friday	Off	Bike Easy: Mid to long distance	Off
Saturday	Off	Brick Hard: race pace	Brick Hard: race pace
Sunday	Morning Swim Easy: Technique and distance	Bike Easy: Long slow distance	Off

By alternating hard and easy days, you will be able to optimize training by adding increased stimulus while allowing added time for recovery. The type of workout on hard days can vary from flat intervals to hill repeats to flat intervals on a track. Intensity can be altered based on current fitness level and training goals. For beginners, your main goal is to complete the race, so do not worry about adding in the hard days. You can keep everything at an easy to moderate intensity level. A fit triathlete who is concerned with finish times can add in or alter hard days. In the program laid out above you could switch the Wednesday bike to a hard day, which will not negatively impact the hard swim day on Thursday because swimming is non–weight bearing and primarily works on the upper body.

Instead of using the terms easy, moderate, and hard, you can also implement the four training zones first introduced in Chapter 4.

- Zone 1 used as a recovery workout
- Zone 2 used for easy and long, slow distance days
- Zone 3 used for moderate to hard
- Zone 4, which is considered a hard workout

The next step in program development is to determine the duration of each workout. The duration is highly dependent on you. What might be a long, slow distance for one individual might be a recovery ride for another. Intensity ultimately determines duration. You cannot run 4 miles at the same speed you can a 400-meter sprint. You have to slow down in order to be able to run 4 miles. Remember by race day you want to be able to complete a longer distance than the race. The example below is for an entry-level triathlete.

	SWIM	BIKE	RUN
Monday	Recovery	Recovery	Recovery
Tuesday	Morning Swim Moderate to hard: Intervals and technique 30–60 mins	Off	Afternoon Run Hard: Intervals or race pace 20–30 mins
Wednesday	Off	Bike Easy: Mid distance 60–120 mins	Off
Thursday	Morning Swim Hard: Intervals and technique 30–60 mins	Off	Afternoon Run Easy: Long slow distance 30–60 mins
Friday	Off	Bike Easy: Mid to long distance 60–120 mins	Off
Saturday	Off	Brick Hard: Race pace 60–80 mins	Brick Hard: Race pace 20–30 mins
Sunday	Morning Swim Easy: Technique and distance 60 mins	Bike Easy: Long slow distance >120 mins	Off

Make changes to duration based on your current fitness level and goals. You will need to adjust the volume of training each week until your ultimate goal is met. Remember not to increase volume greater than 10 percent each week.

Pacing Strategy

To optimally perform during triathlon, it is important to implement the appropriate pacing strategy throughout the race. Research has demonstrated that the most effective pacing strategy is an even pacing strategy, where intensity remains relatively constant throughout the race. Many beginning triathletes will take off too fast and die off before the end of the race, leading to slower race times. You want to find the pace where you are going as fast as you can without blowing up. It is a fine line between an optimal time and dying off prior to the finish line.

When racing attempt to maintain an intensity level that you can continue throughout the race to optimize time. The only way to learn appropriate pacing is through experience. Pacing is set based on known distance and your experience racing that known distance. By working all three sports during a training session, you will develop the ability to appropriately pace yourself.

While it is important to control intensity using heart rate or power during training, do not limit race pace based on either. There is a strong possibility that you may not perform optimally if you use a heart rate or power limit during the race. Instead, race based on perceived exertion. The problem arises when you do not have enough experience racing the distance to accurately pace based on feel. As you gain experience training and racing you will be able to fine tune your race pace based off of the known distance and perceived exertion throughout the race.

STOP
AHEAD

CHAPTER ELEVEN

Off-Season Training

Off-season training is vital for optimizing performance in the upcoming race season. Although you cannot train full force year-round without allowing time to recover, off-season is a misnomer as there is no true "off" period. While you will decrease both volume and intensity and slightly alter how you train, you will still follow a structured training plan. You need to be just as focused on your off-season training as you are on your in-season training. A well planned off-season will lay a strong foundation for preseason training and racing during the competition phase. This chapter will help you develop an off-season training program that will improve performance the following race season.

Recovery from the Race Season

The main reason to incorporate an off-season into your yearly training program is to allow time for you to recover from the grueling race season. Individuals who train at the same volume and intensity year-round will never meet their true potential and often end up overtrained. Decreasing training in the off-season will allow the body to completely repair and be ready to start hard and heavy again in the following preseason.

In addition to your physical recovery, you also need to recover from the previous race season psychologically. The hours of training and the extreme efforts put forth during a race take a mental toll on an athlete leaving them "burnt out" by the end of the season. With all the heavy training and intense racing, we have a tendency to forget why we love the sport. The off-season allows us a chance to take a break and recharge our mental batteries for the upcoming season. If the off-season training is conducted correctly, you will feel rejuvenated and excited to get out and race again.

During the off-season you will reduce your training volume by 20 to 40 percent by decreasing both the duration and frequency of the training sessions. While you will decrease volume, it is extremely important to keep an aerobic base throughout the off-season. If you decrease volume too much, it

Off-season training can make a significant difference in your upcoming race season.

will be extremely difficult to return to race form during the following season. Intensity will also decrease in the off-season. This does not mean that you will not have hard days, but that intensity and frequency of high-intensity days will decrease.

Outdoor and Indoor Training

Off-season for triathlon occurs during the colder part of the year (October to March). Depending on where you live, you may or may not be able to effectively train outdoors during this time. You will need to make arrangements to train indoors when the weather does not permit training outdoors.

Swimming will typically be the least affected by cold weather as most people conduct swim training in an indoor pool. You will give up outdoor open water swims. If you are considering joining a workout facility with a pool for the winter, consider the cost of the facility and the pool hours. Most pools have early morning hours. Find out how crowded the pool is at the times you can train. There is nothing more frustrating than showing up to the pool with a large number of people swimming in each lane and having to wait for a spot to open, especially if you have limited time to swim.

Running can be conducted outside throughout the winter as long as the running surface is clear of ice and snow and the cold is not too extreme. When running indoors there are two basic options: indoor track and treadmill. Indoor tracks are great alternatives to running outside, if you do not mind continually running in a circle. Be careful when running on an indoor track—running numerous laps around a tight track can put undue stress on the joints.

Treadmills allow you to train indoors during adverse weather.

Treadmills also provide an alternative to training in

the cold. Running biomechanics will alter slightly when running on a treadmill. Instead of propelling your body forward you are just keeping up with the belt. This affects both neuromuscular recruitment patterns and energy expenditure. This does not negate the effectiveness of the treadmill, but is something that you should be aware of.

Cycling outdoors during the winter is more problematic than running. The high speeds of cycling along with the resulting wind chill lead to rapid heat loss. Due to wind chill, cycling at 20 mph can drop the temperature by about 10 degrees. As a result I typically stop riding outdoors much sooner than I do running. There are multiple alternatives for cycling indoors.

Bicycle resistance trainers provide altering resistance to enhance training and are the most common choice for indoor cycling. They consist of a stand to hold the bike and a resistance unit with a roller, which is placed against the tire. By placing your own bike in the trainer, you can maintain the neuromuscular adaptations specific to your fit.

Bike trainers allow you to use your own bike for training indoors.

There are four basic types of resistance units found on bicycle resistance trainers: fluid, magnetic, wind, and computer-driven. Fluid trainers contain fluid in the resistance unit that provides resistance as the roller spins. As you ride faster the roller spins the internal impeller faster, which increases resistance. Of the non-computer-driven trainers, the fluid trainer is the most similar to riding on the road. Fluid trainers cost between $200 and $500. Magnetic trainers provide resistance through the alteration of the magnetic field around the spinning metal flywheel located in the resistance unit. These units typically cost between $100 and $300, depending on features. Wind resistance units possess a bladed flywheel that provides resistance as it spins. The faster the flywheel spins the greater the resistance. These units tend to be noisy due to the wind passing over the blades. Wind resistance units typically run around $100.

Computer-driven bicycle trainers, such as the CompuTrainer, are the optimal choice for indoor training. These systems allow you to ride simulated outdoor courses indoor. Resistance is altered through the computer software based on the grade of the simulated course you are riding. You can either ride simulated outdoor courses or create your own. You can even ride your favorite course with your GPS unit and then download the data to create the course for your trainer. These systems provide feedback (power, heart rate, and cadence) that allow you to accurately monitor your training. The software also provides video of you, your avatar, riding the course. The systems run around $1,600, making the units impractical for many triathletes.

The CompuTrainer simulates road riding conditions indoors. *Al Lipping*

Regardless of the type of resistance system, keep in mind that you want to use the skewer that came with the unit. Most modern skewer quick-release levers will not fit properly into the trainer, leaving your bike susceptible to disengaging from the trainer while riding. Most trainers lock your bike rigidly into place, which applies a lot of force on the wheel and rear triangle of the bike. As long as you do not over-tighten the tension knob, risk of damage is minimal. Kinetic makes a trainer that actually moves side to side as you pedal.

Tension has to be created between the tire and the roller in order to keep the tire from slipping too much as it spins the roller. The interaction between the roller and the tire will wear the tread flat relatively quickly. I recommend using old tires that you have retired from service for this purpose in the winter. You can also look at purchasing a tire specifically designed for use in a trainer. These tires do not wear as quickly and dissipate heat created by friction better than the average tire. Do not use these specialized trainer tires outside. They are not designed for use outside and have very poor traction on the road.

Rollers are another option for indoor training. These units allow you to place your bike on top of the rollers, but the rear wheel does not lock into place. Because the bike sits on top of the rollers, resistance is minimal, so they are not recommended for high-intensity workouts. These units do require a great deal of balance and are good for working on a fluid pedal stroke, though they can be somewhat hazardous to you, your bike, and immediate surroundings.

The last option for indoor training is a spin bike. Spin bikes possess a 30- to 50-pound flywheel that provides the initial resistance. Resistance can be increased by adjusting the tension placed on the flywheel. When riding a spin bike, make sure to take measurements from your personal bike and adjust the spin bike accordingly to optimize your training experience. Keep in mind that unlike your road bike, spin bikes are fixed gear; you cannot immediately stop pedaling and must slow down gradually. Spin bikes will cost anywhere from $300 to $3,000, depending on durability and available functions. I recommend visiting a spin class to determine if you enjoy riding a spin bike prior to purchasing one.

Spin bikes are commonly used for indoor cycling training. *Al Lipping*

Training videos designed for riding on an indoor trainer also make riding indoors more tolerable and help the time pass quickly. Most of the training videos are conducted at a high intensity and therefore should not be used every time you train indoors.

Sweat is very corrosive and can damage your equipment. Make sure that you clean your bike and trainer after every indoor ride in order to prevent corrosion. If you have a spin bike, periodically pull the seat and handlebars off and clean inside the frame and lubricate in order to prevent corrosion.

Resistance Training

Resistance training in the off-season is an outstanding tool to improve your triathlon performance. These improvements do not come from increases in aerobic capacity. Instead the increase in performance comes from improved neuromuscular recruitment and subsequent improvement in economy.

You may be concerned that resistance training in the off-season will affect body mass, as body mass does affect performance. But research shows that significant hypertrophy (gain in muscle fiber diameter) does not occur due to off-season resistance training and that there are no increases in body mass. You also want to consider your overall training volume. If you add resistance training on top of your normal off-season training volume, it will most likely be too much. Instead, replace a portion of your off-season training with resistance training—how much should be replaced is highly dependent on your training program and individual needs. Implement the program slowly and watch for overtraining. While an important tool, it is still just one small tool in a large toolbox.

An off-season resistance training program is not a traditional strength or bodybuilding program—don't make the mistake of using this program for that purpose. The goal is not to maximize strength. Instead, the philosophy is to use resistance training to improve endurance performance. This does not require lifting heavy weights for hours in the gym. Instead, you should be in and out of the gym in 30 to 40 minutes.

Adaptation to Resistance Training

The most common adaptation to resistance training is hypertrophy, gain in muscle fiber diameter. Resistance training does lead to an increase in the size of muscles and has the largest effect on strength and power, but there are also other adaptations that occur that are not as obvious to the naked eye and are just as important. These are *neuromuscular adaptations* (adaptations leading to increased muscle coordination).

The largest neuromuscular adaptations occur within the first 8 weeks of training. If you have ever done a weight training program, you probably experienced significant strength gains within the first 6 to 8 weeks and then leveled off. These strength gains were not from hypertrophy, but from neuromuscular adaptations. And since your off-season resistance training program will only last 6 to 12 weeks, the adaptations will be neuromuscular in nature with no noticeable hypertrophy.

There are three primary neuromuscular adaptations that occur. The first is the recruitment of motor units that have not been previously recruited on a regular basis. The second adaptation is the improved synchronization of activated motor units. As synchronization of firing patterns improve, strength increases. The third is a release of *autogenic inhibition.* Autogenic inhibition is a protective mechanism where the contracting muscle relaxes and the antagonist muscle relaxes when the strain on the muscle is too high. This prevents you from placing too much strain on the muscle and causing damage. Through training, the strain threshold for autogenic inhibition to initiate increases, allowing you to lift more weight.

Designing a Resistance Training Program

This section provides you with the general information that you need to design an off-season resistance training program. These recommendations are general in nature; you will need to monitor how you respond to the program in order to optimize adaptation. There is also more than one path you can take to reach the same destination. When initiating the program remember to work into the program slowly in order to prevent undue soreness and injury. To start, you will need to determine volume (frequency, repetitions, and sets) and intensity (resistance).

Frequency

First determine *frequency,* which is based on the length of the program and how many days per week you use resistance training. The typical off-season resistance program should last 6 to 12 weeks. The first 2 weeks of training will be used to slowly work your way into the program, and the last couple of weeks will be used to taper off into the preseason. It is possible to conduct a maintenance phase through the first portion of the preseason. Once you determine the length of your off-season resistance training program, you need to determine how many days per week you will conduct the program.

Resistance training should be conducted 2 to 3 days per week—typically Monday, Wednesday, and Friday. Not all three of those days have to be in the weight room lifting weights. You can work in plyometrics—basically jump training, such as box jumps—or sports-specific resistance training during one of those sessions.

Sets and Repetitions

Sets are the number of times you perform the exercise, and *repetition* is the number of times you lift or perform the movement per set. Research has shown improvements occur with one to three sets. Since you want to get in and out, I typically recommend two sets for the majority of exercises in the program.

Improvements in endurance performance after off-season resistance training have been demonstrated with high weight at low repetitions (4–6 repetitions), moderate weight at moderate repetitions (8–12), and low weight at higher repetitions (up to 30 repetitions). While they all have resulted in improved performance, I typically stay away from high weight and low repetitions due to the increased risk of injury associated with heavy lifting. I recommend 8–15 repetitions. When conducting body management exercises (muscular endurance: push-ups, crunches, etc.) the goal is muscular endurance and therefore do not limit yourself to 8–15 repetitions. Instead, do as many as you can with the goal of conducting at least one more repetition each training session. For example, if you did 16 pull-ups on your first set on Monday, then your goal should be at least 17 reps on the first set during your workout on Wednesday.

Determining Weight

Determine weight based on desired repetitions. For example, if you are conducting two sets with goal repetitions of 8–12, you would set the weight so that volitional exhaustion occurs between 8 and 15 for both sets. This may take you a couple of workouts to figure out, but will work well. If you are able to conduct more than 15 repetitions, then increase the weight. If you cannot conduct at least 8 repetitions, then decrease the weight.

To avoid delayed onset of muscle soreness (DOMS), do not lift until exhaustion during the first 2 weeks. Instead, lift lighter weights, concentrating on technique. After the first 2 weeks, you can increase weight. If you lift too hard too soon, you may lose training days due to soreness.

Choosing Exercises

The next step is to choose the resistance exercises. Below are examples of exercises that you can implement into your resistance training program. Research has shown that improvements occur with lifting, plyometrics, body management exercises, and sports-specific exercises. I typically use a mixture of all of them. These are just a few exercise examples to get you started. If you are serious about your performance, consider hiring a strength and conditioning coach with a background in endurance performance.

Work your entire body, including the upper body, lower body, and core; avoid focusing on one area and ignoring others. The lifts and exercises listed below supply a sufficient program to cover all the major muscle groups that are important to a triathlete. You can replace these lifts with others that work the same muscles or focus more on a specific area by adding more lifts into your program. If you are not familiar with the muscles involved with each specific lift, then I strongly recommend purchasing a book that shows the specific muscles used in each movement, such as *Strength Training Anatomy* by Frederic Delavier.

Start with large muscle groups and then follow up with small muscles. For example, work bench press prior to working triceps. If you fatigue the triceps by conducting triceps extension prior to doing bench, then you will not be able to adequately work the pectoralis major due to triceps fatigue.

Weight Training Log

Follow your progress with a resistance training log in order to mark improvements and keep you on track. The training log should contain the exercises, the weight/resistance for each exercise, and a place to record repetitions. I have provided a sample training log (on the next page) for you to use.

Weight Training Techniques

Learning proper lifting techniques is vital for both optimizing performance and preventing injury. If you have minimal or no lifting experience, work with a *certified* strength and conditioning coach on learning proper technique.

While each lift requires specific techniques there are general guidelines that go with all lifts:

- Maintain proper technique throughout the movements. Don't try to use momentum to get through a lift where the resistance is too heavy. If the resistance is heavy enough to require you to alter proper form, you should decrease the weight to maintain form.
- Movements should be slow and controlled.
- Correctly grip the bar at all times in order to prevent the bar from rolling out of your hands.
- Do not attempt to lift weights that are too heavy for your current fitness level. This is a common source of injury.

Date:

EXERCISE	WEIGHT	SET 1	SET 2	SET 3
Squats				
Lunges				
Leg Extensions				
Leg Curls				
Seated Calf Raises				
Push-Ups	N/A			
Bench Press				
Pull-Ups	N/A			
Lat Pull-Downs				
Seated Rows				
Bicep Curls				
Triceps Push-Downs				
Shrugs				
Crunches	N/A			
Twisting Crunches	N/A			
Leg Raises	N/A			
Back Extensions	N/A			

- Work large muscle groups before working small muscle groups.
- Never hold your breath. Inhale during the eccentric load and exhale during the concentric load.
- For safety always use a spotter with free weights.
- Use collars on the barbells in order to keep the weight from shifting on the bar.

Resistance Exercises

Lower Body

Squat

The primary muscles used during the squat are the quadriceps, hamstrings, gluteus maximus, gastrocnemius, and soleus. When conducting a squat center the bar across the back and shoulders, and grab the bar with both hands. This places you in a comfortable position to control the bar. Lift the bar off the rack and back up into position over the safety bars. Place your feet shoulder-width apart. During the lowering phase do not allow your knees to move forward beyond your feet. Lower into the squatted position until your thighs are parallel to the floor. Next, push up with the legs returning to the standing position. Do not lock your knees at the top of the lift. To maintain proper posture it can be helpful to look up throughout the movement.

Start position of the squat

Down position of the squat

Lunge

Down position on the lunge

The primary muscles involved in the lung are the quadriceps, hamstrings, gluteus maximus, gastrocnemius, and soleus. Lunges can be conducted weighted or unweighted. Start by conducting lunges with no weights and move to weighted lunges only when you are ready.

Place your feet about shoulder-width apart. Step forward with your right leg and lower your body until the thigh of the right leg is parallel to the floor and the knee of the left leg is almost touching the floor. Return to the standing position and then repeat this process by stepping forward with the left leg. Lunges can also be conducted in a walking manner by leaving the lead foot planted and bringing the rear leg forward into a lunge.

Calf raises

Calf raise

Calf raises work the triceps surae, made up of the gastrocnemius and soleus, and can be conducted either seated or standing. Conduct standing calf raises on a raised platform. Stand with the back halves of your feet off the platform. Rise up onto the balls of the feet and toes, then lower your body so that the heels go just below the top of the platform. Calf raises can also be conducted seated. The object here is to put the gastrocnemius on slack and concentrate a little more on the soleus.

Leg extensions

Leg extensions focus on the muscles of the quadriceps. Before beginning leg extensions ensure that the machine you are working on is set up specifically for you. Do not lock your knees out at the top of the knee extension.

Leg curls

Leg curls strengthen the hamstrings (semitenndinosus, semimembanosis, and biceps femoris). Because the gastrocnemius crosses the knee, it will be worked along with the hamstring muscles. Adjust the leg curl machine in accordance with the manufacturer's instruction.

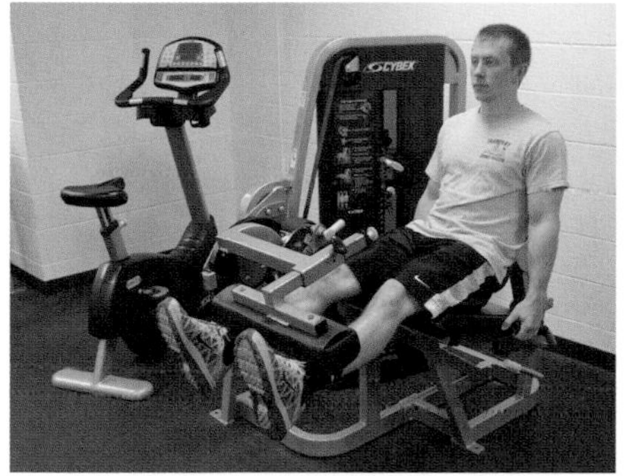

Leg extensions

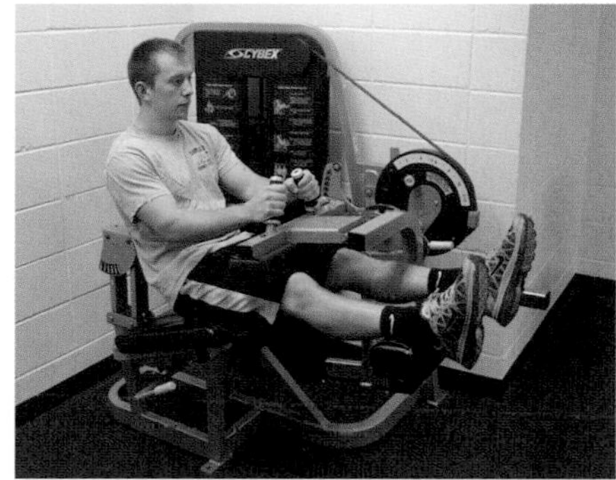

Leg curls

Upper Body

Push-ups

Push-ups increase the muscular endurance of the pectoralis major and triceps brachii. Lie face down on the floor placing the hands just wider than

Push-up start position

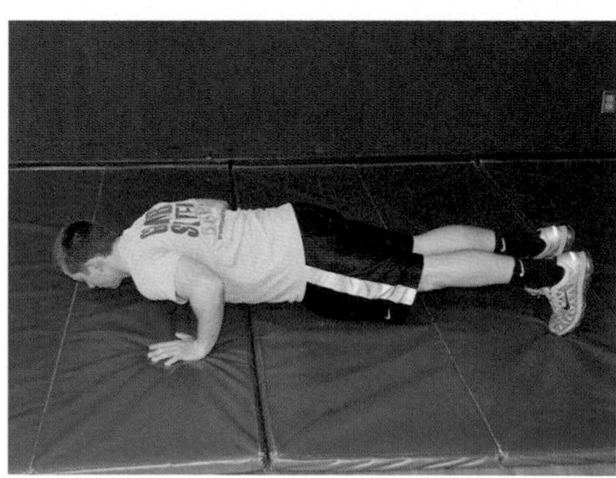
Push-up down position

the shoulders. From this position push up until the arms are straight. This is the start position. From the start position lower your body until the elbows are approximately at a 90-degree angle and then return to the start position. The weight should be borne by the hands and the toes throughout the movement and the body should stay straight as well. If you are just beginning, you can conduct a modified push by changing the contact point from your toes to your knees.

Bench press

The pectoralis major and the triceps brachii are the primary muscles used in the bench press. Synergistic muscles used during the bench press are the anterior deltoids, serratus anterior, and coracobrachialis.

Lie flat on your back with both feet planted on the floor. Place your hands on the bar about shoulder width apart with the palms facing away and fingers and thumb wrapped around the bar. Lower the weight until it is about 1 inch from your chest. Do not bounce the weight off your chest. From the lowered position push the weight back up to the start position.

Bench press start position

Bench press down position

Pull-up

The pull-up improves the muscular endurance of the latissimus dorsi, teres major, and biceps brachii. Grasp the pull-up bar a little wider than shoulder width with the hands facing away from you. Hang with your arms straight and no weight on the ground. Pull your body weight toward the bar until the chin clears the bar and then return to the start position. Do not use a swinging motion during this movement.

Pull-up

Lat pull-downs

The lat pull-down works the latissimus dorsi, teres major, and biceps brachii. Adjust the lat pull-down machine per the manufacturer's instruction. Grab the bar just wider than shoulders with the palms facing away from you and fingers and thumbs wrapped around. Pull the bar down in front of your head and then return to the start position. Do not pull the bar behind your head as this may lead to injury.

Lat pull-down

Seated rows

The latissimus dorsi, trapezius, rhomboid (major and minor), teres major, posterior deltoids, and biceps brachii are worked during the seated row. Adjust the machine per manufacturer's instructions. Bring the bar/handles to your chest and then return to the start position. Maintain proper back posture throughout the movement.

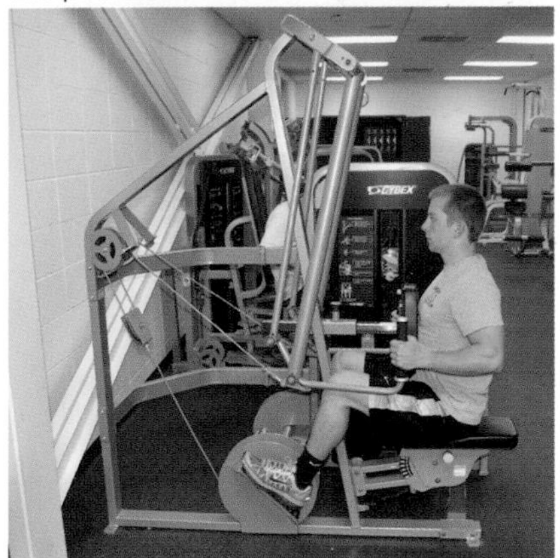

Seated row

Bicep curls

Bicep curls

The biceps brachii is worked during the bicep curl and can be conducted using either a dumbbell or barbell. During the bicep curl keep your back straight and move the weight in a controlled manner. Do not attempt to throw the weight up and get underneath it. Instead move to a lighter weight you can control easily.

Triceps push-downs

The triceps push-down is conducted on a cable machine and is designed to work the triceps brachii. You can use either a triceps rope or close grip bar on the cable machine. Grab the bar in a close grip and pull down until the bar is about chest high and your upper arms are somewhat parallel to your side. This is considered the start position. Push down until the arms are straight and then return to the start position. Keep the upper arms stable throughout the movement.

Triceps push-downs start position

Triceps push-downs end position

Overhead press

The overhead press can be conducted either seated or standing. The deltoid, pectoralis major (clavicular head only), and triceps are the primary muscles used during this exercise. When conducted on a machine, follow the manufacturer's instructions. The overhead press can also be conducted using dumbbells. Grab the dumbbells in an overhand grip and place the dumbbells a little higher than shoulder level with the back of the hand facing you. This is the start position. Press up over the head and then return to the start position. Overhead press can be conducted with a barbell, but I recommend beginners stick with dumbbells. Dumbbells allow more natural joint movement throughout the lift.

Overhead press

Dumbbell shrugs

The upper trapezius (upper and middle fibers) and the levator scapula are the muscles worked during the shrug. These muscles are important as they are responsible for holding your head upright when riding in an aerodynamic position. To conduct the shrug stand with your feet shoulder width apart while holding dumbbells at your side. Shrug upward moving your shoulders toward your ears and then return to the start.

Shrugs

Core

The core muscles work to stabilize the spine and pelvis during the bike, swim, and run. There is a common misconception that the core muscles are primarily just the abdominal muscles and erector spinea muscles. However, the core is correctly defined as the multitude of muscles (approximately twenty-nine) that are designed to stabilize the pelvis and spine. Here are three common exercises that focus on the abdominals and the erector spinea. Those truly interested in developing a workout to develop core muscular endurance should expand this portion of their workout by adding more exercises.

Crunches

Crunches focus on the rectus abdominis and the oblique abdominals.

Crunches

Lie with your back on the floor and place your legs in the air bending at the hips and knees. You can also conduct the crunch by placing your heels on a bench. Place your arms across your chest and curl your body off the floor until the upper back is clear of the floor. Repeat for as many reps as possible. After completing a set of normal crunches you can add in a set of twisting crunches. From the same start position, curl up twisting your right shoulder to your left knee and return to the start position. On the next rep curl up twisting the left shoulder to the right knee and then return to the start position. Repeat this sequence until exhaustion.

Leg raises

The leg raise works the abdominal muscles and hip flexor muscles when performed correctly. Lie on your back with your head off the floor, arms at your side, and feet just off the floor. Lift your legs just past 90 degrees of hip flexion and then return to the start position. Keep your legs straight throughout this process.

Leg raises

Back extensions

Back extension

Back extensions work the erector spinae muscles. Lie face down on the floor with your toes pointed and place your hands behind your head or straight out in front of you. Begin by lifting your upper body off of the floor and then return to the start position. You can either keep your lower body in contact with the floor or lift it from the floor in unison with the upper body.

Sport-Specific Resistance

Sport-specific resistance training can be conducted for swimming, cycling, and running. When conducting this training I typically replace all or a portion of the weight training for that day. Start slowly when adding sport-specific resistance training to your program; adding too much too soon can lead to overuse injuries.

Swim resistance training can be conducted in the pool or on dry land. A common tool used on dry land is the Vasa ergometer. The land-based swim ergometer allows you to perform resistance training that mimics the

Dry land resistance swim training *Courtesy of VasaTrainer.com*

pull of the swim stroke, which works the muscles directly used while swimming. This is a good time to work on stroke technique. Be careful not to get sloppy just to conduct more reps. Due to the cost of the trainer, not every aquatic center will own one. Resistance bands are an inexpensive alternative. By attaching one end of the resistance band to an immovable object, you can mimic your swim stroke.

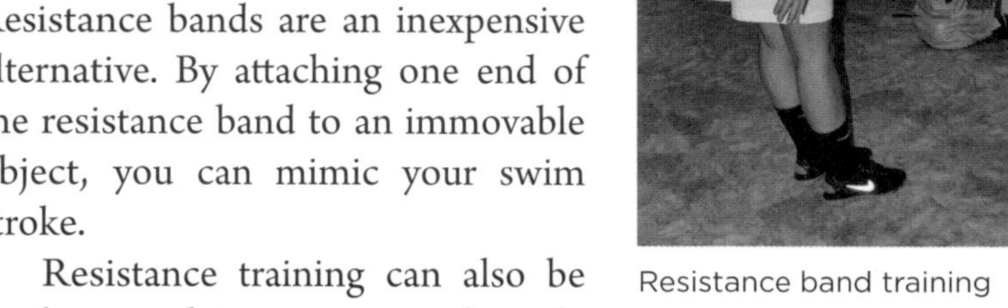
Resistance band training

Resistance training can also be implemented into your pool workouts. Using a swim tether adds resistance to your workout because you are forced to swim against the restraint of the tether. Or, use hand paddles. Hand paddles serve two purposes. The first is to work on technique. If your hand enters the water incorrectly, it will make it difficult for the paddle to correctly catch water and stay firmly on your hand. The second purpose is to catch more water, increasing the resistance. Be cautious when using hand paddles as they can lead to overuse injuries if used improperly.

Common methods for conducting sport-specific resistance training on the bike include hill repeats and tension intervals. With hill repeats find a long hill that you can climb multiple times. Begin by warming up for about 10 to 15 minutes. A sample set looks like this:

- Spin up the hill easy
- Climb the hill seated in a higher gear at a low cadence
- Climb the hill standing
- Climb the hill fast with your normal gearing and cadence

Depending on the length of the hill and your current fitness status, conduct one to five sets. If you cannot find a hill, you can conduct tension intervals. Tension intervals are conducted on flat or relatively flat roads. To conduct tension intervals shift into a harder gear that requires you to pedal at around 60 rpm and conduct intervals.

Sport-specific resistance for running can be conducted as hill repeats or stadium workouts. Find a stadium with stairs that can easily be run. Start by warming up for about 10 minutes and then conduct the following set:

- Run up hitting every step on the way up and then walk back down.
- Run up every other step all the way up and then walk back down.
- Lunge up every other step and then walk back down.
- Double leg hop every other step and then walk back down.

Complete one to ten sets depending on your current fitness level and experience. Keep in mind that this workout contains a very heavy eccentric load, which will make you extremely sore. So go easy on your first run-through. You can also become very seriously injured if you fall. If you feel that you are becoming sloppy as you fatigue, it is time to call it a day.

CHAPTER TWELVE

Nutrition

Nutrition is vitally important for both health and performance. I have seen too many athletes who spend all of their focus on training and completely neglect nutrition. The development of a proper nutritional plan for before, during, and after a workout can go a long way toward increasing performance.

This chapter includes a basic introduction to nutrition and provides general guidelines designed for healthy individuals who do not have dietary restrictions. If you are regularly taking medication or have a known illness, check with your physician prior to altering your nutritional intake. Also consider working with a registered dietitian who has a background in sports nutrition and can establish a detailed nutrition plan tailored to your specific needs and goals.

Nutrients

There are six categories of nutrients: carbohydrates, fats, proteins, vitamins, minerals, and water. These nutrients are responsible for everything from energy transfer to anabolic processes. Each nutrient plays a specific role in normal body function.

Carbohydrates

Carbohydrates are one of the main fuel sources for the human body. Carbohydrates are ingested and then converted to glucose for transportation in the blood and glycogen for storage. Glycogen is not only used for human movement, but is also the only fuel source that is utilized by the central nervous system and the brain. When glycogen stores become low during prolonged exercise, you become fatigued and confused. This is typically termed *bonking*.

The average individual should consume about 50 percent of his daily caloric intake from carbohydrates, and endurance athletes should consume approximately 60 to 70 percent of their daily intake from carbohydrates. To

It's important to stay well hydrated. *Shutterstock*

more precisely determine carbohydrate intake, the average individual should consume 5 to 6 grams of carbohydrates per kilogram of body mass per day, and endurance athletes should consume 7 to 10 grams of carbohydrates per kilogram of body mass per day. The range of 7 to 10 g/kg is highly dependent on the volume and intensity of training. As the volume or intensity increases so, too, will the recommended intake.

The type of carbohydrate ingested is as important as the amount of carbohydrates ingested. Whole grains, fruits, and vegetables are excellent sources of carbohydrates. Try to avoid refined grains, as they typically lose a significant amount of their nutrients during the refining process. Also attempt to limit simple carbohydrates (simple sugars) and instead focus more on complex carbohydrates (whole grains, vegetables, etc.). Except for during a race, avoid foods that are high on the glycemic index.

The *glycemic index* measures the effect of carbohydrate ingestion on blood glucose levels. Foods that are below 50 on the glycemic index have very little effect on blood glucose levels. However, foods that measure above 70 can cause a large increase in blood glucose levels, resulting in a significant spike in insulin (hyperinsulinemia), which in turn results in hypoglycemia (low blood sugar).

Fats (Lipids)

Fats are another primary energy source in the body. They also play other key roles in the body such as thermoregulation, providing protection for vital organs, allowing transport of fat-soluble vitamins, and production of hormones. Fats are stored as triacylglycerol in the body and provide a large amount of energy per molecule. Triacylglycerols are stored in muscle and in adipose tissue, which is found around organs and just under the skin. The average individual stores approximately 70,000 to 80,000 kCals of fats. This number can obviously vary from individual to individual.

There are several different categories of fats. Saturated fats can be found in foods such as meats, eggs, milk, and cheese. Unsaturated fats can be either monounsaturated (found in canola oil, sunflower oil, and almonds) or polyunsaturated (found in meat, eggs, nuts, fish, fruits, and vegetables).

Approximately 30 percent of your daily intake should consist of fats, with the majority coming from unsaturated fats. Less than 10 percent of your dietary intake should come from saturated fats. Stay away from trans fats, as they are detrimental to your health. Also stay away from extremely low fat diets (<15 percent of daily intake), as they can have a strong negative impact on health and performance.

Proteins

Proteins provide very limited energy during exercise and are typically only relied on heavily when glycogen stores are depleted. The main purpose of proteins is for anabolic process in the body, and therefore they are vital in the recovery process. There are no excess protein stores in the body. Proteins ingested in excess of need are converted to either triacylglycerol or glycogen for storage. Meat, seafood, poultry, milk, cheese, eggs, and nuts are primary sources of protein in the diet.

As an athlete, you should ingest 1.2 to 2 grams per kilogram of body mass each day. The amount of protein that you need to ingest will be highly dependent on the volume and intensity of your training program. As volume and intensity increase, you will need to move up on the scale. Taking in very large amounts of protein can place a strain on the liver and result in dehydration and electrolyte imbalance, but there is no great concern as long as you are healthy and not ingesting more than 4 grams per kilogram of body mass per day.

Vitamins

It is a misconception that vitamins provide energy directly. However, they are vital to many of the chemical processes in the body. For example B vitamins and niacin, are a significant part of the chemical process that ultimately results in the production of ATP; vitamin D is important for bone density; and vitamin C assists in iron absorption. There are many more examples of the role of vitamins in the body in relation to exercise and performance.

For most healthy triathletes who maintain a well-balanced diet, there is no need to supplement with vitamins. However, for those who may not be eating an adequate diet, vitamin supplementation may be needed to meet the demand of the body. To establish desired vitamin intake, consult the Dietary Reference Intake chart provided by the United States National Academy of Science.

Minerals

Minerals are inorganic nutrients required for normal body function. The most abundant mineral in the human body is calcium, which plays a key role in many chemical processes in the body. Human bones consist of 60 to 70 percent calcium and, therefore, it is critical for maintaining a healthy bone density. Calcium is also vital for contracting muscles. Calcium is primarily obtained by consuming dairy products.

Iron is another mineral that is necessary to maintain normal body function. Iron is used in the formation of hemoglobin and myoglobin. Iron is not required in large amounts and can be found primarily in meat. Iron can be found in small amounts in plant sources such as potatoes or beans. Unless you are iron deficient or vegetarian, there is no real need to take iron supplements. Supplementing with too much iron can also have a negative health impact.

Iron-deficient anemia presents as a feeling of fatigue due to a decrease in hemoglobin. Certain populations are more susceptible to developing this condition. Females are most susceptible to the development of iron-deficient anemia due to blood loss during the menstrual cycle. Female athletes are even more susceptible due to iron loss through sweat and the high hemoglobin turnover rate associated with heavy training regimens. Vegetarians are at risk due to the limited availability of iron in plants.

Phosphorus is another mineral that is widely used in the body for various chemical processes. Phosphorus binds with calcium to form calcium phosphate, which is vital for bone growth and development. Phosphorus is also important for protein synthesis and responsible for the formation of ATP. Phosphorus is consumed easily in most diets and can be found in meats, dairy products, and cereals.

Fluids

The body is composed of approximately 60 to 70 percent water, which is vital for everyday body functions and sustaining life. Blood plasma consists of approximately 90 percent water and is responsible for transportation of gasses, nutrients, and other compounds. Because heat is transferred rapidly in water, blood plasma is also responsible for thermoregulation. Develop a hydration plan and make sure to stay hydrated.

During exercise blood plasma volumes drop due to water loss through sweating and through respiration. Water loss during exercise can negatively impact both performance and health. A water loss that is equivalent to approximately 2 percent of body mass will negatively impact performance. As the water loss reaches approximately 5 percent of body mass, there will be a negative impact on health. One of the primary health concerns with dehydration is the inability to properly thermoregulate, leading to heat-related illnesses.

Because of the high volume of fluid loss during prolonged exercise, the recommendations for average individuals (1.5 to 3 liters/day) cannot be used with triathletes. Instead focus on replacing the volume of fluid that is lost during a workout.

To determine the volume of fluids lost, weigh yourself before and after the workout (both unclothed). The difference in weight represents the volume of fluid lost. Replace each pound lost with approximately 24 ounces of fluid. This rehydration recommendation assumes that you were properly hydrated prior to the exercise bout.

Nutrition and Exercise

To promote recovery, positive adaptations, and increased performance, you should spend some time developing a sound nutritional strategy. This strategy should not only look at daily intake, but timing of that intake as well.

Before Training and Races

Dietary intake prior to a training bout or race is extremely important and can strongly impact the outcome of either. Training or racing without eating prior to competition can negatively impact performance and possibly health, especially on high-intensity days. Not eating prior to a workout can lead to low blood glucose levels, resulting in feelings of fatigue and dizziness. There is a larger effect at higher intensities due to an increased reliance on glycogen and glucose as a primary energy source. At race pace during a sprint triathlon, you will utilize around 100 percent glucose and glycogen. Low blood glucose levels occur most commonly in individuals who skip breakfast for their morning training.

It is also not a good idea to eat a large meal just prior to a training bout or race. During exercise blood flow will be directed to areas that need it most, such as the working muscles and the skin for cooling. It will also be redirected from areas that need it the least, such as the digestive tract. After eating a meal blood is redirected to the digestive tract in order to properly digest the food. So, if a meal is eaten prior to exercise these two systems are at odds. During exercise inadequate blood flow will be redirected to the digestive system to properly digest a meal, leading to gastrointestinal distress.

Timing, quantity, and type of nutrition must be addressed. Meals should be eaten 2 to 4 hours prior to competition. Eat light foods that will fill you up but do not take a prolonged time to digest. For example, slow-cooked oatmeal, bagels, or fruits make an excellent breakfast, but stay away from the sausage, egg, and cheese sandwich.

Take in carbohydrates that are high on the glycemic index prior to the start of exercise to help spare glycogen during an endurance event. Carbohydrates high on the glycemic index will increase blood glucose levels fairly quickly, which in turn will spare glycogen stored in the liver. Carbohydrates, such as sport gels, can be ingested approximately 5 to 10 minutes prior to the start of exercise. Supplementing with carbohydrates is only recommended for exercise lasting longer than an hour. Do not take in sport gels too far before the start of the event, as this could cause an early blood glucose spike, leading to an overshoot of insulin, low blood sugar levels, and fatigue.

During Training and Races

During training sessions and races that last longer than an hour and a half, you will need to take in carbohydrates. Glycogen stores are limited to around 2,000 kCals and are a limiting factor for energy production through oxidative processes. Ingesting carbohydrates increases blood glucose levels and therefore spares glycogen stores in the liver, offsetting glycogen depletion and the resulting fatigue. Keep in mind that glycogen is utilized at a much faster rate during high-intensity exercise.

You should ingest 30 to 60 grams of carbohydrates every 45 to 60 minutes during exercise. The carbohydrates should be easily digested and high on the glycemic index as to enter the system quickly. Energy gels and sport drinks are typical choices, as they provide both. In comparison, sport bars enter the system at a slower rate. However, taking in solid foods on a long ride can help offset hunger as well as provide the needed carbohydrates.

When choosing what food source to use during training and racing, there are important aspects to consider. First, what is in the supplement? The nutrition label located on the package tells you how much carbohydrates are contained inside and what other supplements it may contain (protein, caffeine, etc.). Another consideration is taste. Simply put, if it does not taste good, you will not take in as much. This is especially true if you use sport drinks. The last thing to consider is how your body reacts to the supplement. If you use a specific brand of sport gel or drink and the race provides another, you may want to find out how your body responds to that specific brand prior to race day. You do not want to end up with gastrointestinal distress during the race. Along this same line of thought, always try a new product on a training day prior to using it in a race.

It is vital to hydrate during the training session or race. Hydrating with water during sessions lasting less than an hour and a half will be sufficient in most cases. High-intensity activities lasting an hour and a half could benefit from supplementing fluid intake with a sport drink. Activities lasting longer than an hour and a half will require use of sport drinks to provide hydration, electrolyte replacement, and carbohydrates.

It is impossible to completely maintain hydration levels during a long training session or race in the heat, so you must develop a hydration plan and stick with it throughout the session. Thirst is a mechanism that lets us know that dehydration is setting in and that we need to drink. During exercise, if you wait until you are thirsty to drink, it is already too late and you have already begun a downward spiral that can lead to decreased performance and the development of a heat-related illness. Try to ingest fluids throughout the session.

There are different drinking strategies for the different parts of the race. Drink water at the start of the race prior to the swim. When swimming laps at the pool, keep a water bottle at the pool edge and drink as needed. For the bike, try traditional water bottles and bottle cages, water containers that attach to the bike and run a drink tube up to the triathlete, or hydration packs that are worn on the back. Ensure that you continually drink water throughout the bike, because drinking opportunities during the subsequent run are somewhat limited. At most races water stops will be located through the run course. In order not to lose time, you do not want to stop and hang out at the water station while you drink. Instead, become comfortable with grabbing a drink on the run and drinking as you go. Know the location of each water station along the course and develop a hydration strategy to optimize your race.

Hyponatremia, a fluid electrolyte imbalance, is not typical in sprint distance races and is much more common in ultra-endurance events. Hyponatremia occurs when electrolyte levels are extremely low, affecting the ration of fluid and electrolytes. The imbalance created by a high concentration of water and low concentration of sodium can result in the following: headache, nausea, cramping, seizures, coma, heart attack, and death. Hyponatremia, as a result of exercise, typically occurs during prolonged events where the athletes ingest large amounts of fluid, fluid retention is occurring due to hormone release (primarily aldosternone and anti-diuretic hormone), and electrolytes lost through sweat. Taking in electrolytes during prolonged exercise can help offset this imbalance.

After Training and Races

Recovery is an important component of any training program, and nutrition is key in the recovery process. What you put into your body after a workout is just as important as what goes in during a workout. Training applies the necessary stress for positive adaptations and eventual performance increases to occur. This stress results in catabolic responses during exercise. It is the anabolic process after exercise that ultimately results in improved performance. Replacing lost fuel sources, including glycogen, after exercise is vital.

You must refuel within 1 to 2 hours after completion of exercise. The typical recommendation to optimize recovery is within 45 to 60 minutes. The four primary nutrients to ingest are water, electrolytes, carbohydrates, and proteins. Replace each pound of fluid lost through sweating with approximately 24 ounces of fluid. Use of a sport drink can be beneficial for both fluid and electrolyte replacement.

Carbohydrates and proteins should be ingested using a 4:1 ratio (4 grams of carbohydrates to 1 gram proteins). Carbohydrates are necessary for replenishing glycogen stores and proteins are vital for supporting the anabolic processes after exercise. Ingesting protein after exercise also assists in glucose and amino acid uptake into the muscles as well as influencing insulin levels. These factors are why the 4:1 ratio has been so successful during the recovery process. Recovery sport drink mixes that provide the necessary 4:1 ratio have been shown to be very effective at aiding recovery. Research has demonstrated that chocolate milk provides the same ratio and the same benefits.

Body Composition

More than 65 percent of Americans are classified as overweight and more than 30 percent are classified as obese. Being overweight or obese can lead to hypertension, high cholesterol (LDL) levels, Type II diabetes, cardiovascular disease, certain types of cancer, gall bladder disease, joint problems, breathing problems, and untimely death.

Periodically measuring your body fat percentage by using one of the methods below is the best way to track changes in your body composition.

For General Health

If you are participating in triathlon for fun or a challenge, you need not worry too much about body composition. By training and eating right, body composition will take care of itself over time. The recommended body fat percent range is 8 to 19 percent for males and 17 to 28 percent for females. Maintaining a healthy body composition within these recommended ranges is idea for promoting optimal health. Classification of overweight begins at a body fat percent greater than 20 percent for men and 30 percent for women. As body fat percent increases beyond the initial classification of overweight, health risk increases significantly. Remember that having too *little* body fat can have a negative impact on your health too. The body requires a minimum amount of body fat to function normally. The essential body fat percentage for males is 4 percent and 12 percent for females.

For Competition

If you wish to race at an elite level, you need to be more concerned with your body composition. Overall body mass has an effect on both cycling and running performance. While cycling is non–weight bearing, weight still has a strong impact on performance. The heavier a person is, the more work required to pedal the bike. This is especially true when cycling hills. Running is a weight-bearing activity in which the ground reaction forces are two to three times the individual's body weight.

The ranges for recommended body fat compositions for competitive triathletes are 4 to 10 percent for males and 12 to 20 percent for females. A low body fat composition is very difficult to achieve and maintain. The closer an athlete gets to the lower end of the recommended athletic range, the greater the risk of decreased performance and compromised health. One of the problems with providing specific numbers to establish a range is that not everyone will respond in the same manner. When you get down to the lower range, you need to make sure that you carefully monitor both performance and health. The goal is to be as light as possible without negatively impacting performance.

Measuring Body Composition

To optimize body composition you should keep track of it by choosing an accurate and reliable method. Different methods for determining body composition are described in this section, along with the advantages and disadvantages of each.

Body Mass Index

The height and weight charts that you see in your local gym or doctor's office are based on a body mass index (BMI) formula. These charts provide a simple and easy way to determine if you are underweight, normal, overweight, or obese. BMI formula requires only that height and weight are measured. BMI is typically measured and calculated using the metric system. However, since most people in the United States use the English system, both formulas have been provided. Once you determine your BMI, you can refer to the chart to determine what category you fall into.

English

$$\text{BMI} = 703 \text{ X weight (lb.)} \div \text{height}^2 \text{ (inches}^2\text{)}$$

Metric

$$\text{BMI} = \text{weight (kg)} \div \text{height}^2 \text{ (M}^2\text{)}$$

Underweight	<18.5
Normal	18.5–24.9
Overweight	25.0–29.9
Obese	>30.0

Body mass index is an excellent tool for estimating body composition for large-scale populations, but not so much for the individual athlete. The reason that BMI is not very useful with athletes is the fact that muscle is denser than fat and therefore weighs more. A professional bodybuilder might have a very low body fat percentage, but would be considered obese when body composition is estimated using BMI. While bodybuilders are an extreme example, the same principle applies to triathletes as well. Body mass index takes into account both height and weight. Height does not drastically change so the main component that would alter BMI is weight.

Bioelectrical

Bioelectrical impedance systems have gained in popularity in recent years. These systems require you to make contact with either the hands or the feet. Once contact is made the system passes an electrical current through the body to measure resistance to flow. Lean body tissue contains high concentrations of water and therefore the electrical current passes easily. Fat contains little water and therefore provides resistance to flow. As fat stores increase, resistance to flow also increases. Unfortunately, these systems are not known for their accuracy or reliability.

Because water is a large factor when using the bioelectrical impedance machine, hydration levels affect readings. Your hydration levels during training will continuously fluctuate, especially in the hotter months, leading to large fluctuations in bioelectrical impedance readings. Due to the large fluctuations in hydration levels and the inherent variability in these machines, I do not recommend them for measuring body composition.

Bioelectrical impedance

Underwater Weighing

Underwater weighing (hydrostatic weighing) has long been considered the gold standard for determining body composition. This method is based on Archimedes' Principle, which states that the weight of water displaced by the body is equivalent to the buoyant forces acting on that body. Lean body mass (muscle, bone, organs, etc.) has greater density than water and therefore sinks. Fat, on the other hand, is less

Hydrostatic weighing is used to measure body composition.

dense than water and therefore floats. The amount of lean mass and fat mass will determine how buoyant an individual is in water.

Hydrostatic weighing requires large specialized equipment and trained professionals to conduct. Dry weight is taken prior to you entering the tank. Then you enter the tank and sit in a sling that is attached to a large scale. Next you bend at the waist and completely submerge your body while maximally exhaling air from the lungs. Once you have exhaled maximal air and are still, a reading can be taken from the scale. This process is repeated three times and then the numbers are averaged and placed into a formula. This methodology is not recommended for those who are uncomfortable underwater.

Dual-Energy X-Ray Absorptiometry

Dual-Energy X-Ray Absorptiometry (DXA) determines body composition through the use of two low energy x-ray beams. Research has demonstrated that DXA has the ability to determine density and accurately distinguish between fat and fat-free mass. Due to this method's accuracy and reliability, it is now often considered the best way to determine body composition. The issue with this method is that the equipment is extremely expensive and requires very specialized skill to operate.

Calipers

Skin fold calipers are an accurate and inexpensive method for determining body composition, far more accessible to most triathletes than DXA or hydrostatic weighing. Fat deposits are stored under the skin and calipers allow you to measure the thickness of the skin fold, which includes the skin and fat stores. From the skin fold measurements, total fat stores are estimated using simple formulas. Basic skin fold calipers cost anywhere from $25 to $200. The major differences between a lower- and higher-cost caliper is accuracy and durability.

Conducting skin fold testing is relatively simple, but does take some practice. There are different tests used to measure skin folds, but the three-site test is the one that is most widely used. The most common sites used for men are the chest, abdomen, and thigh. The three most common sites for females are the triceps, iliac, and thigh. The following pictures and instructions will provide you the necessary information to conduct a simple three-site test.

The chest is located along the outer edge of the pectoralis major at the midpoint of the muscle. The skin fold should be in line with the outer edge of the muscle.

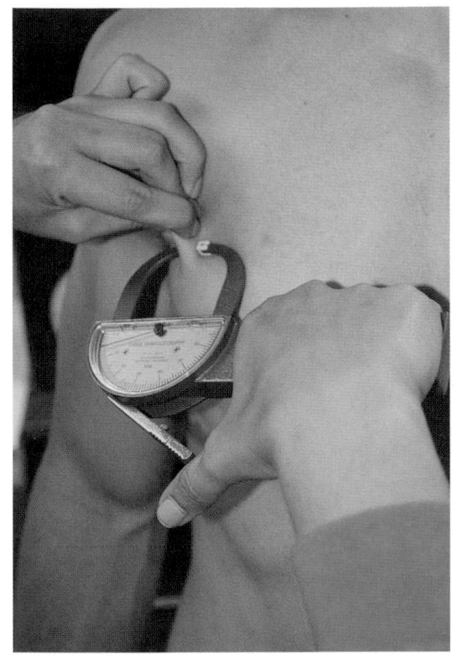
Chest

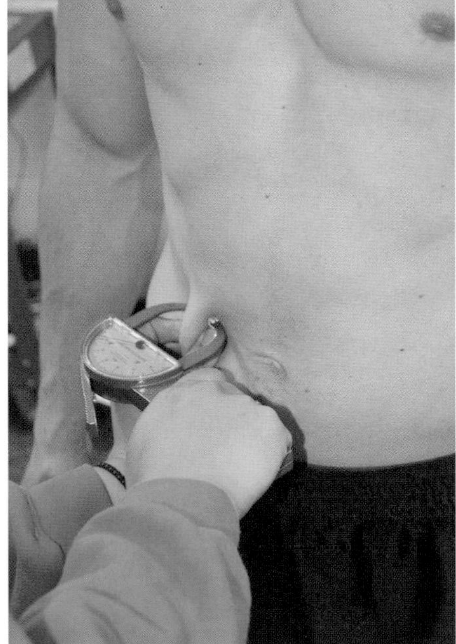
Abdomen

Iliac

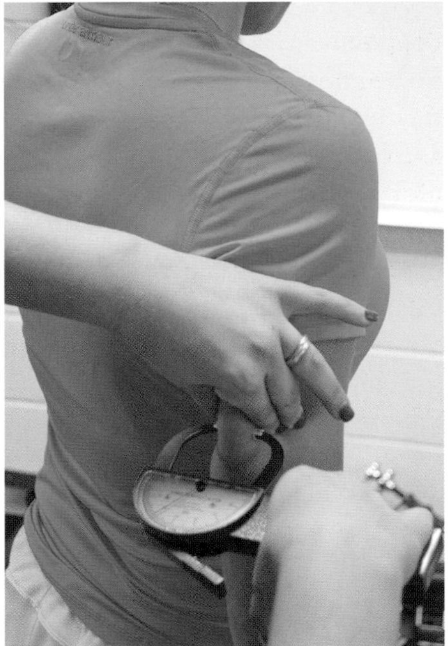
Triceps

The abdomen is located in line with the navel and one inch toward the side. Fold the skin vertically, not horizontally.

The iliac is located just above the hip bone. Fold the skin in line with the natural crease at the hip bone.

The triceps are located at the back of the arm, centered and halfway between the shoulder and elbow. Fold the skin vertically.

The thigh is located on the centerline of the thigh halfway between the hip and the patella. Fold the skin vertically.

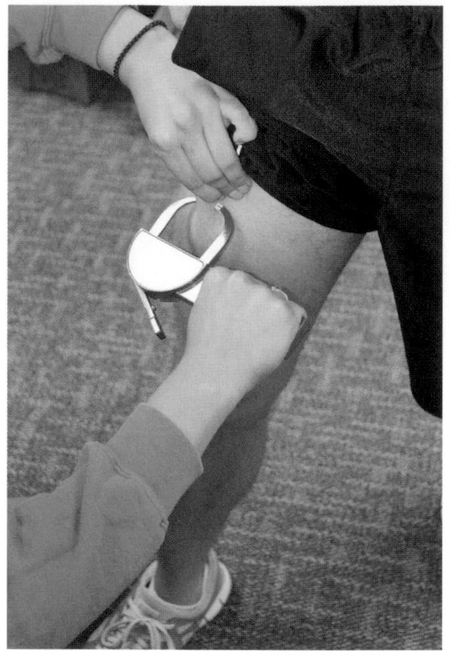

Thigh

When conducting skin fold measures, it is important to accurately measure each site as described. Position the hand so that the fingers point down and fold the skin between the thumb and index finger as shown in the photos. Once your fingers are positioned over the correct spot, pinch the skin, bringing it up into a fold. For an accurate measurement, pinch skin and fat only. Too large of a pinch typically results in getting muscle, which results in an inaccurate measurement. Next, place the caliper pincers directly below your thumb and index finger with the gauge facing up so that you can read it. Once the caliper is in position, allow the calipers to close on the fold by slowly releasing the lever. Do not release the skin fold with your fingers until you record the measurement and remove the calipers. If you release the skin fold prior to the calipers, it can be slightly painful. Take three to four measurements at each site to ensure consistent readings. Once you have recorded all three sites, take the sum of the readings and plug the necessary data into the following equations:

Men

Body Density = 1.10938 – (.0008267 X sum of skin folds) + (.0000016 X [sum of skin folds]2) – (.0002574 X age)

Women

Body Density = 1.0994921 – (.0009929 X sum of skin folds) + (.0000023 X [sum of skin folds]2) – (.0001392 X age)

Once body density has been established, the next step is to determine body fat percentage using the following formula:

Body Fat% = (4.95 ÷ Body Density) - 4.50 X 100

Example Equation

Male: Age = 31; Iliac = 6, Triceps = 9, Thigh = 14 (Total = 29)
Body Density = 1.0994921 - (.0009929 X 29) + (.0000023 X [29]2) - (.0001392 X 31)
BD = 1.0665162
Body Fat% = (4.95 ÷1.0665162) - 4.50 X 100 = 14.13%

Weight Management

Many people get into the sport of triathlon to improve their health and lose weight. Keep in mind a few things while on the path to achieving weight loss. The first is patience. You did not put on excess weight overnight, so it is unrealistic to believe that you can lose it overnight. Remain patient, avoid undue frustration, and stick with the plan. When things get frustrating ask yourself: Do I want to be standing here a year from now having lost weight or do I want to be standing here a year from now saying I wish I would have stuck with it and lost weight?

Second, recognize that there will be hard, physical work to achieve your goal. Not everyone responds to weight loss in the same manner, due to genetics. Additionally, you will need to implement a healthy diet to accomplish your goal in a safe and productive manner. Failure to take into account these simple facts is what leads to unsuccessful weight loss.

Genetics

Genetics play a major role when it comes to body composition. Research shows that children of overweight parents are much more likely to be overweight than children of non-overweight parents. How body fat is distributed in the body is also strongly affected by genetics. It is easier for some people to lose weight while others continuously struggle. However, this does not mean that you are fated to be overweight just because you have a genetic predisposition toward weight gain. All it means is that you need to be more careful of how you eat and that you need to exercise on a regular basis.

Lifestyle

Lifestyle is probably the biggest determinant of an individual's body composition. While genetics is a key factor, it is the lifestyle choices people make that have the largest effects on body composition. The two key lifestyle choices that affect body composition are physical activity and diet.

Often food offered at sit-down and fast food restaurants provides more calories in one meal than people need in one day. While it is unrealistic to think that you will never eat out, there are strategies that you can implement to help when you do. The first requires a little bit of pre-planning and a little work. Prior to going out to eat, look up the menu and choose low-calorie, healthy foods. The other option is to decrease your portion size. Just because you order the meal does not mean that you have to eat all of it in one sitting. If you do not have the willpower to stop eating when you are full, then ask for a "to go" box at the beginning of the meal and place the portion that you do not plan to eat in the box to take home. If you are eating with someone who has similar taste, you can also consider sharing a meal.

The best option is to eat at home and prepare meals from fresh foods that have not been overly processed. Eating healthy is not expensive and does not necessarily require hours in the kitchen slaving over a hot stove. If you are not familiar with healthy cooking, consider buying a cookbook that focuses on the subject. You will soon find healthy, tasty meals that are easy to prepare.

Even when eating healthy at home, you need to be aware of portion sizes. Modern dishware has gotten larger over time and if you fill your plate you will probably take in more calories than you need. Most of us were raised on "cleaning" your plate before leaving the table in order not to waste food. While the logic behind this practice is understandable, it is much better to listen to your stomach and stop eating when you are full.

Eating healthy begins when you go to the grocery store. If you do not buy junk food, it will make it that much easier not to eat it. I have a serious sweet tooth and if sweets are brought into the house they will not last very long. So instead of buying cookies and ice cream I buy oranges, peaches, and apples. Fruit is sweet and can fulfill the same cravings but is much better for you. Make a list of what you need prior to going to the grocery store and buy only what is on the list. This helps prevent those impulse buys just because something looks good. It is also not a good idea to grocery shop after a hard workout when you are tired and hungry. When I do that, my grocery basket always seems to be fuller and filled with not so healthy foods.

When purchasing packaged foods always look at the nutrition label. From the package you can determine cholesterol, sodium, sugar, and total calories. When looking at calories always look to see not just how many calories per serving, but to also determine how many servings there are in the container. There is a big difference between 120 kCals per serving with only one serving in the container and 120 kCals per serving with ten servings in the container.

Keep a nutrition log to help track caloric intake and for weight management. Record what you eat throughout the day and add up the calories that night. You may be surprised by how many calories that you take in just from sodas alone. This is a very effective tool for demonstrating the need for a lifestyle change. Keeping a nutrition log is tedious work and may not be something that you want to maintain on a permanent basis, but try to keep a log until you have made the proper adjustments to your eating habits.

Setting Goals

The first step in developing a weight management program is to set goals. Ideally goals should be challenging yet realistic. Losing 10 pounds in a week of training is extremely unrealistic, whereas losing 10 pounds over an 8 to 10 week period would be both challenging yet realistic. If your goals are unrealistic, you will set yourself up for failure and will become discouraged. Because weight loss occurs over a long period of time, you want to set both short- and long-term goals. The safe rate of weight loss is no more than 1 pound per week. To compensate for the extended period of time required to lose that amount of weight, short-term goals should be established. While it will take a long while to lose 20 pounds, you can lose 5 pounds more quickly, so try setting up your short-term goals in 5-pound increments.

First, you need to know where you are and where you want to go. The first step is to determine your current body weight and body fat percentage. Next, decide your goal body fat percentage. Your goal does not have to be the low body fat percentage of most elite triathletes, which is an unrealistic goal for most individuals. For the majority of those reading this book, the goal of 8 to 19 percent for males and 17 to 28 percent for females is a good and achievable goal. This is a wide range and where you would like to be in that range is a personal choice. Once you have all of the necessary information, use the formulas below to determine weight loss.

(Current Weight) x (Current Body Fat Percentage) = Weight of Fat in the Body
Current Weight - Weight of Fat in the Body = Weight of Fat Free Mass
1 - Desired Body Fat Percentage = Percent Fat Free Mass
Weight of Fat Free Mass ÷ Percent Fat Free Mass = Desired Body Weight
Current Body Weight - Desired Body Weight = Desired Weight Loss

Example

Male: 200lb: Currently 18% Body Fat; Desires 10% Body Fat
(200lb) x (.18) = 36lb
200lb - 36lb = 164lb
1 - .10 = .90
164lb ÷ .90 = 182.22lb
200lb - 182.22lb= 17.78lb

In the example above a 200-pound male with a body fat percentage of 18 was able to determine that his desired body weight would be 182.22 pounds and that he would need to lose 17.78 pounds to reach the desired body fat percentage of 10 percent. Remember, the goal is really about body composition and not weight. If you have just started training, muscle will hypertrophy over time, which increases weight as muscle is denser than fat. If your goal is to lose a lot of weight, you will need to periodically measure and run the formula again.

Caloric Balance

Weight management is all about caloric balance. If you consume the same amount of calories that you used during the day, then weight will not alter. It is not possible to take in the exact amount of calories that you use every day. Some days you will take in slightly more than you use and others you will take in slightly less than you use. So it balances out over time. If you take in more calories than you use, you will gain weight. Typically it is not that you take in drastic amounts over expenditure on a daily basis, but that you take in slightly more than is used and weight builds up over time. If you take in less than you use, then weight will drop over time. Caloric intake should not be drastically lower than usage. If caloric intake is too low for too long, metabolism can decrease, which is counterproductive to weight management. Too low a caloric intake can also lead to catabolism of lean tissue, primarily muscle, in the body, which is also counterproductive.

The most commonly recommended caloric intake is between 2,000 and 2,500 calories per day for males and 1,500 to 1,800 calories per day for females. On the surface it appears that these recommendations would make life simple. However this is not the case. These common recommendations are for the average male and female who do not participate in regular athletic training and therefore represent insufficient calories for most athletes, especially triathletes. A triathlete can burn over twice the number of recommended calories during a long race or training day. To determine how many calories that you need to take in, you must first estimate how much you utilize.

The first step in determining caloric balance is to measure *basal metabolic rate* (BMR), which is the minimum energy required to properly maintain normal body function at rest. BMR generally ranges from around 1,100 kCals to 2,100 kCals/day. It is the energy required just to exist. Any physical activity conducted throughout the day will add to BMR. Basal metabolic rate is measured using a metabolic cart after a good night's sleep and a 12-hour fast. Exercise should be avoided for 24 hours prior to testing.

A linear relationship exists between heart rate and VO_2 and therefore heart rate can be used to estimate basal metabolic rate. In order to estimate BMR using heart rate, you will need a heart rate monitor that estimates kCals at rest. Record caloric expenditure at rest for 10 minutes and multiply by 6 to determine caloric expenditure for an hour. The resultant number is then multiplied by 24 to determine caloric expenditure for an entire day (BMR).

Formulas that estimate basal metabolic rate are often used in place of testing. These formulas are not as accurate as direct measures but will work.

Male

kCals/day = 66 + (13.7 X body weight in kg) + (5 X height in cm) - (6.9 x age)

Female

kCals/day = 665 + (9.6 X body weight in kg) + (1.7 X height in cm) - (4.7 X age)

Example Problem

Male, 165lbs (74.83 kg), 72" tall (182.88 cm), age 41

kCals/day = 66 + (13.7 X 74.83) + (5 X 182.88) - (6.9 X 41) = 1722.67 kCals

After basal metabolic rate has been determined, caloric expenditure due to activity will need to be added to the equation. If you had a morning run that used 550 kCals and then an afternoon bike that used 600 kCals, you would add 1,150 kCals to your basal metabolic rate. Any physical activity above resting needs to be added on top of BMR. This methodology is not 100 percent accurate and only gives you a ballpark number; therefore, it is important to monitor weight. If you lose or gain too much weight, you need to adjust caloric intake accordingly.

When training for triathlon make sure to replenish the calories used throughout the day. This process is vital for energy replenishment as well as for driving anabolic processes for recovery. As mentioned previously it is all about manipulating caloric balance in order to reach your specific weight management goals. If you know how many calories you burned throughout the day, you know how many you need to replace. This is where your nutrition log can be helpful. By reading the caloric content of the food you consume and keeping track of the totals, you can compare caloric expenditure to caloric intake. Keep in mind that it is not just about the volume of nutrients but the quality of the nutrients as well.

Fad Diets

Stay away from fad diets—they do not work. When it comes to weight loss, if it is too good to be true then it is. Fad diet programs result in no change in body composition at best and lead to health-related problems at worst.

Low-carbohydrate diets have been pushed in the media and lay population as a healthy way to lose weight. However, there is nothing healthy about a low-carb diet. The only source of fuel that the central nervous system and the brain can use for fuel is glycogen (storage form of carbohydrate), so inadequate supplies of glycogen result in mental confusion and fatigue. As a survival mechanism the body will produce glycogen through protein degradation. Excess protein is not stored in the body and therefore the protein that is degraded comes from tissue, primarily muscle.

Lipid catabolism will also be compromised due to low glycogen stores. As stated earlier, lipids require glycogen in order to be completely catabolized for energy. Low glycogen stores and compromised lipid catabolism results in a decrease in pH. Other common complications of a diet are dehydration, electrolyte imbalance, strain on the liver, and strain on the kidneys.

A low-carbohydrate diet will negatively impact triathlon training and performance. Glycogen stores are extremely important when training or racing at high intensities. Because glycogen stores are limited to around 2,000 kCals, you do not want to start off the session with low glycogen stores. Feeling fatigued and the inability to think clearly will also negatively impact your performance. While you will lose weight on this diet, the weight that is lost is not entirely due to decreased lipid stores leading to improved body composition. The weight loss will be a result of significant lean tissue loss, water loss, and lipid loss. Loss of muscle mass will have a strong negative impact on triathlon performance.

Use of diet pills for weight loss has increased greatly in recent history and has developed into a multibillion-dollar industry. Diet pills are considered a supplement and therefore fall outside of FDA regulations. This allows companies to make any claim that they like without fear of prosecution.

Never use diet pills as a source of weight management Diet pills contain stimulants that increase metabolism. This greatly increases resting heart rate and can cause heart palpitations and other medical complications and can even result in death. Because exercise naturally increases heart rate, diet pills can exasperate the problem. On hot, humid days when blood plasma volume drops significantly due to sweating, the use of diet pills can apply excess strain on the heart.

Ergogenic Aids

The word "ergogenic" means work enhancing. In the arena of sport performance, ergogenic aids are any aid that increases performance. There are three basic ways in which ergogenic aids work. They directly increase performance during an event, they promote recovery for improvements in later performance, and they allow you to increase the amount of training in order to improve later performance. When considering ergogenic aids it is important to examine their effectiveness, known and possible side effects, ethics, and legality.

Ethics, Legality, Regulations

Triathletes are very focused on finding ways to improve performance. Ergogenic aids can be a pathway for improved performance, but you have to first

Ergogenic aids are used to increase sport performance.

look at the legality and ethics of using those aids. While ethics are more subjective and based on your individual morals and sense of right and wrong, there is no such gray area if you violate the law, and you can end up being fined or even incarcerated.

In sports there is a basic premise that all competition is conducted on an even playing field and that there are no unfair advantages. Any differences in performance should be based strictly on genetics, training, tactics, and ergogenic aids that are permitted by the sport's governing body. If an ergogenic aid is illegal, such as steroids, then it is also against regulations and hopefully counter to the established ethical guidelines of the athlete.

The sport of triathlon takes decisive steps in the effort to keep the sport clean. The International Olympic Committee created the World Anti-Doping Agency (WADA) in order to regulate the use of ergogenic aids in sports. The charge of this committee is to develop a list of banned substances, develop rules, test for banned substances, and enforce rules. The United States Anti-Doping Agency (USADA) is signed on to WADA and is responsible for implementing WADA regulations in this country.

When determining if a substance should be banned or not, WADA examines three main areas during deliberation:

- Is the substance illegal?
- Does the substance pose a serious health risk?
- Does the substance give the triathlete an unfair advantage over their competitors?

An answer of "yes" to one or more of these questions can result in the substance being placed on the banned substance list. You should know what is and is not on the banned substance list, which can be found on the WADA, USADA, and USAT websites. Make sure you know what is in the supplements and medications that you take, because they may contain banned substances. If you have to take a medication that contains banned substances, you can file for a therapeutic use exemption.

Supplements

Due to the Dietary Supplement Health and Education Act of 1994 (DSHEA), supplement companies are legally allowed to lie and mislead in advertisements. They can make claims without scientific proof, be intentionally vague, remain outside of the Food and Drug Administration (FDA) control, and remain outside of Good Manufacturing Practices (GMP). As long as supplement companies do not claim to cure or mitigate a disease, they can claim whatever they want. The GMP requires that all drugs be within a very strict limit (typically within 1 to 2 percent) of what is stated on the label. Because supplements are not regulated by the FDA, they are outside the GMP and therefore do not have to have the exact amount of the stated ingredient in the product. Scientific studies have examined supplements and found that some have exactly what is stated on the package while others have little to none of the advertised product.

Due to the way that supplements are marketed, it can be difficult to determine what works and what does not. It should go without saying that you cannot take the supplement companies at their word and must look to other sources. Testimonies from professional athletes are also suspect. Many times these athletes are paid by the companies and therefore may not actually even believe that they work. The athlete may also truly believe that the supplement is the secret to their success, when in reality it is not. Magazines are also not a valid source for information on the effects of ergogenic aids. The magazine may be reluctant to print an article that a supplement does not work when that company is advertising in its pages. Peer-reviewed scientific journal articles are the best source of information because the reviewed studies are conducted under strictly controlled settings and in an unbiased manner. If you decide to try a specific ergogenic aid, make sure that you know the possible side effects and pay attention to how your body reacts to the supplement. Most supplements are expensive; you do not want to waste money on something that will not work for you.

There are a few ergogenic aids that can be beneficial for triathlon. The primary ergogenic aids were mentioned at the beginning of the chapter (water, carbohydrates, proteins, and sport drinks). Here are a couple more:

Caffeine

Caffeine is the most widely used supplement in the world. It is a naturally occurring stimulant found in plants (coffee beans, tea leaves, cocoa nuts, etc.). Caffeine is found naturally in many products such as coffee, tea, and soda, but is often added to other products as a stimulant. Because of this it is often used as an ergogenic aid. Research strongly supports the use of caffeine for improving human performance in sport.

Caffeine can easily cross the blood/brain barrier, acting as an ergogenic aid by decreasing feelings of pain and fatigue during exercise. A lower feeling of pain and fatigue allows you to race or train at a higher intensity level. Caffeine stimulates and increases mobilization of free fatty acids into the blood, resulting in an increased availability for energy production and, thus, conserving glycogen stores. Caffeine increases the muscles' ability to contract by also increasing activity at the neuromuscular junction and increasing motor unit recruitment.

While caffeine is widely used by a large portion of the population, there are potential side effects. The most common include muscle tremors, gastrointestinal distress, headache, nervousness, elevated heart rate, arrhythmia, and high blood pressure. Thermoregulatory complications are more likely to occur when caffeine ingestion occurs in a hot environment. Side effects are more likely to develop at high levels of ingestion and in individuals who do not normally consume caffeine. While it is commonly stated that caffeine acts as a diuretic, research has shown that caffeine does not act as a diuretic during exercise. This is primarily due to the release of anti-diuretic hormone and aldosterone that occurs during exercise in order to retain water.

Caffeine does not have to be taken in large doses to increase endurance performance. Caffeine ingestion equivalent to 2.5 cups of coffee has been found to be sufficient to improve performance. Caffeine peaks in the system around 1 hour after ingestion and therefore should be taken an hour prior to competition.

Illegal Aids

Two ergogenic aids commonly used in triathlon are illegal and against WADA regulations: anabolic steroids and blood doping. This section discusses these ergogenic aids so that you can have a better understanding of how they work when the topic is brought up in the news.

Anabolic Steroids

Anabolic steroids (synthetic testosterone) are unfortunately prevalent in most sports. Steroids promote anabolic process in the body and improve performance by increasing the speed of recovery, by repairing damaged tissue, hypertrophy and reducing the catabolic effects of exercise. The ability to recover faster between training bouts allows an athlete to train harder more often, which in turn leads to improved performance. Steroids are typically administered through injection, oral doses, patches, or cream.

There are reversible and irreversible side effects that occur with steroid use. Reversible side effects include acne, depression, increased rage, infections at injection sites, and high cholesterol. These side effects dissipate once steroid use has stopped.

The irreversible side effects of steroids occur due to prolonged use and are typically more serious. They include cancer, liver disease, cardiovascular disease, and baldness. Side effects that are specific to males are testicular atrophy, impotence, developing mammary glands (breasts), and a permanent decrease in natural testosterone production. Women run the risk of developing facial hair and a deeper voice. Steroid use in pregnant women can also lead to birth defects. Due to the lack of research, it is not possible to truly know the negative impact steroid use has on health.

Blood Doping

The term *blood doping* covers any method that increases red blood cell count. If red blood cells increase, then your ability to transport oxygen to the working muscles also increases and, therefore, performance increases. There are three primary methods used for blood doping: autologous, homologous, and erythropoietin. Autologous blood doping involves removing blood from the athlete and spinning the blood in order to separate plasma from hemoglobin. The plasma is then injected back into the athlete and the red blood cells are stored for later use. It takes approximately 4 to 6 weeks for hemoglobin levels to return to normal. The hemoglobin is then reinfused prior to competition in order to increase red blood cell count. The downside to this method is that the athlete will be weak for a period of time, which affects training.

To prevent the period of weakness following blood removal during autologous blood doping, some athletes choose to use homologous blood doping instead. Homologous blood doping involves infusing red blood cells from a matched donor just prior to racing. This method carries a high risk of transmitting disease, may lead to infection, and the triathlete's body may reject the donor blood. Due to antigens found in blood differing between individuals, this method is easily detectable.

Erythropoietin is a naturally occurring hormone that is produced in the kidneys and is responsible for stimulating red blood cell production in the bone marrow. Epoetin (synthetic erythropoietin) is injected in order to increase red blood cell production. The problem with epoetin is that it can drastically increase red blood cell production, leading to a large increase in hematocrit, which can strongly impact health. It is recommended to supplement with iron when using epoetin.

Blood doping is banned not only because it gives the athlete an unfair advantage, but also due to the serious health complications that can occur when implementing this process. All three of these methods significantly increase hematocrit levels. If hematocrit gets too high, it will result in an increase in blood viscosity, which in turn could lead to a stroke or heart attack. The sport of triathlon requires endurance performance over a prolonged period and on a hot day dehydration can easily occur. When an athlete becomes dehydrated, plasma volumes are significantly decreased, which increases blood viscosity. Blood doping combined with dehydration is a deadly formula.

CHAPTER THIRTEEN

Special Considerations

Previous chapters discussed training principles, training plans, and how to apply both to the average population. This chapter covers specific populations that require special considerations when applying the accepted training principles: women, the elderly, and children, as well as those who are overweight and/or have diabetes or asthma. Due to gender differences females do not respond to training precisely the same as males. As we age the body's ability to adapt to training stimuli alters and should be taken into consideration when developing a training program. Certain conditions can also alter the body's ability to adapt and may require special care and consideration.

Women

Since the implementation of Title IX, female participation in sports has increased dramatically. While still not equivalent in all sports, support for female athletes has grown tremendously. USA Triathlon and the triathlon world in general strongly support female participation. In 2012 USA Triathlon had 155,198 annual members with 38.18 percent of those memberships being held by females. USA Triathlon–sanctioned races require that the prize purse be equal between genders, which is not the case in all sports. To further support female participation in triathlon, women-only races have been established recently. These races are designed to provide females with an opportunity to compete in a less intimidating environment. Manufacturers are also beginning to realize the need to develop triathlon products specifically with females in mind.

When developing a training program for females, the same training principles discussed earlier can be applied without alterations, with the exception of during pregnancy. Women adapt to training stimuli in ways that are very similar to male athletes. However, there are some factors that females should understand and take into consideration when training.

RUDY
ØVAL
ØVAL

Gender Differences

The physiological gender differences between males and females should be considered when developing a training program. One of the primary differences involves hormones, primarily testosterone and estrogen. Males produce approximately ten times more testosterone than females, which leads to a larger increase in muscle mass. Men can produce a faster contraction than females due to a greater speed of signaling. Muscle mass distribution also differs between males and females. A greater percentage of muscle mass is distributed in the upper body in males. However, there are no physiological differences between muscle tissue found in males and that found in females. The main difference in muscle mass is directly related to hormone levels.

Females produce a much greater volume of estrogen, which affects the way females develop physiologically. Estrogen is responsible for increasing lipid storage, particularly in the thighs and hips. This is why women tend to store greater amounts of lipids in those areas. This is also the reason that essential body fat in females is 12 percent as opposed to 4 percent in males. Scientists have theorized that this increased lipid storage is essential for the reproductive process. Estrogen is also responsible for bone growth in females, resulting in a wider pelvis.

Males possess a higher aerobic capacity due to a number of factors. The first is that males possess a larger blood volume and increased hemoglobin count per unit in relation to females. This greatly increases the ability to transport oxygen, which in turn increases performance. To help offset lower levels of hemoglobin, females typically have higher levels of 2,3-DPG, which helps release oxygen into the tissue. Women also tend to have smaller hearts, which in turn decreases stroke volume. All of these factors lead to a lower aerobic capacity, resulting in lower VO_{2max} scores. At any given fitness level, females will produce VO_{2max} scores that will be 5 to 10 ml/kg/min lower than their male counterparts.

All of this, however, does not mean that all males can outperform all females. The key is that males possess a higher aerobic capacity at any given level of competition. The average male age grouper would most likely receive a VO_{2max} of around 50 to 55 ml/kg/min on a graded exercise protocol while the average female age grouper would receive 40 to 45 ml/kg/min, whereas, a female professional triathlete would receive >60 ml/kg/min and a professional male triathlete would achieve >70 ml/kg/min. From this set of data, you can see that the average age-group male outperforms the average

Female participation in triathlon has grown exponentially over recent years.
Nathan Kortuem

age-group female. However, a professional female triathlete can outperform the average amateur male.

Female Athlete Triad

The female athlete triad, as the name suggests, consist of three distinct, but interlocking components: inadequate caloric intake, amenorrhea, and osteoporosis. The first step in the triad is inadequate caloric intake. When caloric expenditure consistently exceeds caloric intake, it places the body in negative balance leading to the development of an unhealthy body composition. Essential body fat, the minimum body fat necessary to maintain normal body function, is considered 12 percent in females. Those who drop below this percentage run the risk of developing the female athlete triad as well as other health discrepancies. This caloric imbalance is commonly brought on by the desire to optimize performance as well as concerns with body image.

Many times the desire to optimize body composition for performance and body image can become an obsession and lead to eating disorders such as anorexia nervosa and bulimia. You do not have to have an eating disorder to be in a constant negative caloric balance. Triathlon training requires high volume, which in turn requires a high caloric intake to replace expended energy. A female may appear to eat normally, but still be in a negative caloric balance. When eating disorders are present, there is a strong psychological aversion to food or what food represents to that individual. In this case the psychological aversion does not exist; they are just not eating adequately. It is a good idea to monitor caloric expenditure as well as caloric intake. Another way is to monitor body composition to ensure that you maintain essential body fat.

The next step in the female athlete triad is the development of abnormalities in the menstrual cycle, ultimately leading to amenorrhea (cessation of the menstrual cycle). Prolonged negative caloric balance and unhealthy body composition has a negative impact on the hypothalamus, reducing the release of gonadotropic hormones, which in turn impacts estrogen production and the menstrual cycle. An unhealthy body composition does not have to exist for amenorrhea to occur. Serious training has also been shown to lead to amenorrhea.

The last step in the female athlete triad is the development of osteoporosis, where bone density is lost and the bone becomes brittle and susceptible to fracturing. Estrogen is responsible for the absorption and retention of calcium. When estrogen production greatly decreases with the cessation

Maintaining a healthy body composition is extremely important for female endurance athletes. *Shutterstock*

of the menstrual cycle, calcium absorption and retention greatly diminishes, leading to a decrease in bone density. While the female athlete triad is a serious concern for females of all ages, special attention should be paid to those in their developmental years when bone growth is paramount.

Female Biomechanics

One of the main structural differences between males and females is the pelvic girdle. Women have a wider pelvic girdle, wider sacrum, and the pelvis is shaped slightly differently. These differences are necessary to accommodate the birth process. These factors also lead to altered lower extremity biomechanics compared to males. During running females tend to have increased hip adduction leading to greater inward force placed on the knee, which greatly increases the risk of injury. One method for decreasing the risk of injury is to strengthen the knee extensors (quadriceps) and the knee flexors (hamstrings). Typically the quadriceps muscles will be significantly stronger than the hamstring muscles. Research supports that the less of a strength difference between the extensors and flexors the less likely an injury will occur.

The width of the pelvic girdle also affects saddle choice during cycling. Bike saddles are designed so that the ischium (sit bones) contact the saddle at the back and the nose of the saddle comfortably fits between the legs. Due to the width of the pelvic girdle, female saddles are designed wider where the ischium makes contact. A thinner male saddle may not be wide enough to support the female pelvis, causing the ischium to slide off one side or the other. You also do not want an extremely wide saddle. Test out a few saddles until you find one that accommodates your ischium.

Pregnancy

Research has demonstrated that there are many benefits for women who exercise during pregnancy, from a decrease in excessive weight gain to decreased labor pains, decreased risk of developing gestational diabetes, and easier return to pre-pregnancy weight and fitness level. Exercise during pregnancy should only be conducted by females who are experiencing a normal pregnancy and have their doctor's permission. Remember, only your doctor can determine if you are healthy enough to exercise and at what level you can train.

Once you become pregnant sit down and have an honest and detailed conversation with your doctor concerning exercise. Once it has been established that you are experiencing a normal healthy pregnancy, then discuss your goals and training plan with your doctor. The doctor will establish your training limitations, which you should follow precisely. Throughout the pregnancy continue to maintain a continuous and open dialogue regarding your training.

Once you become pregnant your training and racing goals will need to change. Intensity will need to be significantly lowered in order to accommodate pregnancy. Blood flow is redirected during exercise to the working muscles and skin for cooling, which in turn reduces blood flow to the fetus. At mild to moderate intensity, reduced blood flow does not impact fetus health. However, as intensity increases a greater amount of blood is redirected from the uterus. It is for this reason that vigorous high-intensity exercise should be avoided during pregnancy. When training it is okay to exercise until you feel slightly fatigued, but never exercise to exhaustion. Due to alterations in blood flow during pregnancy, heart rate becomes an unreliable tool for determining exercise intensity. Instead, use perceived exertion to determine intensity.

Due to reduced blood flow to the skin and increased insulation, your ability to dissipate heat is greatly compromised during pregnancy. A significant increase in the fetus's core temperature can negatively impact development. Do not train in the heat, stay well hydrated, and be mindful of any significant increase in core temperature. Train during a cooler part of the day or inside to avoid overheating.

Activities that put you at risk for impact should be avoided. As pregnancy progresses balance becomes compromised. As the baby grows and the belly protrudes the body's center of gravity shifts. During pregnancy a hormone, relaxin, is released in order to relax the pelvis to prepare for birth. Unfortunately, relaxin also causes other joints in the lower extremities to loosen too, which leads to decreased stability and balance. Due to this significantly decreased balance and the speed of cycling, do not ride outdoors during pregnancy.

Exercise in a supine position, on your back, is also not recommended during pregnancy, as it lowers cardiac output and can restrict blood flow to the fetus. Find an alternate exercise to replace those that you typically conduct in a supine position.

Aging

As we age our ability to adapt to training stimuli is somewhat diminished. There is a theoretical curve that we are on where physical abilities increase through life until they peak somewhere between the ages of 25 and 30 and then begin to gradually decline at 35–40 years of age. If someone remains sedentary his entire life, he will be on the same shaped curve as someone who remains active his whole life. The difference between the two curves is that the active person is at a higher fitness level at any given point throughout the curve. At 70, the active person can still ride his bike while the sedentary person may have trouble walking to the mailbox.

Fitness level along this curve can be altered by increasing or decreasing physical activity. If a collegiate athlete, who has been active his entire life, stopped training after college his fitness level would drop back down to the level of someone who is sedentary. The reverse is true for someone who has been sedentary his whole life and decided to start training. However the basic principle still remains true in that his ability to adapt to training will begin to diminish around the age of 35 with a significant decline starting around 45 years of age.

There is a greater decline in aerobic capacity in those that are sedentary compared to those who remain active. Much of the decrease in aerobic capacity is due to lack of physical activity and the loss of muscle mass that occurs with aging (sarcopenia). Sarcopenia occurs with everyone. However, the extent of the decline in muscle mass is highly dependent on your individual fitness level. Those that remain active throughout life have less of a decrease than sedentary individuals. While physical activity goes a long way toward preventing loss of muscle mass, it cannot completely offset sarcopenia. During the aging process hormone production greatly decreases, which results in a decrease in protein synthesis and, therefore, a decrease in muscle mass.

Triathlon is an excellent way to offset the effects of aging.

With age there is a naturally occurring decrease in bone density. There are two distinct stages: osteopenia and osteoporosis. Osteopenia is a decrease in bone density that occurs prior to the development of osteoporosis, which is a severe decrease in bone density and strong susceptibility to fractures. Both occur due to age-related decreases in hormones. In males there is a link between a decrease in testosterone production and a decrease in bone density. Females are more susceptible to the development of osteoporosis, especially post-menopause when estrogen production is significantly reduced. One of the responsibilities of estrogen is the absorption and retention of calcium. Since estrogen production is greatly diminished, the absorption and retention of calcium decreases, leading to a reduction of bone density.

There are two main things that you can do to help prevent a decrease in bone density. First, consistently maintain a healthy, well-balanced diet. Second, participate in weight-bearing activities. Bones respond to stress in the basic manner that muscle does. If you apply adequate stress to the bone, then bone density increases. If inadequate stress is applied to bone, then bone density decreases. Weight-bearing activity is the only way to increase bone density. Unfortunately, swimming and cycling are non–weight bearing activities and will not apply enough stress to increase bone density. Running is a weight-bearing activity and will lead to increased bone density. The problem with running is that it does nothing to increase the bone density of the upper body. This is where off-season resistance training comes in. Resistance training is weight bearing and allows for adequate stress to be applied to almost all bones in the body. Research has demonstrated that cyclists and swimmers who do not participate in resistance training have bone densities similar to sedentary individuals.

These recommendations are not guaranteed protection against the development of osteopenia and osteoporosis. There is also a genetic component for the development of these disorders. However, a proper diet and weight-bearing activities go a long way to help offset a decrease in bone density.

Cardiac output decreases with age as a result of a decrease in stroke volume and maximal heart rate. There is a slight decrease in stroke volume due to a reduction in the left ventricle's ability to expand and contract. And as we age there is an estimated decrease in maximal heart rate by 1 bpm each year. The decrease in maximal heart rate is believed to be attributed to age-related changes to the cardiac conduction system (electrical signaling for contraction) combined with decreased sensitivity of the myocardium to specific hormones, primarily epinephrine and norepinephrine. A decrease in cardiac output results in a decrease in your ability to perform aerobically.

Another key factor in an age-related decline in performance is the ability to recover between training bouts. Monitor your response to training as you age and adapt the triaging program accordingly. There will come a point where both intensity and volume will need to be adjusted to allow time for adequate recovery. The exact timing is variable and will be highly dependent on your age, training status, health, and training goals.

Increases in fitness levels can occur at any age and therefore should not hinder anyone from starting a program. The fitness gains for someone starting a training program at 60 will not occur as quickly or be as large as the individual who started a program at 20. Aerobic training can lead to increases in muscle mass, decreases in body fat, increases in bone density, and lower blood pressure, and can positively impact cholesterol levels and provide many other health benefits. While medical clearance is important for all ages, it is vitally important that older individuals consult a physician prior to beginning an exercise program (slowly and gradually).

Children and Adolescence

In this discussion, childhood is defined as age 6 to puberty and adolescence is defined as the time period from puberty to age 18. Getting our youth involved in physical activity at an early age is extremely important. I currently have two wonderful boys (ages 5 and 7) who are typically going at everything 100 miles per hour. I am lucky in that I never have a problem getting them active. As a matter of fact, I typically have a problem slowing them down. I look forward to doing races with both of my boys, assuming they want to.

The minimum age to participate in triathlon is 6. Kids' triathlons are held at shorter distances. The swim is typically 50 to 200 m, the bike 2 to 4 miles, and the run 400 to 1600 m. The shorter distances allow kids to participate without overtaxing themselves during the race. The most important aspects of a kids' triathlon are to introduce kids to the sport and ensure that they have fun. Kids' triathlons follow the same basic rules as adult triathlons, with a few alterations. One major alteration is that youth are not permitted to race with aerobars. Moving from traditional handlebars to aerobars requires increased balance and bike-handling skills, which kids may not be able to master at their current developmental stage.

Kids will need to possess basic skills in the areas of swimming, cycling, and running in order to participate. Verify that they can comfortably complete the distance prior to participating in a triathlon. You want your child to enjoy the experience. If the swim scares them, they will be less likely to participate in the future. They should comfortably be able to ride and control their bike prior to their first race. USA Triathlon rules prohibit the use of training wheels during a race. Other than learning to correctly pace, running comes more naturally to kids and does not require a lot of training on technique. One point that I cannot stress enough is that triathlon for kids should be about fun only and not true competition. I believe that kids learn as much from losing as they do from winning, but the key is that they have fun.

Children and adolescents differ from adults both physiologically and psychologically. Because of these differences they should not be trained as small adults. The main physiological difference involves hormone levels. Prior to puberty children produce very small amounts of hormones and therefore cannot adapt to training as effectively as adults. Research shows that performance gains in prepubescent children occur in aerobic performance, anaerobic performance, muscular endurance, and muscular strength. However, the mechanisms behind these changes are not as straightforward as they appear.

With training children can experience significant gains in aerobic performance. However, with these gains there is little to no change in VO_{2max}. The

Triathlon provides a great outlet for children.

changes that occur are attributed to improved neuromuscular recruitment patterns. As the child's technique improves, he becomes more economical and aerobic performance improves dramatically with no alteration to aerobic capacity. The same basic concept applies to resistance training as well. With resistance training children see an increase in strength. This increase in strength is not due to muscle hypertrophy, but instead occurs due to neuromuscular adaptations that occur with training. The take-home message here is that training should not focus on attempting to alter aerobic capacity or strength. Instead the training programs should focus on producing proper technique, leading to optimizing recruitment patterns.

More important, training should focus on having fun. At this stage training should not feel like a chore, and children should look forward to it. The biggest mistake people make is forcing training on children and working them too hard. Watch and listen to your child and he will let you know when he is tired and needs a break.

During puberty hormone levels begin to increase, but still not quite to the level of adults. As a child reaches adolescence, his ability to adapt to training improves dramatically. At puberty testosterone production in males increases by around ten times that of prepubescent levels. This leads to a substantially increased rate of growth. At this time joints are not as stable and can lead to pain and injury during sports. During this period volume and intensity can increase, but not yet to the level of an adult. An adolescent should hold off on beginning an entry-level adult program until the age of 16, which is an average number as some adolescents mature faster or slower than others.

Another aspect to consider is that kids are still developing psychologically and therefore cannot be treated like an adult. Children and adolescents may not be able to readily grasp complicated concepts. So keep the explanations simple and expressed in terms that they can understand. This will not only get the concept across to them, but also prevent the child from becoming frustrated.

Do not allow kids to train at too high an intensity or volume. Sports-related injuries have drastically increased in children due to improper training. Doctors are reporting overuse injuries that typically do not occur in athletes until their collegiate or professional careers. One of the problems is that adult training programs are being applied to children and adolescents. Another problem is that kids are playing sports at a high volume and intensity year-round. It is good if a child stays active year-round, and it is also good if a child plays multiple sports, but you have to look at the overall training volume and intensity and ensure that your child is not overtraining. Take into account your child's other sports when developing his training program.

Overweight and Obesity

One reason that people become involved with triathlon is to become healthy and lose weight. This is an excellent goal and triathlon is a great format to support healthy weight loss. There is one important fact that I stated earlier in this book that I will restate now: Research shows that individuals who are overweight and physically active are significantly less likely to develop cardiovascular disease than thin, inactive people. You do not have to look like one of the people on the front of a fitness magazine to be healthy. In some races USA Triathlon has a Clydesdale (males weighing more than 220 pounds) and Athena (females weighing more than 165 pounds) division for those that choose to participate. You do not have to participate in those divisions and can choose to compete as an age grouper instead. There are certain key points you should consider when training and racing while overweight or obese.

If you are overweight you are much more susceptible to the development of heat-related injuries, as fat storage acts as insulation, reducing the body's ability to effectively dissipate heat. While this can be beneficial on cold days, it is counterproductive on hot, humid days. Make sure to read the section on training in the heat in Chapter 16.

Cycling equipment has become lighter over the years, adding a strong performance benefit. For individuals who are overweight, lighter is not always better. When purchasing a bike you want to make sure that the bike can support your current weight. Most midrange frames will be fine and only extremely lightweight frames should be a concern. If in doubt contact the manufacturer and ask if there are weight restrictions. The largest concern when purchasing a bike is the wheel set. Do not purchase lightweight race wheels with a low spoke count. Race wheels can have spoke counts as low as sixteen on the front and twenty on the rear (this statement does not take into account the large molded three-spoke wheels). To err on the side of safety, use a spoke count of thirty-two or higher.

Running is a weight-bearing activity where two to three times your body weight is expressed through the ground reaction forces during a run. If you are severely overweight or obese, you will want to slowly work your way into running. Jumping into running too quickly can lead to the development of overuse injuries, such as stress fractures or joint injuries. Listen to your body and progress your training accordingly. It is okay to feel soreness, but you should not feel pain. The development of sharp pains is a sign of damage and should be evaluated by a physician.

Diabetes

Diagnosed diabetics are typically well versed on their disease, treatment, and symptoms. While you may be confident that you can manage your diabetes, you should still consult with your doctor when beginning a training program for triathlon. You must ensure that your diabetes is under control and discuss how to alter diet and insulin injections, if needed, to accommodate training.

This section is not intended to provide medical advice or treatment. Prior to beginning a training program it is important to seek medical clearance from your regular physician. Diabetes can also lead to the development of other health complications such as high blood pressure, cardiovascular disease, compromised peripheral vascularization, and peripheral neuropathy. For this reason obtaining a physician's clearance prior to starting a training program is vital. While exercise is recommended for individuals with diabetes, it is important that diabetes is under control prior to starting a program and that control is maintained throughout training. Once cleared to participate in physical activity, you must monitor blood glucose levels before, during, and after training and adjust accordingly.

There are two basic pathologies for the occurrence of diabetes. The first pathology occurs when the insulin-producing cells located on the pancreas are damaged, which ultimately limits insulin production. This usually occurs due to an auto-immune dysfunction where the body's immune system attacks the cells. Because the pancreas cannot produce adequate amounts of insulin, many diabetics will need to inject insulin into their system. This type of diabetes is typically referred to as Type I or early onset diabetes.

Type II diabetes occurs due to a decrease in insulin sensitivity. Whereas Type I diabetes is a result of a decrease in insulin production, insulin production is not negatively impacted in Type II diabetes. Instead insulin receptor sites are down regulated (reduction in hormone receptor sites) in response to chronic high levels of insulin being released into the system. The two primary risk factors for the development of Type II diabetes are being sedentary and overweight.

Exercise and proper diet has a strong affect on both Type I and Type II diabetes. Due to the permanent damage to the islet beta cells of the pancreas, exercise and proper diet do not provide a cure for Type I diabetes, but both are strong tools used to keep Type I diabetes under better control. However, proper diet and exercise do provide a strong means for alleviating Type II diabetes by increasing insulin receptor sites.

If you have diabetes, work with a registered dietitian who is familiar with sport performance. It is unlikely that the average coach would have sufficient knowledge to adequately assess and prescribe proper nutrition to a diabetic, and some state regulations even prohibit giving nutritional advice to those with diabetes.

Low blood sugar (hypoglycemia) is of great concern for diabetic triathletes. The central nervous system and brain require glycogen for fuel. Glycogen (storage form of blood sugar) and glucose are the only sources the brain can utilize for energy, and therefore when blood glucose levels are low the brain and central nervous systems are severely affected. The initial response to low blood sugar is the release of epinephrine (commonly referred to as adrenaline) in an attempt to increase blood sugar. The release of epinephrine results in a significant increase in heart rate, the development of muscle tremors, anxiety, and an increased appetite. These are common early symptoms of hypoglycemia. As the brain is affected by lack of glycogen, symptoms of hypoglycemia worsen. Symptoms that occur as a result of lack of glycogen to the brain are: headache, dizziness, fatigue, irritability, slurred speech, blurred vision, confusion, lack of coordination, and unconsciousness. If the hypoglycemia becomes too severe, it could even result in coma or death.

Hypoglycemia can progress very quickly and therefore training should stop at the first presentation of any symptom. The triathlete should immediately measure blood glucose and respond accordingly. Diabetics will typically keep foods high on the glycemic index available for situations like this. The athlete should eat, recheck blood sugar levels, and then make an educated decision on whether or not to continue training. If blood sugar levels are not within the normal limits or the athlete does not feel well, the training session should be canceled.

Training for triathlon places a heavy strain on glycogen stores and blood glucose levels and therefore adjustments to both diet and insulin may need to be considered. Insulin-dependent triathletes may need to adjust insulin timing and dosage. The injection site can also affect insulin uptake. During the run and the bike, blood circulation is greatly increased to the muscles of the legs, which can speed up insulin uptake. Any alteration to diet or timing, dosage, and location of insulin injections should be thoroughly discussed with a physician prior to implementation.

Asthma

Asthma is the most common chronic disease faced by athletes. Asthma is characterized by difficulty breathing and wheezing. During an asthma attack the air passage constricts and mucus builds up interfering with normal breathing.

The severity of asthma attacks vary and can range from slight discomfort while breathing to a life-threatening blockage. Diagnosed asthmatics with a prescribed inhaler must have it available at all times.

Some asthmatics only present with symptoms 5 to 10 minutes after the cessation of exercise. This form of asthma is commonly referred to as exercise-induced asthma. While incidences usually occur after exercise, it is not uncommon for symptoms to start during exercise. Any asthma trigger (pollen, carbon monoxide, etc.) can increase the risk of exercise-induced asthma. Environmental factors also play a role. Cold, dry environments greatly increase the risk of an incident, whereas warm humid environments reduce the risk.

A slow, gradual, and longer warmup is recommended for those diagnosed with asthma. If you have frequent or severe asthma, pay close attention to your warmup protocol. If prescribed by a physician, an inhaler can be used prior to competition in order to help prevent an occurrence. Inhalers contain banned substances (primarily albuterol) and therefore use of an inhaler in USAT–sanctioned races requires a medical waiver. Most age-group triathletes do not bother to seek the medical waiver because typically only elite-level triathletes are ever tested.

Chiropra
Stabilit

CHAPTER FOURTEEN

Health and Injury

Health and injury are two main concerns for athletes. It is often said that there are two types of triathletes: those that are injured and those that are about to be. The general advice in this section should not be considered medical advice or be substituted for medical advice from a licensed health care provider. If in doubt on any health or injury complication, consult your physician.

Research has frequently demonstrated that endurance activities have a positive impact on cholesterol levels, blood pressure, cardiovascular health, and Type II diabetes. Some research even indicates a decreased risk for developing certain cancers.

Physical Exam

When starting any physical activity, make sure you are healthy enough to safely participate. While a physical exam is time consuming and does cost money, it is a good idea to have one prior to starting any exercise program.

It's especially important to get a medical exam if you have not participated in regular physical activity prior to starting triathlon. Being sedentary is a major risk factor for developing cardiovascular disease, Type II diabetes, high cholesterol, high blood pressure, and other medical problems. If you have one of these conditions, your doctor may recommend exercise as a way of controlling or improving your health. However, exercising, especially at high intensities, can also increase the risk of an adverse incident in individuals with these conditions.

When starting a new training program, age is another area for concern. Unfortunately, as we age the risk for developing cardiovascular disease, as well as other diseases, increases significantly. Older individuals (males >45 and female >55) should seek medical clearance first.

Any individual with signs or symptoms of cardiovascular disease should seek medical clearance prior to starting an exercise program. Read through the following list of signs/symptoms of cardiovascular disease to determine

Unfortunately injury is a common occurrence when training for triathlon.

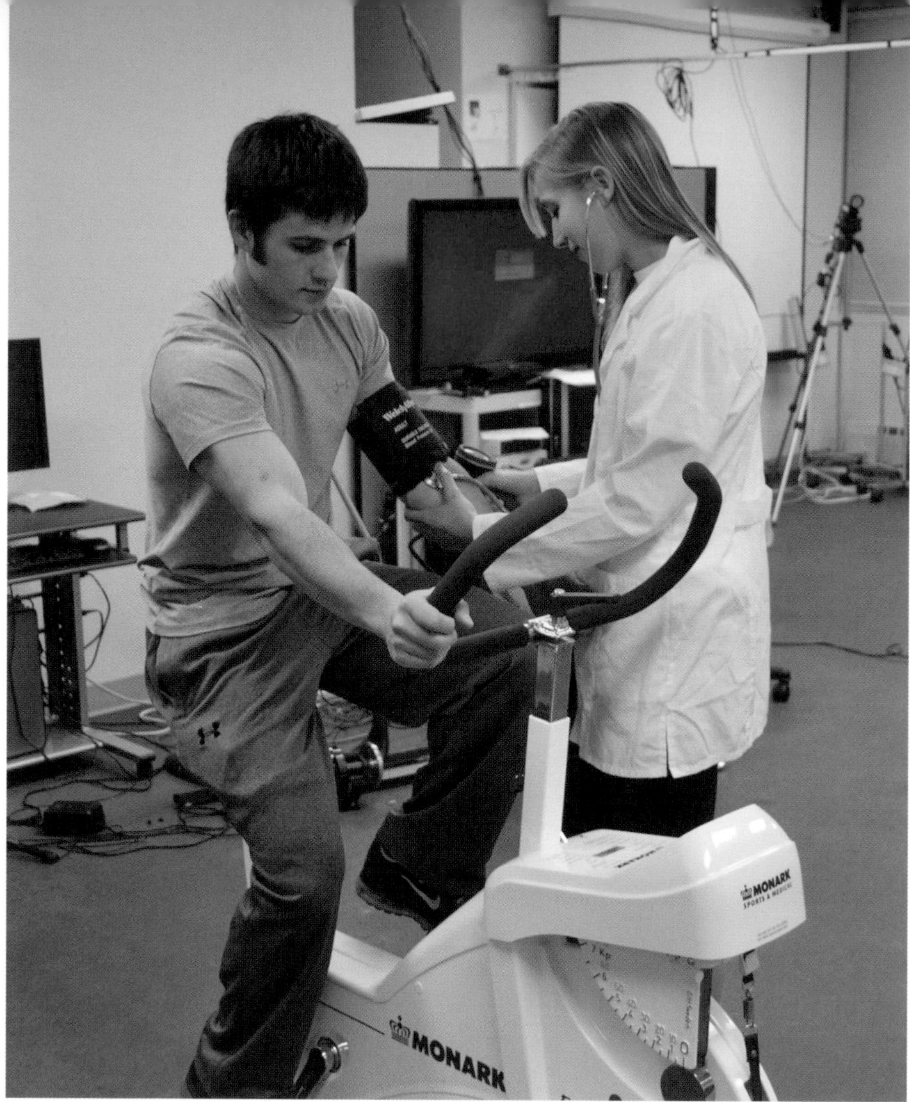

Ensure that you are healthy enough to begin a triathlon training program.

if any apply to you. If you have any of the following symptoms, you should contact your physician immediately. The signs/symptoms only indicate the possibility of cardiovascular disease. Only your physician can diagnose it or rule it out.

- chest pain at rest or during exercise
- pain in the arms, shoulder, neck, or jaw regions
- abnormal shortness of breath
- irregular heartbeat (speed or rhythm)

- edema in the ankles
- cramping in the calf muscles
- unusual fatigue
- dizziness
- fainting
- difficulty breathing when lying down

When choosing a doctor consider using a sport-specific doctor as your physician, someone who works with athletes on a daily basis and will have a better understanding of what it takes to train and think as an athlete. A physician who has a specific understanding of triathlon or endurance training will be able to properly assess your training load and provide insight.

When dealing with overuse, muscular, connective tissue, or bone injuries, ideally you should seek medical advice from an orthopedic sports medicine specialist, someone with a strong background in sports medicine and who will understand the common reasons that injury occurs in a specific sport. An orthopedic sports medicine specialist will attempt to keep you training as much as possible without leading to further damage and allowing for recovery.

Illness

In general, chronic exercise results in improved immune function within the body. A bout of exercise challenges the immune system, leading to a positive physiological response that increases immune function. Athletes who train correctly will generally possess greater immunity than their sedentary counterparts. Note, however, that frequent or persistent illness is a sign of overtraining.

For the most part training should be avoided when ill in order to prevent the illness from becoming worse. However, it is okay to train under certain conditions. Follow this rule of thumb: If the illness is above the shoulders (not including headaches), you are okay to train. If the illness moves below the shoulders, then you should not train. For example, if you have a cold and your only symptom is a stuffy nose, then it is okay to train. If you have a headache, fever, or aches and pains throughout the body, then it is not okay to train. If the cold moves into your chest, training should also be avoided. When the immune system is already fighting an illness, it makes no sense to decrease its ability to fight infection by exercising.

No matter what your symptoms are, do not train with a fever, as it is an indication that the immune system is attempting to fight an infection. Virus and bacteria can thrive at the normal body temperature (98.6°F), but do not survive well at higher temperatures. In order to fight off the infection, the body begins to increase core temperature. Attempting to train with a fever will only further reduce the body's ability to fight off the infection.

If you are ill you will be better served by taking a day or two off in order to recover. Missing a couple of days will not greatly alter your training and progression. However, trying to work through the illness could make matters worse and result in a longer period of time off from training. Remember the recovery phase is a very important part of training.

Be cautious when taking over-the-counter or prescribed medicine. Know how the medicine interacts with your training. For example, decongestants act as a stimulant, leading to a significant increase in resting and submaximal heart rate. They can also result in dehydration and drowsiness.

Psychological Stress

Psychological stress can be either good or bad, depending on the type of stress, the level of stress, and your reaction to that stress. Physiologically we are designed to handle stress. In severe stress the sympathetic nervous system (fight-or-flight) is activated, releasing hormones to optimize situational response. In athletics we often refer to good stress as a challenge.

It is the bad stress that you need to be concerned with. High levels of stress suppress immune function and increase recovery time. It takes much longer to recover between bouts when stressed. However, exercise is a great way to relieve psychological stress.

Preventing and Addressing Specific Injuries

There are specific injuries that can occur when participating in triathlon training and racing. This section discusses a few of the most common issues, including causes, treatment, and prevention. The best way to deal with an injury is to do your best to prevent it from occurring.

Chafing

Chafing is one of the most common issues triathletes face. Chafing presents as sore red skin and, in serious conditions, can bleed. During the swim it

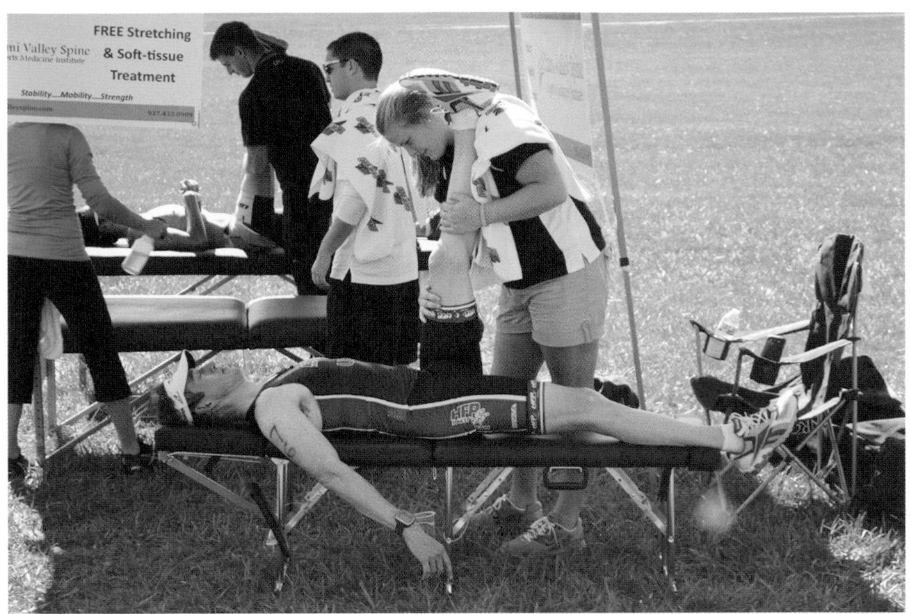

A massage upon completion of a race is ideal for keeping muscles loose.

typically occurs under the arms due to your triathlon or wetsuit top rubbing as you swim. To prevent chafing ensure that your triathlon top or wetsuit fits properly and apply body glide or a similar lubricant over the area prior to the start of the swim. Another common site for chafing is the back of the neck where the wetsuit zipper is located. Make sure that the protective flap is down and between you and the wetsuit. Apply lubricant to that area as well. After wearing your wetsuit one or two times you will find out where all the chafing spots are located. Be sure to lubricate all of the spots prior to swimming. A well-fitting wetsuit will not have too many hot spots.

In cycling chafing has the potential to occur at any point where your skin moves across the saddle. Chafing often leads to the development of saddle sores, which are formed when bacteria interacts with abrasions. Saddle sores can be as mild as a small pimple or as serious as a cyst that must be surgically lanced. The development of a cyst is not that common and typically only occurs in those who put in a lot of miles on the bike. The first step to preventing chafing in cycling is to ensure that you have the correct equipment (proper saddle and a good pair of bike shorts). A good pair of bike shorts goes a long way toward preventing chafing. The chamois (pad) in cycling shorts is designed to both relieve pressure and to reduce chafing.

Place chamois cream in the cycling shorts to add lubrication and further prevent chafing.

An ill-fitting bike can also lead to chafing. If the saddle is too high, then you will rock back and forth across the saddle. If the saddle is tilted nose down, which is a common mistake in triathlon, then you will slide down the saddle to the nose and then push back up the saddle repeatedly on a ride. Both situations can result in serious chafing.

As mentioned above saddle sores are created through a combination of chafing and bacteria, so it is important to address the bacteria issue as well. Bacteria thrive in warm, moist environments, such as in cycling and triathlon shorts. At the end of the training session, remove the wet shorts as soon as possible and change into something dry. This should go without saying, but always wash your shorts before training in them again.

Chafing can also be a huge problem on the run. Chafing during the run is caused by skin rubbing against skin or skin rubbing against clothing. As run distance increases so too does the risk of chafing. Make sure your clothing fits right and that there are no rough seams. Clothing should be made of lightweight, breathable material designed for running. Cotton is not a good choice as it retains water and increases chafing. I typically eliminate anything from my running wardrobe that chafes. Common places for chafing are under the arms, between the legs, and the nipples. To prevent chafing under the arms and between the legs, use lubricant prior to starting the run. Lubricant may or may not work for the nipples. For long runs I recommend you place Band-Aids over the nipples in order to prevent chafing. Women may need to lubricate the band around their sports bra.

Running shoes can lead to chafing that results in blisters. The most common cause of blisters on the foot is shoes that do not fit right or are tied too tight, which leads to increased friction. When purchasing a pair of running shoes, ensure that they are large enough to allow the foot to swell during the run, but not so large that the foot moves within the shoe a great deal. The typical rule of thumb is to purchase a half size larger than your normal everyday shoes. Running in improper socks can also lead to increased friction and blisters. Socks should be breathable, not retain water, and have no noticeable seams. To prevent chafing you can lubricate hot spots or use moleskin at the location of the hot spot to prevent the formation of a blister.

Urinary Tract Infections

Urinary tract infections are a common problem for females. Unfortunately, training and racing triathlon create a moist, warm environment and increase the risk of an infection. Change out of wet clothing and into dry clothing as soon as possible.

Numbness and Cycling

Cycling in triathlon places you in a relatively fixed position for a prolonged period of time. You make contact with the bike in three primary locations: aerobars (or handlebars), saddle, and pedals. A lot of weight is placed on the saddle, resulting in pressure being placed on the groin region. This pressure pushes on nerves located in the groin region and can result in penile numbness in male triathletes. While less studied, saddle pressure has also been shown to result in female numbness as well. Numbness occurs during the ride, and once pressure is relieved from the groin area feeling returns fairly quickly. If numbness persists contact your doctor immediately. In many cases numbness can be rectified through altering bike setup, changing saddles, or purchasing new shorts.

Bike setup for triathlon can be challenging due to the aggressively forward cycling position. This position causes the pelvis to rotate forward, placing more pressure on the groin region. You may want to slightly tilt the nose of the saddle down to relieve the pressure. Do not lower the nose of the saddle too much because it will cause you to slide forward on the saddle, which is counterproductive and makes matters worse. Find a saddle that fits you appropriately to help alleviate pressure and numbness in the groin area. Unfortunately, there is not one saddle that fits everyone; it may be a trial and error process.

During long rides the toes and part of the feet can also become numb. The most common cause of numb feet is shoes that are too tight, too small, or shoe straps that are too tight. Make sure that your shoes fit snug but not tight. One of the problems with cycling shoes is that the toe box is often too narrow, especially for those with wider feet. If your shoes are the right size and your feet go numb, try loosening the straps for relief.

The interaction of the shoe and the pedal can also lead to foot numbness. If the sole of the shoe is not stiff enough, then the pedal can create a hot spot and lead to numbness. Aftermarket insoles may help add foot support and relieve numbness. Cleat placement may also apply pressure that will result in numbness. Make sure that the pedal axle is centered on the ball of the foot.

Sometimes the problem may just be the way in which the shoe fits your specific feet. I had a pair of shoes that would make my toes and feet numb after about 25 to 30 miles of riding. The shoes fit properly, the straps were not too tight, and the sole was stiff. I ended up just getting new shoes and the problem went away.

With a triathlon bike the risk of hand numbness occurring is minimal due to spending very little time riding with the body's weight supported on the hands. Hand numbness is more of an issue for those with a traditional road bike. The weight to the upper body is supported by the hands on a narrow bar, which places pressure on the ulnar nerve located in the palm of the hand. The effect is amplified by road vibrations that are sent up through the bike and into the hands. There are a few things that you can do to alleviate hand numbness, which typically occurs in the fourth and fifth fingers. First, buy a good set of padded cycling gloves. This adds a layer of cushioning between the handlebar and your hands. Installing padded bar tape is another method that increases cushioning. Also have your bike fit checked to ensure that you do not have too much of your weight distributed toward the front of the bike.

Regardless of the location of numbness, any persistent numbness is cause for medical concern and should be examined by a physician. Repetitive numbness could result in damage to that area and steps should be taken to rectify the situation.

Overuse Injuries

Unfortunately, overuse injuries are very common in endurance sports. Repetitive motion places stress on the muscles, connective tissue, bone, and joint structure. This repetitive motion can result in an injury to the mechanical systems of the body. The benefit of triathlon is that you don't train the exact same sport all week long. An overuse injury presents as chronic pain that can occur during or after a training bout. This pain may be mild to severe, depending on the injury.

Attempting to increase volume or intensity too quickly is the most common reason for the development of an overuse injury. This is especially true for beginning triathletes who are excited about training. Always slowly increase volume prior to increasing intensity in order to decrease the risk of developing an overuse injury. Intensity takes a greater toll on the body.

Overtraining can also cause overuse injuries. Recovery is a very important part of the training program, but it is often ignored. If you do not allow enough time for recovery between bouts overtraining occurs, leaving the body in a weakened state that is susceptible to the development of an overuse injury.

The use of improper technique in all three sports can lead to the development of an overuse injury even when all other factors are accounted for. The most common overuse injuries to swimmers who concentrate on the front crawl involve the shoulder joint. Improper stroke angles can add undue stress, resulting in increased torque at the shoulder joint. Movement of the neck during the swim can also lead to overuse injuries. While overuse injuries of the knee do occur when swimming the front crawl, they are not very common (they are more common in the breast stroke). The most common overuse injuries seen in swimming include:

- **Shoulder pain.** The rotator cuff muscles are small and fatigue easily, making it easier for the humerus to subluxate (partially dislocate). Between the increased range of motion required for swimming and the fatigue that occurs during training, shoulder joint stability is greatly compromised. Due to a decrease in shoulder stability, subluxations are not uncommon. Another common overuse injury is shoulder impingement, which occurs when the scapula (shoulder blade) presses on the muscles of the rotator cuff as the arm rotates, resulting in inflammation and pain.
- **Biceps tendonitis.** A lot of force is applied to the long head of the biceps tendon at the point of entry to the catch and from the mid stroke to just before exiting the water. The movement and the forces applied during the stroke place a lot of force on the tendon causing irritation and inflammation.

In cycling, overuse injuries due to technique are often a result of improper bike fit. The human body and machine must work together flawlessly in order to optimize performance and prevent overuse injuries. When cycling you ride in a relatively fixed position with very little movement. An average cyclist will work on maintaining an rpm of 90 throughout his ride. If a triathlete cycles for 1 hour at 90 rpm, he would pedal 5,400 revolutions, which places repeated load on the joints. A saddle height that is too high, too low, too far forward, or too far back can result in the development of an overuse injury. Correct bike fit for performance and injury prevention is detailed in Chapter 2. Cycling in too high a gear or increasing intensity too quickly can also lead to overuse injuries in cycling. The most common overuse injuries in cycling include:

- **Knee pain.** During cycling knee pain either presents on the front of the knee as pain at the patella (kneecap) or just below it on the patella tendon. Patellar tendonitis occurs when too much stress is placed on the patellar tendon. Anterior knee pain typically occurs when you cycle in too high a gear, train at too high of an intensity, or the saddle height is too low. Knee pain can also occur on the back of the knee, typically due to a saddle height that is too high.
- **Achilles tendinopathy.** The foot acts as a very important lever during cycling. All of the force generated through the hips and legs must be applied through the feet and into the pedals. During the pedal cycle the foot plantar flexes, which requires strong activation of the triceps surae, which places a large amount of force on the Achilles tendon and can lead to tendon damage and inflammation. Achilles tendonitis usually occurs due to riding in too large a gear, increasing intensity too quickly, or if the overall training volume is too high.
- **Plantar fasciitis.** Presents as pain on the bottom of the foot at the heel and occurs when the plantar fascia, the connective tissue that runs from the heel to the toes, becomes damaged and inflamed. The plantar fascia is responsible for maintaining the longitudinal arch of the foot. The pain typically occurs after the run, but can also occur during. There is typically pronounced pain when getting out of bed in the morning. This is due to sleeping with the foot plantar flexed during the night and then placing weight on it without stretching first. This is why physicians typically recommend sleeping in a night splint, which keeps the foot neutral and pulls the toes slightly upward. Because of the large amount of force placed on the foot during the pedal cycle, it is important to have shoes with a rigid sole. Shoes with a flexible sole place a lot of strain on the plantar ligament, resulting in plantar fasciitis. Plantar fasciitis can also occur due to the pedal axle being located too far forward on the ball of the foot, which effectively increases the moment arm of that foot.
- **Iliotibial (IT) band syndrome.** Presents as pain along the lateral (outside) portion of the upper leg. The tensor fascia latae is

Two to three times your body mass goes into the ground reaction forces that propel you forward.

responsible for ensuring that the leg moves forward in a straight manner. During cycling the IT band can become tight and result in inflammation. One of the best ways to prevent IT band syndrome is to work on flexibility.

Running places the greatest amount of strain on the body due to the ground reaction forces. Each time the foot strikes the ground the reaction force is two to three times your body mass. Another reason that overuse injuries are common in runners is biomechanical insufficiencies. The ground reaction force is sent up the kinetic chain and if there are any biomechanical abnormalities then a greater amount of stress is applied along the chain. Due to ground reaction forces and biomechanical insufficiencies, overuse injuries of the lower body are very common. The most common overuse injuries include:

- **Shin splints.** Present as pain in the lower leg area around the tibia due to damage to the soft tissue (primarily connective tissue). Shin splints often occur due to increasing intensity too quickly, but can also occur due to increased volume. Shin splints can also occur due to biomechanical abnormalities, such as severe overpronation. Lack of flexibility and joint instability also contribute to shin splints. If you have persistent shin splints, see a specialist. Often stress fractures and compartment syndrome are misdiagnosed as shin splints. Both of these conditions can deteriorate quickly if not properly addressed.

- **Knee pain.** Presents as pain located around the knee joint and is typically referred to as "runner's knee." There are two common pathologies that lead to runner's knee. The first is when pain occurs behind the patella due to improper tracking of the patella or pressure on the patella as it passes across the femur. The second pathology is patella tendonitis. This presents as pain of the patellar tendon just below the patella. Runner's knee occurs as a result of muscular imbalances, patella tracking issues, and repetitive strain placed on the knee while running.
- **Plantar fasciitis.** Plantar fasciitis also occurs during running. The large ground reaction forces place a heavy strain on the plantar fascia. Plantar fasciitis is common in individuals with abnormal arches (too high or too low). Plantar fasciitis is typically caused by long runs, excessive downhill running, and lack of flexibility.
- **Achilles tendinopathy.** Presents as a pain located in the Achilles tendon. When running the triceps surae is used heavily during plantar flexion of the toe off phase. This movement places a lot of strain on the Achilles tendon and can lead to Achilles tendinopathy, most commonly caused by too high of an intensity or volume, lack of general flexibility, poor biomechanics, or heavy uphill running.
- **Iliotibial band syndrome.** The tensor fascia latae is responsible for ensuring that the leg swings forward in a straight manner during running and the gluteus maximus is used strongly to extend the hip when running, placing a lot of strain on the IT band. Work on flexibility to decrease the risk of problems involving the IT band.

If caught early enough, most overuse injuries can be remedied before they become too severe. Rest, ice, and elevation can go a long way toward recovery. If approved by your doctor, over-the-counter anti-inflammatory medications can also help alleviate the pain. Do not ignore persistent pain as overuse injuries can progressively worsen over time. If pain worsens or does not go away, visit your doctor immediately.

Road Rash

Road rash is the common terminology for the friction burns and lacerations that occur on your skin as it slides across the concrete during a crash. It is common in cycling. While not as common, road rash does occur during running as well.

If the road rash is serious or you have deep lacerations, seek medical attention immediately to avoid the onset of infection. For most simple cases of road rash, you can take care of it at home. When sliding across the pavement, small rocks, dirt, and other debris get embedded in the wound. To clean, simply wash and scrub the wound. Be cautious using a washrag as it can leave lint in the wound. I keep a medical scrub brush around just for this purpose, but typically only use one for deep abrasions. If you are unable to clean the wound properly at home, seek medical attention.

Once the wound has been properly cleaned, the next step is to put a light coating of antibacterial ointment on the wound. Keep the wound covered until it is beyond the oozing stage. Then leave the wound uncovered for better healing. Seek medical attention if you suspect an infection.

Common Signs of Infection

- the wound becomes hot
- pain increases
- red swollen skin around the edges
- lines radiating from the wound
- pus and oozing
- foul odor

Part III
RACING

Maintaining flexibility is an important step in preventing overuse injuries in triathlon.
Shutterstock

CHAPTER FIFTEEN

Racing

During the off-season you need to spend time carefully choosing races for the upcoming season. The races will determine how you schedule your training sessions as well as the details of each training session. This process allows you to use periodization (discussed in Chapter 6) to optimize your training in order to ensure that you are ready for the races; you'll need to prioritize the races to peak appropriately.

To set your race schedule, first look into available races. Local triathlon shops and clubs are great places to find information on races. All triathlons will typically advertise through these venues in order to attract locals to the race. Locals will be able to give you honest feedback on the race course and organization.

USA Triathlon is another excellent source for finding local races. Most triathlons are USA Triathlon–sanctioned and therefore can be found on the organization's official website (www.usatriathlon.org). The organization provides insurance coverage, race publicity, USA Triathlon ranking for those racing, safety, and other benefits.

TriFind.com and Active.com are two Internet sources for triathlon race information. These sites have both sanctioned and not sanctioned races listed. TriFind.com focuses solely on multisport events. Just go to the site, click on your state, and find a race. Active.com is a sporting event registration site that covers many different sporting events. Click on triathlon to filter your search. You can register directly through Active.com for any race that you find on its site.

When choosing a race first consider the length of the course. You should focus on the sprint distance races and get a few under your belt before attempting longer distances. Schedule ultra-endurance events (half to full ironman distance) sparingly.

Also consider the date and location of the site to allow for travel to and from the race, and to ensure that you can comfortably work the race into your training, work, and family schedule. Carefully consider races held early in the competition season as you may not have the training volume necessary

After all of your training and hard work it is race time.

to comfortably complete the course at that point in time. This is especially true if it is your first triathlon. While you do want to challenge yourself, you want to finish the race winded but thinking that it was an amazing experience and looking forward to the next race.

Local races are typically less expensive (no lodging and minimal travel), require less planning, and are typically less stressful overall. You will be more familiar with the area and therefore more comfortable planning the race weekend. Local races also allow you easy access to train on the course in order to optimally prepare for the race. Traveling to a race adds significant cost to the overall budget (hotel, travel, food).

When looking at the races, you should develop a budget. Unfortunately, races are expensive and the cost can add up if you are not careful. Entry fees for sprint distance races range from $35 to around $100 with the average cost of a race being about $55. However, entry fees are not the only expenses you have to consider. Factor travel, lodging, and food costs into your budget. Put money into a race fund throughout the off-season to support the cost of racing during season.

The size of the race is another key consideration. You may prefer to participate in a low-key event with few participants or you may get more excited about a large race with a lot of participants. Both have their advantages and disadvantages. The smaller races have fewer people and therefore are typically less crowded on the swim, bike, and run. A smaller group of people racing may also be less intimidating for those just starting out. The downside to smaller races is that they may not be as well supported on the course. Large races have a big wow factor that brings with it a lot of excitement and energy. When you have 1,000-plus triathletes competing in an event, it creates a festive atmosphere that takes on a life of its own, providing a great experience for everyone involved.

Registration

Most races have early registration, which will save you money. Take note of the dates that registration fees increase and plan to register accordingly. One downside of registering too early is being unable to recoup your money if something such as work, family, or injury interferes with your ability to attend the race. Most races will not refund registration fees or will only provide a partial refund if requested by a specific date. Some of the popular races fill up quickly; if you wait too long there will be no open spots available. You

Be sure to know when and where to pick up your race packet.

can always contact the race director to get a feeling of how quickly the race fills.

USA Triathlon–sanctioned races require you to have a USA Triathlon license. You have two options: You can purchase an annual license (currently $45) or a 1-day license (currently $12). If you plan to do more than a couple of races, it makes sense to go ahead and purchase the annual license. If you are unsure and purchase a day license, you can mail in the receipt for credit toward the purchase of an annual license. Some races require you to provide your USAT license or purchase a 1-day license at the time of registration. You may want to purchase an annual license prior to registration in order to provide your USAT number at registration. However, the majority of races will let you purchase a 1-day license the day of the event.

Keep a copy of the registration receipt in a folder to take with you to the race. While rare, there have been occasions when the race director does not have confirmation of your registration at the race site. Also remember to take your USAT license with you to the race as you will be required to show your USAT license along with picture ID at packet pickup.

You will need to determine when and where packet pickup occurs. Most races have packet pickup the morning of the race near the transition area.

However, some races require packet pickup the day prior to the race, which may or may not be at the race site. Most races will have packet pickup both on the day prior and on race day. Also read the race flyer for any specialized information concerning the race.

Logistics

To save headaches come race day, make sure you cover all aspects of race weekend logistics. The first step is to determine your method of transportation. Will you fly or drive? Flying has specific challenges due to having to transport your bike and equipment to the race. When flying you basically have two options: flying with your bike or shipping your bike. Over the last 10 years, flying with your bike has become expensive, and the risk of the airlines damaging your bike seems greater than the possibility of damage occurring during shipping. I prefer to ship my bike to a race that requires flying. You can either ship your bike to a local bike shop or to the location where you are staying. Whether you take your bike on the flight or ship it to the race, pack your bike correctly by following the instructions in the Packing Your Bike for Travel section below.

Prior to race weekend go over the race schedule and plan your weekend based on the schedule. Determine when and where packet pickup will occur and schedule accordingly. You will also need to know when the transition area opens and closes for pre-race staging. You typically want to show up as soon as transition opens to allow for a greater choice of where to stage your equipment and ensure that you can comfortably set up and prepare for your race. Typically you will have to get body marked prior to entering the transition area.

Scout out the transition area. In most cases this will be difficult to accomplish the day prior as the transition area may not be completely set up until race morning. Take note of the swim in, swim exit, bike out, bike in, run out and finish line. Most races will have a bike mount and dismount line. If you mount your bike prior to the mount line or dismount past the dismount line, you will be assessed a time penalty. Knowing the rules and the setup ahead of time will allow your transitions to run smoothly on race day. Some race directors will provide a race map with complete course directions. The race map can typically be found on the race website and at the registration booth on race day. It is also advisable to examine the swim course prior to race start.

Water start

Beach start

Become familiar with the transition area prior to the start of the race.

Equipment Check

Prior to leaving home it is important to conduct an equipment check so you don't leave equipment behind. Create a checklist, laying everything out and visually marking everything off the list. Below is a generic checklist of the equipment you would typically take to a race. Feel free to use this checklist and modify it to fit your needs.

- ❑ Bike
- ❑ Helmet
- ❑ Cycling shoes
- ❑ Water bottle
- ❑ Tire pump
- ❑ Tools
- ❑ Spare tube
- ❑ Swim goggles
- ❑ Triathlon suit
- ❑ Socks
- ❑ Wetsuit
- ❑ Running shoes
- ❑ Race belt
- ❑ Sunglasses
- ❑ Sunscreen
- ❑ Nutrition
- ❑ Towel

Consider packing two bags. The first bag is your transition bag where you place all of the equipment that you use during the race. This way you can grab your bag and go to transition on race day and know that you have everything you need. The second bag will contain clothing, travel supplies, and any extra gear that you may need. If you have a set of bike tools, bring those along as well. It is better to have the tools and not need them than need the tools and not have them.

Packing Your Bike for Travel

When traveling to a race by plane, you need to make sure that your bike is packed properly in order to ensure that it is not damaged during transit. You have two basic options when packing your bike. The first involves using a cardboard bike box, which you can get from your local bike shop. The second involves purchasing a hard plastic bike case, which provides greater protection.

If you do not know how to pack and unpack your bike, you can pay a bike shop to do it for you. Have your local bike shop pack and ship your bike to a bike shop at your race destination, who will then have the bike put together and ready to roll when you arrive. For the return trip simply reverse the process. This is a costly process and you may want to consider learning how to pack and unpack your bike on your own.

Here are the basic steps to prepare your bike to ship:

- Remove the front and rear wheel from the bike. Remove the skewers from both wheels.
- If you have them, place plastic protectors into the front and rear drop-outs to help prevent damage to the fork and rear stay.
- Remove the stem from the fork steer tube and place the handlebars along the side of the frame. Place a towel between the handlebars and the frame and then attach the bars to the frame with zip ties so that they do not move.
- Remove the pedals from the bike.
- Remove the rear derailleur and attach it to the rear stay with a zip tie.
- Remove the seat post and seat from the bike (no need to remove the seat from the seat post).
- Pack the bike, wheels, and parts into the case or box. If using a case pack the wheels per the instructions of the case manufacturer.

Race Day

Body marking prior to race start

On race day arrive early enough to find parking, pick up your race packet, set up transition, and arrive at the start line on time. To ensure that there are no unforeseen complications with registration, go to the registration table to pick up your race packet. The race packet will contain a race number for you that will go on your body, on your bike and sometimes on your helmet. Race officials and photographers use the number to identify you during the race. You will use the race number to pick up your race chip and to get body marked for the race. The race officials will typically write your number on your arms and legs and place your age group on the back of your calf.

The race numbers must be worn at all times during the race. The bike number can be attached directly to the seat post or top tube of your bike using twist ties, tape, or staples. The second race number that you receive is to be worn during the bike and the run. Place this number onto a race belt that can be quickly donned during transition one after the swim. The helmet number is a small sticker that is placed on the front of the helmet where it is easily visible. While most races have a number for your bike and your person, not all have helmet numbers.

Some races require a safety inspection prior to the start of the race. During the inspection the race official will check to ensure that your helmet is in working order and that it meets safety requirements. He will also inspect your bike to ensure that you have bar end plugs and that the bike meets minimum safety requirements.

It is inevitable that you will have to go to the bathroom prior to starting the race. Nerves have a tendency to press the issue. Do not wait until the last minute as the lines are typically long.

Transition

Setup

The transition area is the hub of a triathlon race. The swim leg will end at the transition area (after a short run from the water), the bike will begin and end at the transition area, and the run will leave the transition area and end somewhere within the vicinity of the transition area. Setting up in the transition area is a very important part of race day preparation. Some races require bikes to be racked in a specific location designated by race number—racking your bike and staging your transition in the wrong place can result in a penalty. Most races do not have designated locations and it is first come first serve, which is why it is important to arrive early to set up in transition. Know when the transition area opens and closes prior to race day.

Arrive early enough to find a good spot in transition.

Lay out your gear for easy access.

When setting up your transition area, do not take up more space than is necessary. Place your bike on the rack using either the handlebars or the seat. There is no right or wrong way as long as the bike is secure. I recommend placing the bike on the rack using the seat. Lay the rest of your gear out on one side of the bike or the other (it should be barely wider than a pair of shoes).

As transition becomes full it will be harder and harder to find a spot to place your gear. There are times when triathletes take up too much space with their gear. Never move anyone else's bike or gear. If someone is incorrectly racked in your designated spot or there do not appear to be any open spaces, speak with a race official. If someone is incorrectly racked in your spot, then the race official can ask that person to move to the correct spot so you can set up. If it appears as if there are no more open spots, the race officials can find a spot to make room for you to set up your transition area.

Remember that there is limited space to set up and therefore excess equipment should not be brought into the transition area. For example, many people recommend using a water bucket in transition in order to clean debris from the feet prior to putting on socks or shoes. A water bucket takes up too much space—a quick wipe of a towel works well enough.

Here is the beginning method you should use for setting up transition: First, rack your bike and determine which side to lay out your gear. Place a towel down with enough of it sticking forward that you can easily wipe your feet prior to putting on socks or shoes. Place your cycling shoes down on the towel facing away from you. Ensure that the shoe closures are open or loose so that you can easily slide them onto your feet. If you are going to wear socks, then place the socks on top of the shoes for easy access. Place your race belt and number on top of the cycling shoes. Next, place your running shoes just in front of the cycling shoes, so that they will be there and ready after the bike leg. Your sunglasses and helmet should be on the handlebars for easy access and so that you do not forget to put them on prior to the bike leg.

Remember where your bike and equipment are located within the transition area. When the transition area is full, it is somewhat difficult to immediately locate your bike as you enter the transition after the swim. Identify the row and the rack number of where you are located. If the racks are not numbered, then simply count. Also, notice any landmarks that will allow you to quickly find your bike. Do not rely on other triathletes' racked bikes as a landmark because they may or may not be there when you enter the transition area.

Transition One

Transition one begins as soon as you leave the water. As you exit the water take off your swim cap and goggles and hold them in your hands as you run. If you are wearing a wetsuit, begin removing the wetsuit by stripping the top down as you run. Once you reach the transition area, finish removing the wetsuit. Drop your swim gear into your area, making sure not to cover your cycling or run gear. Next put your socks (if you wear them) and shoes on. I recommend taking the little extra time it requires to put socks on in order to prevent blistering on the bike and later on the run. Lastly, put on your helmet and sunglasses and grab your bike. Be sure to don your helmet prior to cycling as you can be penalized or disqualified for riding without a helmet.

Run with your bike out of the transition area and then mount the bike beyond the bike mounting line. Almost all triathlons have a bike mounting

Begin removing your wetsuit as you leave the water.

Do not mount your bike until after you have crossed the bike mount line.

line so that triathletes do not ride their bike in the transition area and so that the transition area does not become congested. Mounting your bike prior to the line will result in a time penalty. Be careful running in your cycling shoes in the transition area. Cycling shoes' cleat systems are designed to interact with the pedal and not for running, so they may be a little slick.

Transition Two

Transition two consists of transitioning from the bike to the run. When returning to the transition area be sure to note where the bike dismount line is located. Dismounting beyond this line can result in time penalties. Approach the dismount line at a speed that you can control, dismount just prior to the line, and run your bike to the transition area.

To dismount, try this method: Remove your feet from the shoes prior to reaching the dismount line and leave the shoes attached to the pedals as you run to your transition area. The problem with this method is that if a shoe hits the ground as you are running it will disengage from the pedal, requiring you to backtrack to pick it up. I prefer to leave my shoes on and run to my transition area.

Here's another method: Unclip your right leg and bring it behind the seat and wheel of the bike while placing your weight on the left leg. Bring the right leg forward between the left leg and bike until it is in front of the left leg. Slow to a comfortable speed, place the right foot on the ground, remove the left foot from the pedal, and then run into transition. This method requires practice and skill.

Once at your transition area, rack your bike, remove your helmet, and place it on the bike. Make sure that you rack your bike back in the correct spot so as not to interfere with other triathletes. Remove your cycling shoes if you have not already and replace them with your running shoes. After donning your running shoes, head out of the transition area to finish the race.

Drafting

Drafting is when a cyclist rides behind another to gain an aerodynamic advantage. During cycling, up to 90 percent of the work required is used to overcome aerodynamics. When drafting behind another cyclist, the second will typically do 30 percent less work than the first. To ensure that triathletes are racing against each other with no advantage, and for safety reasons, USAT rules prohibit drafting during racing.

Dismount prior to the dismount line and then run your bike into transition.

USA Triathlon regulations require that you keep three bike lengths between you and other cyclists. If you overtake another cyclist, you have 15 seconds to pass that cyclist. If you cannot pass within 15 seconds you need to drop back and then try again. When you decide to pass another triathlete, speed up and pass with authority, as this will limit those who try to speed up to prevent you passing. Once your front wheel passes their front wheel, they are required to drop back out of your draft zone three bike lengths. Always pass to the left of the cyclists without crossing the center line. To help avoid a collision, always let the person know that you are passing by yelling "on your left" as you come up on him.

CHAPTER SIXTEEN

Heat, Cold, and Altitude

Environmental factors such as heat, cold, and high altitude have a strong potential to alter performance. The body's acute response to training in these environments differs from the response that occurs when training in a thermo-neutral environment or at sea level. Significant adaptations occur due to chronic exposure to heat and to altitude. Understanding the body's response to exposure and adaptation to these environments allows you to optimize both training and racing under these conditions.

Training in the Heat

Training in the heat can be very demanding. As mentioned previously, only 30 to 40 percent of metabolic energy is used for energetic processes and the remainder is degraded as heat. This internal heat generation coupled with heat intake from the environment creates a very precarious situation.

External heat is typically brought into the body through *radiation* and *conduction*. Radiation is the transfer of heat through electromagnetic waves. Heat is transferred to the body from the sun directly or through the sun's radiation reflected off of objects, such as asphalt. Thermal ground radiation also sends radiation to the body. Conduction requires direct molecular contact in order for heat to transfer. The most common form of conduction is when the foot makes contact with the hot ground.

When training in a hot environment, you need to remove excess heat from the body in order to prevent a heat-related illness. Heat can radiate from the body to the environment only when the body is at a higher temperature than the environment. Conduction is not a typical method for cooling the body during exercise but can be purposefully implemented to help dissipate heat. For example, placing cold towels across your neck during a run helps dissipate heat. The two main sources for heat dissipation during exercise are *convection* and *evaporation*. Convection is the transfer of heat through a fluid medium. As the air travels across the body the boundary layer of air next to the skin is continuously replaced with cooler air. The faster the boundary

Precautions should be taken when training in the heat. *Shutterstock* layer is replaced the faster the body can dissipate heat. There will be greater heat dissipation through convection while cycling at 24 mph than while running at a 6-minute-per-mile pace (10 mph). When you stop at a stoplight, you can feel your body temperature rise and then lower again as the light turns green and you take off.

Evaporation is the primary mechanism for heat dissipation during exercise. As sweat evaporates on the skin, heat is transferred to the environment. The key to evaporative cooling is that the sweat must evaporate on the skin in order for the cooling process to occur. One of the main factors that influences the effectiveness of evaporative cooling is the *relative humidity* (the ratio of water contained in the air compared to the amount the air could contain). If the relative humidity is 60 percent, then 40 percent more water can be taken in. If the relative humidity is 90 percent, then only 10 percent more can absorb water. In the second example there would be very little room for evaporation to occur and therefore cooling during exercise would be greatly compromised. Air moving across the skin during motion will continually replace the boundary layer with less saturated air to aid in cooling.

For cooling to occur heat must be transferred from the working muscles and core and dissipated into the surrounding environment. During exercise blood flow is redirected toward the skin in order to transfer heat from the core to the environment and, as temperature increases, so too does blood flow to the skin. Blood makes an excellent transporter of heat as roughly 50 to 55 percent of the blood consists of water. Heat is transferred from the blood to the skin where it is dissipated through evaporation, convection, and radiation. The cooled blood then is eventually circulated back through the body where it picks up more heat to transfer to the skin for cooling.

Because blood is vital in the process of heat dissipation, hydration status strongly impacts the body's ability to cool. To make a long story short, sweat is filtered plasma, and as you sweat plasma volume decreases. The decrease in plasma volume results in dehydration and impaired cooling. Core temperature then begins to steadily rise, resulting in the development of a heat-related illness. Water loss equivalent to 2 to 3 percent of body mass will negatively impact performance, whereas a loss equivalent to 5 percent or greater will negatively impact health.

Heat-Related Illness

Heat-related illness occurs when the body's ability to dissipate heat has been compromised due to high internal and external temperatures and dehydration. Heat-related illnesses can be very serious and result in death if untreated. While there are many discomforts or pains that you can push through, this will not be one of them. The primary heat-related illnesses are heat cramps, heat exhaustion, and heat stroke.

Heat Cramps

Heat cramps present as very strong and painful muscle contractions, which occur due to dehydration and sodium loss. The best way to counter heat cramps is to stop exercising, get to a cool environment, rehydrate, and ingest electrolytes.

Heat Exhaustion

Heat exhaustion occurs when the thermoregulatory system fails to regulate temperature due to an inability to effectively dissipate heat. Heat exhaustion is defined by its symptoms. They are headache, dizziness, nausea, feeling of weakness, tingling sensation in the skin, chills, pale moist skin, and rapid weak pulse.

Heat Stroke

Heat stroke occurs as symptoms progress beyond heat exhaustion and can lead to serious health issues, including death. While some symptoms of heat stroke are the same as heat exhaustion, there are key symptoms that differ, the most important of which is the development of a core temperature of 104°F or higher. Of course you probably will not have a thermometer with you while training. Instead, look for cessation of sweating and hot, red, dry skin as signs that you have moved from heat exhaustion to heat stroke. Symptoms of heat stroke:

- core temperature greater than or equal to 104°F
- hot, red, dry skin
- cessation of sweating
- rapid, strong pulse
- headache
- confusion
- chills

At the first sign of a heat-related illness, you should stop exercising immediately, get to a cool area as quickly as possible, and drink plenty of fluids. Heat-related injuries can escalate very quickly from mild to severe symptoms, which is why it is very important to stop activity immediately. Once core temperature starts to increase beyond the body's ability to control it, it will continue to increase as long as you exercise and generate metabolic heat in a hot environment.

Once you stop exercising and have moved to a cooler environment, continue working to bring the core temperature down. Take a cool shower or bath, apply cold towels, or use ice packs. It is also very important to ingest fluids in order to bring hydration levels back to normal. This becomes problematic if you are nauseous and cannot keep fluids down, in which case a trip to the doctor and an IV will most likely be required. If you suspect that you have heat stroke, seek medical attention immediately.

Prevention

The best way to treat a heat-related illness is not to have one in the first place. With the proper precautions a heat-related illness can be avoided altogether. Try to avoid training during the hottest part of the day during the really hot days of summer. Instead, attempt to go out early before the temperatures get too high.

Clothing can also help prevent the development of a heat-related illness. Clothing should be breathable so that sweat is able to evaporate on the skin in order to cool the body. Don't wear dark colors as they will absorb radiation and make you hotter.

Proper hydration is important to maintain the body's ability to regulate a functioning core temperature. Unfortunately, most triathletes are chronically dehydrated during the summertime due to long hours training and inadequate hydration strategies. It is not possible to maintain hydration during exercise on a hot day, so it is very important to start a training session fully hydrated.

One of the most important steps in preventing a heat-related illness is to become acclimated to the heat. It typically takes approximately 2 weeks for the majority of the physiological changes that result in acclimation to occur. These adaptations are key to preventing a heat-related illness. During early season races the weather is typically much cooler in the north as compared to the south. If you live in New York and have a big race in Florida, there will be a large temperature difference. The ideal situation would be to travel to Florida for two weeks in order to acclimate to the hotter weather. While ideal, this may not be practically feasible.

As the body adapts to the heat, more blood will be directed to the skin for cooling and there will be a more efficient distribution of blood throughout the body. You will begin to sweat more, sweat will start at a lower core temperature, and sweat will be better distributed across the body to optimize cooling. While sweat does increase with adaptation, sodium within the sweat will decrease in order to offset an electrolyte imbalance.

Glycogen usage significantly increases when exercising in the heat. After acclimation glycogen usage will not be as high as prior to acclimation. This will spare glycogen stores, which are limited and can negatively impact performance when diminished.

Training in the Cold

You will need to train year-round in order to be optimally prepared for triathlon season. Because of this you will need to train outside when the weather provides opportunity for safe winter training. If proper precautions are taken, winter training can be safe and effective, although not overly comfortable.

Open water swim training in the colder parts of the year can lead to the development of a cold-related illness. Because heat can transfer through water up to twenty-five times faster than air, the water temperature does not have to be very cold to result in hypothermia (core temperature <95°F). Most lap pools are kept somewhere between 78 and 82°F. If you were to stand in a pool with 80°F water and do nothing, your core temperature would continue to drop until hypothermia sets in. However, when conducting a swim workout 80°F would feel comfortable due to the metabolic heat generated while swimming.

Wind chill is another key factor that you must be aware of when training in the cold. Wind chill is determined by the ambient temperature and the speed of the wind: The faster the wind the lower the wind chill at any given ambient temperature. When looking at wind chill, the relative velocity of the body also plays a role. With cycling speeds being much greater than running, wind chill goes up exponentially.

The body responds to the cold environment in three basic ways. The first is *peripheral vasoconstriction,* which significantly decreases blood supply to the extremities, keeping warm blood at the core. The second method is *non-shivering thermogenesis,* where metabolism is increased in order to increase core temperature without actually producing shivers. The last method is

To prevent a cold-related illness, always dress appropriately when training outdoors. *Shutterstock*

shivering thermogenesis, where heat is produced through muscle rapidly contracting and relaxing to generate metabolic heat.

Cold-Related Illness

Hypothermia is the most common cold-related illness. It occurs when core temperature drops below 95°F. Symptoms of hypothermia are:

- shivering (begins before core temperature reaches 95°F)
- weakness
- mental confusion
- impaired speech
- loss of dexterity and coordination
- pale, gray-tinged skin color
- muscles become stiff and movement sluggish
- breathing and heart rate slow
- loss of consciousness

When hypothermia occurs it is very important to move to a warm environment as soon as possible. The key to getting warm is to remove all wet clothing, dry off, and put on dry warm clothes. Water on the skin or in clothing will continue to allow the core temperature to drop, even if in a warm environment. If you present with some of the more serious symptoms, seek medical attention as soon as possible.

Prevention

The human body does not acclimate to the cold as significantly as it does to a hot environment. Prolonged cold exposure leads to small adaptations (earlier onset of shivering and increased blood flow to the extremities), but does not dramatically offset hypothermia. Due to the lack of adaptation, proper clothing choice is the primary method for preventing cold-related illness.

On cold days layer clothing in order to keep the body warm. The first layer of clothing, the base layer, should be made of breathable material that allows moisture to be wicked away from the skin. The next layer, the insulating layer, is designed to keep heat in while allowing moisture to pass through and away from the body. Polyester fleece makes the best insulating material as it has both abilities. The last layer, the shell, is designed to block wind and prevent heat loss through convection. The shell is typically vented to allow moisture to escape through the vents while preventing too much heat loss. Be sure not to overdress, as you can develop a heat-related illness even in the winter.

Wetsuits can be used to decrease the risk of developing hypothermia in the water. There is no magic number that indicates at what temperature you should wear a wetsuit. Most swimmers start using wetsuits when the water temperature reaches the low 70s. USAT rules allow wetsuits to be worn below 78°F without penalty. Wetsuits can be worn between 78 and 84°F, but you cannot win prizes or awards. Wetsuits are not permitted at water temperatures greater than 84°F as it can result in the development of a heat-related illness.

Training at High Altitudes

As altitude increases, atmospheric pressure decreases, resulting in a decrease in the partial pressure of oxygen (PO_2), calculated by multiplying barometric pressure by .2093. Air consists of 20.93 percent oxygen, 79.04 percent nitrogen and .03 percent carbon dioxide. These percentages do not change even when barometric pressure decreases with increases in altitude. In a simplistic manner barometric pressure can be considered the pressure of the atmosphere. As you move up in altitude there is less atmosphere pushing down on you and therefore less pressure. As altitude increases barometric, pressure decreases, resulting in a lower PO_2. The chart below demonstrates the difference between the PO_2 at sea level and at the top of Mt. Evans in Colorado.

	BAROMETRIC PRESSURE	CALCULATION	PO_2
Sea Level	760 mmHg	760 mmHg x .2093	159.07 mmHg
Mt. Evans, Colorado	460 mmHg	460 mmHg x .2093	96.28 mmHg

Dropping from a PO_2 of 159.07 mmHg to 96.28 mmHg has a strong negative impact on oxygen transfer in the body. If you remember from Chapter 5 gas exchange is driven by the pressure differential across the respiratory membrane. If the PO_2 decreases in the atmosphere then the PO_2 also decreases in the lungs, resulting in less of a pressure differential between the lungs and the capillaries. Due to this, the PO_2 decreases throughout the body, significantly lowering the available oxygen for metabolic demand and leading to a chronic hypoxic state at the altitude. With less oxygen available the ability of muscles to produce work aerobically is significantly diminished.

The body responds to the hypoxic state created by altitude through various physiological means. In response to the decreased PO_2 both rate and depth of breathing increase. Increased ventilation leads to an increased release of CO_2 from the body. On the surface this may seem like a good thing, but it does have negative consequences. As CO_2 levels drop pH increase, leading to an alkaline state. To offset this increase in pH the kidneys excrete more bicarbonate ions, which results in two negative effects. The first is that the increase in urination (in combination with increased water loss through increased ventilation) leads to a significant decrease in plasma volume. This is why it is very important to take in fluids in order to remain hydrated at altitude. The second is that the significant reduction in bicarbonate ions significantly reduces the body's ability to buffer hydrogen during anaerobic bouts, which significantly decrease anaerobic training and performance.

Cardiac output also increases in response to a decrease in PO_2 and the decrease in stroke volume. There will be an increased release of norepinephrine and epinephrine to increase heart rate in order to increase cardiac output. Since there is less oxygen per volume of blood the body adjusts by increasing blood flow.

Due to the decreased PO_2 and the body's response to this decrease, endurance performance significantly decreases at altitude. Lack of sufficient oxygen delivery to the muscles caused by the thin air decreases the muscles' ability to perform aerobically. At altitude there will be a feeling of sluggishness and a feeling of strained breathing during training. This is especially true for those who have not acclimated to the environment. There will also be a decrease in your ability to perform high-intensity bouts.

Altitude Sickness

When traveling from sea level to altitude, there is a significant risk of developing altitude sickness. The severity of altitude sickness is determined by how high you travel and how fast you reach high altitude. Naturally, the higher you go the greater the risk of developing altitude sickness. Altitude sickness typically presents at around 7,000 to 8,000 feet or higher. The faster you travel to altitude, the higher the risk of developing altitude sickness. Ideally, you want to gradually increase altitude over days to allow acclimation to occur. However, this is typically not a practical approach for triathletes. Some develop altitude sickness more easily than others. Unfortunately, there is no way to predict how you will respond until you experience it. Symptoms of altitude sickness are:

- increased rate and depth of breathing (happens at altitude regardless of altitude sickness)
- fatigue
- loss of appetite
- headache
- mental confusion
- nausea
- insomnia

Descending and acclimating to the altitude changes are the only methods to counter altitude sickness. Most of these symptoms subside as you become acclimated to altitude. If altitude sickness occurs it is ideal to descend to a lower altitude and slowly work your way back up to altitude.

There are two more conditions that can occur at altitudes greater than 9,000 feet: high-altitude pulmonary edema and high-altitude cerebral edema. Both of these conditions can become life-threatening and medical attention should be sought immediately if either condition is suspected. Here are the symptoms:

High-Altitude Pulmonary Edema

- wheezing
- coughing up pink phlegm
- excess mucus in the lungs
- severe headache
- severe weakness
- skin discoloration (blue or gray)

High-Altitude Cerebral Edema

- neurological symptoms
- loss of coordination
- mental confusion
- slurred speech
- severe drowsiness
- loss of consciousness

Prevention

Take training and racing at high altitudes very seriously to prevent negative physiological consequences. Acclimation is the only way to help prevent the onset of altitude sickness. It takes approximately 3 weeks to see noticeable adaptations to moderate altitudes. If going to extremely high altitudes, you need to acclimate in stages at different elevations.

There are numerous physiological adaptations that allow for acclimation. Ventilation increases upon arrival at altitude and continues to increase for about 3 to 4 days before leveling off at an elevated rate. Erythropoietin, responsible for red blood cell production, increases within hours of arriving at altitude and levels off after about 3 days of exposure. Once red blood cells have increased significantly, after about a month, then erythropoietin levels return to normal while red blood cell count remains elevated. This increase in red blood cell count leads to an increase in hematocrit readings.

All of these adaptations allow you to acclimate to altitude. However, they do not completely offset the negative impact of altitude on both the body and on performance. If you do not have time to travel and acclimate to the altitude, I recommend that you compete in the event within 24 hours of arriving at altitude.

Altitude is often used as a method to improve performance during endurance sports. The rationale is that using altitude to increase red blood cell count increases hematocrit and, therefore, performance. While this method may look convincing on the surface, there are some underlying issues that prevent it from actually increasing performance, mainly the significant decrease in PO_2 and your inability to train at high intensities while at altitude. Even though adaptations occur that increase oxygen delivery to the working muscles, it will still be lower than at sea level and, therefore, negatively impact your ability to train. You will be unable to train at high intensities and therefore will be unable to race at high intensities when traveling to sea level. The vast majority of races are not held at altitude.

Because of the inability to train at high intensities while at altitude, I recommend the "live high/train low" approach to altitude: By living at altitude you get the desirable physiological adaptions. Training low allows you to train at much higher intensities than when training at altitude.

SPEEDY FEET
FINISH
HFP
USA

Index

Remember to enjoy your triathlon experience.

About the Author

Will Peveler, PhD, is a noted exercise physiologist who has coached at the university level and ridden bicycles competitively since 1994. In addition to his work as a bicycle-fitting specialist, he writes about performance cycling and biomechanics. The author of *The Complete Book of Road Cycling and Racing* and a seasoned triathlete, he is assistant professor of exercise science at Northern Kentucky University.